Liturgy ᵒᶠₜₕₑ Hours

Its history and its importance as the communal prayer of the Church after the Liturgical Reform of Vatican II

Father Dominic F. Scotto, TOR

Franciscan University Press
1235 University Blvd.
Steubenville OH 43952

Acknowledgment

Excerpts from the various documents from Vatican II are taken from *Vatican II—The Conciliar and Post-Conciliar Documents*, ed. A. Flannery. Dublin: Dominican Publications, 1975

Censor Deputatus	Reverend Quentin L. Schaut, O.S.B. February 8, 1986
Imprimatur	Most Reverend James J. Hogan, D.D., J.C.D. Bishop of Altoona-Johnstown February 25, 1986

The *Imprimatur* is an official declaration that a book is considered to be free of doctrinal and moral error. It is not implied that those who have granted the *Imprimatur* necessarily agree with the contents, opinions, or statements expressed.

LIBRARY OF CONGRESS CATALOGING-IN-PUBLICATION DATA

Scotto, Dominic F.
  The Liturgy of the hours.

  Bibliography: p.
  Includes index.
  1.Catholic Church. Liturgy of the hours. 2. Divine office.
  3.Catholic Church – Liturgy. I. Title
  BX2000.S36 1986   264.0201   86-17821

1987 Published by St. Bede's Publications
2001 Revised cover and reprint by Franciscan University Press

Franciscan University Press
1235 University Blvd.
Steubenville, OH 43952
Printed in the United States of America

Cover design and photography: Lori Bortz Design

ISBN 1-888462-11-6
UP 217

Contents

Foreword

When I entered the Franciscan Third Order Regular, I experienced the Liturgy of the Hours as only prayed by priests and religious. Today, that has greatly changed.

This week I was invited to a home dinner, and the hostess suggested we "pray vespers" before eating. This morning three lay students joined the friars for morning prayer. Every day in our University chapel, lay students pray liturgical morning and evening prayer.

Fr. Dominic Scotto is a scholar and leader in the movement for lay participation in liturgical prayer. This book presents the foundation for this movement and the inspiration to participation in the prayer of the "Whole People of God."

FR. MICHAEL SCANLAN, TOR
Chancellor
Franciscan University of Steubenville

Introduction

On November 1, 1970, Pope Paul VI promulgated the Apostolic Constitution on the Breviary, *Laudis Canticum*,[1] a document which was to have a profound and lasting effect upon the entire future of Christian prayer in the Roman Catholic Church. As the official introduction to the renewed Liturgy of the Hours, this Constitution represented the culmination of the reform of the Divine Office called for by the Second Vatican Council in the Constitution on the Sacred Liturgy.[2] While this reform embraces the entire Divine Office in its many differing aspects, the principal object of this study concerns that aspect involving the renewed stress now placed upon the Liturgy of the Hours as a prayer involving the entire People of God.

> Since the Office is the prayer of the whole People of God, it has been drawn up and prepared in such a way that not only ecclesiastics but also religious and even laymen can take part in it. By introducing various forms of celebration, the attempt has been made to meet the specific requirements of persons of different order and degree. The prayer can be adapted to the different communities that celebrate the Liturgy of the Hours, according to their condition and vocation.[3]

For many centuries, the Church had, at least on the practical level, almost completely lost sight of the Liturgy of the Hours as a public act of worship of the whole Christian community. It became commonly known as the breviary, or priest's daily prayer book, in effect the exclusive, and principally private prerogative of the clergy and religious. The liturgical reform of the Second Vatican Council has directed that the Divine Office be once again restored to its original purpose, namely, as a prayer for the entire community of the faithful. These thoughts have been well summed up by Archbishop Anibale Bugnini, former secretary of the Sacred Congregation for Divine Worship, in the following statement:

The awareness of the Liturgy of the Hours as something belonging essentially to the whole Church has, regrettably, hardly been in evidence for many centuries. It had come to be considered as the preserve of religious and clergy. Liturgical services, however are not private functions, or reserved to groups of elites; they are celebrations of the Church which is the sacrament of unity. They pertain to the whole body of the Church in different ways according to the diversity of holy orders, functions, and degrees of participation.

As can be seen from the very structure of the Hours, with their psalms, reading, hymns, responsories and prayers, they are designed for celebration in common. Individual recitation came in only when this communal celebration was not possible.[4]

Consequently, in the midst of the great liturgical renewal effected by the Second Vatican Council, one of the most significant liturgical reforms has been the rediscovery of the Liturgy of the Hours as a prayer for all the People of God.

Perhaps many would not agree with this statement feeling that the Liturgy of the Hours is not that important in the liturgical life of the Church, or feeling that the laity would simply not be interested in this archaic practice any longer. The few instances in the modern times where people had been participating in the Liturgy of the Hours in a limited way had been for the singing of Tenebrae during Holy Week celebrations, and for Sunday Vespers. However, with the restored Easter Liturgy and the introduction of the evening Masses, this ancient practice was just about eliminated.[5] What purpose would then be served in reviving a very ancient practice of the Church which has, to all intents and purposes, slowly but surely died?

Certainly one of the principal reasons would seem to be that this exalted prayer of the Church belongs by its very origin and nature to all the People of God and not solely to cleric and monks.[6] Thus, although the obligation for the celebration of the Hours concerns some of the faithful in a special way,[7] nevertheless, the entire Church, that is, all the People of God, share in a certain sense in that very same obligation.[8] For the celebration of the Divine Office is not simply a peripheral or optional activity of the Church, but it is rightly considered to be among the first duties of the entire Church.[9]

On the other hand, the communal celebration of the Hours constitutes an invaluable source of grace and strength for both our pastoral and apostolic lives, whose overall goal is to bring the entire community of the faithful to that necessary praise and worship of God in prayer. Next to the Eucharist itself, it is the Liturgy of the Hours which provides the most efficacious means for achieving both the glorification of God and the sanctification of men.[10] However, at the same time, the Church insists upon the necessity of the communal dimension of this prayer, a dimension which must include the commitment of the entire community of faith.[11]

We know, we understand, and we reverence the Eucharist as the heart and the fount of the liturgical life of the Church through which Christ, together with the faith-filled community, offers the Father an unending sacrifice of praise. "The Church not only satisfies this precept by celebrating the Eucharist, but also in other different ways, especially the Liturgy of the Hours."[12]

> The Liturgy of the Hours was gradually developed until it became the prayer of the local Church, where, at established times and places, with the priest presiding over it, it became a necessary completion, as it were, of the whole divine worship contained in the Eucharistic Sacrifice, to be poured forth and spread at every hour of man's life.[13]

Thus we can see that while the Eucharist is certainly central to the Christian life, the Liturgy of the Hours is an essential complementary prayer by which the sacrifice of praise and adoration may be made to effectively consecrate the entire day of the Christian community.[14] Therefore, outside of the Eucharist, and yet intimately related to it, it is the communal celebration of the Liturgy of the Hours by all the People of God which is viewed by the Church as the outstanding means whereby the relationship within the life of every Christian between life and prayer, between service to man and worship to God, may be reestablished, developed, and strengthened.

It is certainly true that in its pre-Vatican II form the Liturgy of the Hours was hardly a vehicle by which the faithful could readily pray, find spiritual fulfillment and draw communal strength and support in the face of their everyday needs and aspirations. However, with the new reformed Divine Office, adaptation and facility of use for the entire People of God has been very prominent in the minds of the reformers. For example, the revised Liturgy of the Hours may now be celebrated in the living language of the people; the psalms are more numerous and varied; there is a more liberal use of biblical texts and of the other writings of the Church; the use of the homily, the prayers of intercession and petition, the hymns and other sung forms of prayer, all help to make the reformed Office more rewarding, more interesting and more conducive to communal participation. All of these meaningful changes serve to effectively demonstrate to all participants the theological and spiritual richness of the Liturgy of the Hours. It is only in this manner that we are able to maintain that this magnificent prayer of the Hours is truly the public and communal prayer of the entire Church for the greater glory of God and for the spiritual growth and development of the life of prayer of the faithful. This is exactly what Pope Paul VI so strongly affirms in his Apostolic Constitution on the Breviary.

> The prayer of Holy Church having, therefore, been renewed and completely restored according to her earliest tradition, and in consideration of the necessity of our time, it is highly desirable that it should deeply penetrate all Christian prayer, become its expression and effectively nourish the spiritual life of the People of God.
>
> For this reason we hope and trust that there will be a new awareness of the prayer to be recited "without interruption," which Our Lord Jesus Christ laid upon his Church. In fact the book of the Liturgy of the Hours, distributed in the right time, is intended to sustain prayer continually and help it. The very celebration, particularly when a community meets for this reason, manifests the true nature of the Church in prayer, and appears as her marvelous sign.[15]

THE LITURGY OF THE HOURS

Abbreviations

AA	Apostolicam Actuositatem, Decree on the Apostolate of Lay People
AAS	Acta Apostolicae Sedis
ASS	Acta Sanctae Sedis
CC	Corpus Christianorum
CSEL	Corpus Scriptorum Ecclesiasticorum Latinorum
EL	Ephemerides Liturgicae
GILH	General Instruction on the Liturgy of the Hours
GS	Gaudium et Spes, The Pastoral Constitution on the Church in the Modern World
LG	Lumen Gentium, The Dogmatic Constitution on the Church
LMD	La Maison-Dieu
PG	Patrologia Graeca, ed. J. P. Migne
PL	Patrologia Latina, ed. J. P. Migne
PO	Presbyterorum Ordinis, Decree on the Ministry and Life of Priests
SC	Sacrosanctum Concilium, The Constitution on the Sacred Liturgy

I

A Historical Survey of the Liturgy of the Hours as the Communal Prayer of the Church

On November 1, 1970, Pope Paul VI, in the Apostolic Constitution *Laudis Canticum—The Canticle of Praise*[1]—approved the revised Liturgy of the Hours for use by the Roman Catholic Church. One of the most significant aspects of that renewal has been the restoration of this treasured prayer to all the People of God. Before proceeding to explore the significant pastoral implications of this singular feature of the reform it will be necessary for us to first have a clearer understanding of the origin and subsequent development of the Hours as communal prayer involving the entire Christian community.

This chapter will be concerned primarily with this particular aspect, namely, a historical survey of the Liturgy of the Hours as communal prayer, from its origins to the modern liturgical movement, as it evolved principally in relationship to the Latin Church of the West. Hopefully, this study will serve to broaden our vision and understanding of the Hours and at the same time will help us to realize more fully the need for this reform as well as its great importance for the life of the Church. However, this chapter would hardly be complete in its scope without dealing in some degree with the entire question of the influence of Jewish communal prayer upon the public prayer of the early Christian Church.

The Judaic Heritage—Biblical Origins

Few scholars today would reject the idea that the origins of Christian liturgical prayer are, in a certain sense, deeply rooted in the Judaic heritage, principally the Synagogue tradition. The Judaic characteristic of the sacralization of time through daily, weekly, and yearly cycles had a profound and marked influence upon the prayer life of the early Christian communities.[2] Nevertheless, despite these conclusions, this is a question which needs careful examination and prudent consideration in order to avoid arriving at overly facile and accommodating answers.

First of all, we need to establish the fact that the Liturgy of the Hours, as we have come to know it, was clearly a later, uniquely Christian, development as our historical survey will try to demonstrate. The point which we now wish to investigate is how the seeds of this development were initially embedded in the soil of Judaic communal prayer as exemplified primarily in the Synagogue services. The principal source for our investigation of this interrelationship will be, of course, the Sacred Scriptures which contain the common ground for both traditions. However, both the fragmentary state of the sources as well as the many critical problems which they pose make it particularly difficult to trace the origins and subsequent development of Jewish public prayer with any kind of precise certitude.

While we may safely conclude that the elements of spontaneity and right intention are essential to an expression of true prayer, nevertheless, we can also affirm the necessity of some type of ordered expression in worship for an individual or for a community. The practice of praying at specific, preordained times of the day, principally in the morning and evening, is a practice which is neither originally Judaic nor Christian since it springs from the very naturally religious instincts of man as clearly demonstrated in many recent studies of natural religions.[3] However, Judaism does represent a first and decisively creative adoption of this natural pattern of prayer which is discernible throughout the life of the Jewish people in their personal piety, in the elaborate public cultus of the Jerusalem Temple, and in the simple but much more durable liturgy of the Synagogue.[4]

While much confusion continues to exist both within rabbinical writings and among modern scholars concerning the origins and growth of the Synagogue services and their relationship to the Temple services, certain areas presently call for our careful consideration. One of these areas would be that of the Jewish ritual practice of sacrifice, in particular that of the daily holocaust or perpetual sacrifice.[5] The established practice of offering a burnt holocaust each day of the year in the Temple at Jerusalem was a custom based upon the command contained in Exodus 29:38-42. This daily cultic service was called the perpetual (tamid) sacrifice.

> Now, this is what you shall offer on the altar: two yearling lambs as the sacrifice established for each day; one lamb in the morning and the other lamb in the evening twilight. With the first lamb there shall be a tenth of an ephah of fine flour mixed with a fourth of a hin of oil of crushed olives and, as its libation, a fourth of a hin of wine. The other lamb you shall offer at the evening twilight, with the same cereal offering and libation as in the morning. You shall offer this as a sweet-smelling oblation to the Lord. Throughout your generations this established holocaust shall be offered before the Lord at the entrance of the meeting tent, where I will meet you and speak to you.

An essentially similar text may be found in Numbers 28:1-8. The general rule in these two passages calls for a daily burnt-offering of an unblemished male lamb and a cereal oblation of flour and olive oil each morning and evening. Exodus 30:7-8 adds that these sacrifices must be accompanied by an offering of incense upon the altar of perfumes. The ritual is referred to in the Book of Chronicles as pertaining to the monarchic period, but it is certainly of post-exilic origin.[6]

The morning holocaust was offered between dawn and sunrise signaling a reawakening of life and activity; and the evening sacrifice was offered between sunset and dark, signaling the close of one day and the beginning of another. The person who was making the offering had to do so while in a state of ritual purity. Laying hands upon the victim's head, the offerer made a solemn attestation that the victim being presented was his personal offering; that the sacrifice which was going to be presented to God by the priest, whose primary office was to offer sacrifice, was being offered on his behalf and that all the benefits derived from the sacrifice would be his. The prescriptions of the Priestly Code given for ceremonies of the holocausts are found in Leviticus 1:13-17. Distinct from other sacrifices, the holocaust was wholly destroyed by fire and none of it was eaten either by the priest or by the victim's donor. The primary purpose of this complete gift was to render glory and praise to God.[7]

A study of the vocabulary and context of these basic texts will clearly demonstrate that they are the result of a historical development which embraced the fusion of various cultic practices, essentially similar to each other but emanating from diverse cultural backgrounds, namely, pastoral and agricultural, nomadic and settled. The holocausts, therefore, served to demonstrate and to strengthen the harmony and concord of God's Chosen People, as they consecrated each day to the Lord from sunrise to sunset, turning to him in worship.[8]

While the very action of the Temple holocaust was itself seen as a prayer in act, these accounts do not provide us with the actual prayer formulas to be used during the offering of the sacrifices. However, sacrifices in Judaism were normally and naturally accompanied by prayer.

> Although the ritual does not contain any prescription for the prayer formulas to be used during the offering of sacrifices, such formulas certainly existed and were in common use. They are found in every religious ritual throughout the world. Amos 5:23 refers to the singing of the hymns to instrumental accompaniment, but only in a general way. We may assume that the development of liturgical chant kept pace with that of the ritual and of the increasingly specialized priesthood. There were official chanters in Solomon's Temple from the beginning (2 Chr. 5:11-14), and the importance of this group grew steadily until, in the post-exilic Temple, it enjoyed great prestige. The official hymnbook of the new Temple was the Psalter, and several of its clearly liturgical hymns had already been in use during the royal period.[9]

An examination of the text of the Psalter underscores the use of the psalms in connection with worship, usually a sacrificial service to which certain psalms would be sung as an accompaniment (Ps. 20:4; 26:5; 27:6; 66:13-15; 81:4; 107:22; 116:17). Other psalms, however, specifically refer to the Temple as the locale in which they were sung (Ps. 48; 65; 95; 96; 118; 134; 135).[10] Biblical prayer was therefore intimately bound up with cult, both giving their distinctive stamp to the Judaic faith. The Temple of Jerusalem occupied the principal position within Jewish piety for it was seen as the chosen dwelling of God (Dt. 12:11), and as the house of prayer for all the People of God (Is. 56:7). It was judged to be the center of Israel's legitimate worship and eventually as the only place of worship in Israel. However, with the destruction of the Temple in 586 B.C., and the subsequent exile and separation from Jerusalem, the Chosen People began to realize more fully the true value and limitations of the Temple.

In the face of this great adversity, Israel continued to preserve her Mosaic faith with tenacity and vitality, thereby managing not only to survive the ordeal of foreign captivity, but actually being immeasurably enriched by the experience. Encouraged by such prophets as Jeremiah, who assured them that although bereft of the Temple and in exile, they could still have access to God through prayer (Jer. 29:12-14), and Ezekiel, whose account of the great vision of Yahweh's arrival upon his throne among his people in exile continued to assure them of God's availability to them (Ezek. 1:1-28), those faithful Jews who did not succumb to absorption into the Babylonian culture continued to hold steadfastly to their Jewish faith and brotherhood. Possessed by this spirit the Israelites were able to understand that in reality they could approach God anywhere with complete confidence in his proximity and availability, as their spiritual sanctuary in a strange and foreign land (Ezek. 11:16). Undoubtedly it was during this period that these faithful Jews would come together informally in small groups in order to receive instruction in their scriptural traditions and to pray together.[11] Some have viewed these gatherings as most probably the origin of the phenomenon of the synagogue in Judaism,[12] although there does not seem to be strong enough evidence to support such a view with any degree of certitude.

> There is no evidence, however, that there were any organized local assemblies. All that can be safely said is that the later synagogues which came to be scattered throughout the countries of the dispersion, arose in response to a need that was first experienced during the Exile, when Jews were separated from their land and their Temple.[13]

Therefore, despite the uncertainty surrounding the precise origins of Synagogue worship, we are inescapably certain of their gradual emergence and spreading sometime after the demise of the Temple in 586 B.C.[14] Although by 516 B.C. the Temple had been rebuilt by the returning Jewish exiles, it never regained the total command of the centrality of Jewish worship that it once enjoyed. This was so because the heart of the Temple, the Ark of the Covenant, God's visible presence in the midst of his people, was no longer present. Coming out of the traumatic watershed of the destruction of the Temple and the Babylonian captivity, a certain transformation began inevitably to take place within Jewish worship which eventually expressed itself as the distinctive worship of the Synagogue.[15]

The Synagogue Service

While Synagogue worship seemed to have grown out of the vacuum created by the destruction of the Temple in 586 B.C., it in no way was seen to be a substitute for it, at least not until the final destruction of the Temple by the Romans in 70 A.D.

> Far from taking the place of the Temple, the synagogue only reinforced the unique significance of the Temple in the cult of Israel. There were synagogues even in the precincts of the (rebuilt) Temple and in the humblest villages. These "houses of prayer" were used for meetings at which Jews prayed and listened to the reading of the Bible.[16]

At this point it is important for us to try to understand to the best of our ability the composition of the pre-Christian Synagogue service and its true significance in the everyday life of the Chosen People. However, this is a complicated and difficult task to achieve with any degree of certitude. Besides not possessing any of the original texts from the ancient Synagogue service, we are also dealing with a liturgical form which has undergone a great degree of growth and development over the centuries with the gradual accretion of later material. Nevertheless, we do possess enough early, indirect evidence to enable us to arrive at a fairly reliable, composite understanding of both the ritual and purpose of the early Synagogue liturgy.[17]

In general, it seems that we are justified in stating that the daily Synagogue service was composed of two principal elements, namely, the reading of Scripture and Prayer.[18] Concerning the element of Readings, it was from very early times, most certainly pre-Christian, that a central place was reserved for the reading of portions of the Pentateuch and the Prophets in the Synagogue service, not only on Sabbaths and other holy days, but at other prescribed times as well. These readings were followed by an explanatory exposition which assumed a homiletic character and which was meant to promote the absorption of the Law into the very heart and soul of the attending community which remained passive throughout the service.[19] Eventually, prayers were added to the service composed of extracts from the Torah as well as from other edifying texts. This additional element of prayer was composed of two principal parts: a) the *shema*, and b) the *tefillah* or the *amidah*.[20]

Being one of the most ancient and important prayer formulas of the Synagogue service, the *shema* was in reality more of a creed than a prayer, wherein the pious Israelite would confess his steadfast faith in the one, eternal and true God both privately and publicly.[21] As embodied in Deuteronomy 6:4-9, this creed is evidently a stereotyped formula (Dt. 9:1; 11:13-21; 30:3; 27:9; Nm. 15:37-41), and contained the fundamental and all-inclusive stipulation of the covenant—the command to love Yahweh with one's entire being. Since Yahweh is one, man's love of him must therefore be undivided. Twice a day the Jews would pray in the words of Deuteronomy 6:4, believing that the eschatological era would bring a great revelation of God's oneness to the world.[22]

> Listen, Israel: Yahweh our God is the one Yahweh. You shall love Yahweh your God with all your heart, with all your soul, with all your strength. Let these words I urge on you today be written on your heart. You shall repeat them to your children and say them over to them whether at rest in your house or walking abroad, at your lying down or at your rising; you shall fasten them on your hand as a sign and on your forehead as a circlet; you shall write them on the doorposts of your house and on your gates (Dt. 6:4-9).

It is significant that originally the heart of this prayer (Dt. 6:4-5), was probably the traditional summons with which in the old days the assembly for worship of the tribes, the *Qahal*, was opened.[23] However, not only does rabbinical literature attest to the fact that in its fuller form (Dt. 6:4-9), it was used as an integral part of the Temple liturgy, but also that it eventually was adopted from the Temple into the Synagogue liturgy.[24]

Besides the reading of the Torah and the Prophets, and the recital of the creed, the *shema*, there was another principal element which was part of the Synagogue liturgy, namely, that element of prayer primarily centered in the formula known as the *tefillah* (prayer). This formula has been described as the prayer *par excellence* of the Synagogue liturgy.[25] It was composed principally of rabbinical texts which took the form of blessings or benedictions, adding a further name to this prayer, the *Shemoneh Esreh*, or the Eighteen Blessings. The benedictions themselves seem to belong to different periods of composition, however, most of them seem to be substantially attributable to pre-Christian times with a few marked exceptions.[26] Being composed essentially of three separate groups of prayers or benedictions (*berakoth*), "it is the formula which gave gradual definition to the totality of the objects of prayer to which the Israelite was commanded and obliged to give his full attention."[27] The first and last groups respectively, were oriented to the offering of praise and thanksgiving to Yahweh, lauding and thanking him for his majesty, for his justice, for his mighty works of creation, and for his special benevolence and protection toward his Chosen People throughout the course of salvation history as exemplified in their deliverance from bondage in Egypt. The doxology which ended each prayer further emphasized the element of praise. Both of these groups of prayers were invariable and were recited daily forming a fixed framework for the intermediate group of blessings. This middle group consisted of petitionary prayers originally not of a fixed character, but were left to be formed spontaneously by the individual leader in prayer according to the particular needs of the Chosen People or, significantly, the needs of others. Eventually even these variable prayers became themselves fixed in form.[28] Aside from these most significant aspects of Judaic liturgical prayer as embodied in the *Shemoneh Esreh*, a further though less prominent element was a corporate sense of sinfulness expressed through a liturgical confession and a plea for forgiveness.[29]

Accompanying these prayers was the singing of various psalms and canticles at least most likely at the Sabbath Assembly. While the precise origins of the liturgical use of psalms in the Synagogue services remains obscure, we are able to gain a better understanding of their liturgical evolution from Temple to Synagogue liturgy through a brief overview of their place in Judaic worship.

Although the Psalter received its final formation at the hands of the staff of the second Temple of Jerusalem, most of the psalms seem to reflect the official, pre-exilic worship of Israel.[30] This is to say that the majority of the psalms seem to have been specifically composed for use in the actual liturgical services of the Temple. Internal evidence strongly points to this cultic origin and use of most of the psalms.[31] "The frequent allusions to Jerusalem, to the Temple, to the sanctuary, to God's mountain, to his abode, to his footstool and to the holy feasts indicate that, in one way or another, a great number of psalms originated in relationship with the Temple."[32]

Essentially the psalms seem to be reducible to two major categories: the Psalms, or Hymns of Praise, wherein the worshiping community praises God for his person and for his mighty works,[33] and the Psalms of Supplication or Lament, either personal or collective, in which God's help is sought in the face of man's dire needs.[34] While it seems that the majority of psalms were originally composed for use in Temple worship, especially on the great festivals,[35] there are certain psalms which do not seem to fit into this category. These particular psalms, such as Ps. 1; 19:7-14; and 119, reflect another ambient since they possess a central theme dedicated to meditation upon and delight in the Torah. Most likely, they were composed in later, post-exilic times, at a period when the synagogue began to exert increasing influence upon Judaic worship.[36]

That the psalms, primarily under the influence of the liturgy of the Temple, eventually became part of the pre-Christian Synagogue service while Temple and synagogue coexisted, seems to be a well accepted opinion.[37] Despite the final destruction of the Temple and the cessation of all its services, the psalms did not fall into disuse. Rather, becoming detached from their original setting, they continued to maintain their significant position in the community's religious life.[38] Within this religious life, the family always enjoyed a very central position, but it was the synagogue and its worship which emerged as the principal religious institution of Israel at this time.[39]

The leader of the local community usually assumed the role of the president of the synagogue, and presided at all the meetings. Commensurate with his position he was the one who opened the services and who pronounced the formulas of benediction. He was also the first to read the Sacred Scriptures although one of the Scribes usually offered an explanation of the sacred texts. In general, the leader presided over the entire performance of the liturgical rites, which were closed with his concluding prayers. The other ministers or officers of worship were selected from among the other male members of the community.[40] With the development of Synagogue prayer services a new cult comes to light in the Judaic religion, a cult in which the sacrifice of blood and burnt offerings was replaced by a sacrifice of praise in prayer. "The liturgy was more democratic, more independent of the priesthood and the laity played an important part in it. The synagogue plunged Jewish life deep in prayer."[41]

With the full flowering of the Synagogue services we have the establishment of an institution which has continued to exist and flourish in Judaism down to our own day. Springing out of a milieu of deprivation, destruction, and exile, the Synagogue sacrifice of praise filled an essential need of the Jewish people to declare their oneness with Yahweh and their continued fidelity to the Covenant. Linked to the cult of the Temple in its spirit of offering praise and thanksgiving to Yahweh on behalf of all the people, it served both as an extension and further development of the Temple. Looking to the Temple for continued inspiration and leadership, whether physically present or not, it sought to preserve everything that the Temple stood for in the lives of the people. Drawing its inspiration from the centralized Temple cult, the liturgy of the Synagogue gave its own sacrifice of praise a unique character, rhythm and universal spirit embodying the entire community of the Chosen People of God. Now the deeper meaning of the Temple cult was presented to the people and they were able to share in it in a way they had never been able to experience before.

For about four centuries both Temple and Synagogue worship coexisted surviving one crisis after another until the final destruction of the third Temple in 70 A.D. and the overthrow of the Jewish state in 135 A.D. However, Jewish worship contined to survive in the now well-established Synagogue liturgy not only in Palestine but throughout the Graeco-Roman world as well.[42]

With the emergence of synagogues throughout Palestine, their services were closely linked to that of the daily services offered in the

Temple since time immemorial. The duty of officiating at these Temple services fell upon the priests, Levites, and other Temple officials. While a small number of superior priests and officials resided permanently at the Temple in Jerusalem the vast majority resided throughout the towns and villages of Palestine. Born into the class of priest or Levite through heredity, after the exile they were divided into twenty-four classes representing twenty-four districts and each class took a turn in going up to the Temple of Jerusalem in order to officiate in a week of service.[43]

Hebraic ritual law not only forbade the cultic offering of the sacrifices outside of the Temple in Jerusalem, but it also did not permit the people to assist directly at the daily burnt oblations because they took place within the holy, internal sanctuary of the Temple. Since the representation of all the people at these same cultic celebrations was guaranteed as well by the same Hebraic cultic law order, a certain category of laymen was attached to each of the twenty-four priestly classes and was deputed to represent the people at each morning and evening sacrifice.[44] Some of these laypeople would accompany their priests and Levites to Jerusalem in order to represent their people directly at the week of service while the rest of the group would remain at home. During the week of services allotted to their particular district, they would gather with the people in a local synagogue at the same time the sacrifices were taking place in the Jerusalem Temple. Turning toward Jerusalem at the time of the sacrifices, they would read from the Sacred Scriptures and offer prayers and in this way would represent their people from afar.[45] In addition, whenever the priests, Levites and the *ma'amodat* (people's representatives) found themselves not involved in the Temple services and consequently outside of Jerusalem, they still "had to perform within their cities the same prayers which accompanied the perpetual sacrifices."[46]

The important thing for us to note is that whenever synagogues did arise in the towns and villages of Palestine, the institution of the *ma'amodat* served to link closely the services of the synagogue with those of the holocausts offered twice daily in the Temple both in the morning and during the evening twilight.

Therefore, although it may be true that not every village community was able to go en bloc daily to the synagogue, at least in the larger towns, where it would be easier to obtain the requisite minimum of ten males and where the homes of the people were grouped more closely around the synagogue, daily attendance at the public worship of the community would be the practice of every devout Jew. In such a milieu the Christian community arose. Moreover, it is worthy to note that the great centers of the infant Church, in which the Gospel tradition was formulated, were among the larger towns of which we have spoken. Daily services of prayer, morning and evening, would almost certainly be held in the synagogues at Jerusalem, Caesarea, Antioch and Rome. And although it is true that large numbers of Gentile converts joined the Church in its early years, necessitating successive modifications of Church practice and the fusion of Semitic with Hellenistic thought, they joined a Church which was essentially Jewish in origin and nucleus.[47]

It is in the light of this overall development, therefore, that it becomes all the more understandable to find the Gospel narratives abounding with the spirit and substance of Jewish customs, prayers, and rituals, and it is in this context that Jesus lived and prayed.[48] His love and respect for the sanctity of the Temple as well as his frequent presence and actual participation in the Synagogue services are verified by many Gospel references.[49] The rich milieu of prayer within which the young Jesus grew to maturity as part of the Father's mysterious design of salvation helped to shape each aspect of his personality and was always present in every element of his teaching.[50] This legacy which Christ left to his diciples and to his Church helped to insert the unique character of Christian prayer into the entire saving plan of God, finding in its Jewish heritage not only a principle for its own specific nature, but a source of rich, ongoing nourishment as well. It is only in the light of this development that we will be able to more fully understand and appreciate not only the strong sense of continuity in God's loving plan for mankind, as exemplified by the growth of Christian prayer out of Jewish liturgical prayer, but also the unique character of Christian prayer itself. In Jesus the organic union of Temple, sacrifice, and prayer was to be fully realized.

The Development of Public Prayer in the Early Church

The passion, death, and resurrection of Jesus signaled a dramatic point of demarkation for the lives of all of the disciples. Suddenly, the Lord was no longer physically present in their midst, giving them the guidance and the example upon which they had relied so heavily and which they now needed so badly. From this point on, however, they had to learn to continue to live as his followers in the light of the resurrection and of the parousia, on the strength of his continued sacramental presence in their midst, as well as on the basis of the rich heritage in word and deed which he had left them. This was to be the basis for the growth and development of their daily lives of prayer.

Although the early sources are few and not beyond the realm of much questioning and debate, we do know that within the early Church Christians prayed continuously both privately and communally after the example and teaching of Jesus Christ.

> The ideal of the Christian life was that of a constant communion with God, maintained by as frequent prayer as possible. A Christian who did not pray every day, and even frequently, would not have been considered a Christian at all.[51]

The heart of this prayer was rooted in the Resurrection of Jesus, an event for which they constantly praised God in eternal gratitude.

Like Jesus his followers were also good practicing Jews and remained such even after his Ascension. For instance, before its final destruction the Temple continued to play a prominent role in the religious lives of these first Christians.[52] Similarly the synagogue most certainly remained an important religious institution in their lives as well, especially as exemplified in the life of St. Paul,[53] just as it had been in the life of Jesus himself as we have already noted. But it was the liturgy of the Synagogue rather than the worship of the Temple which exerted the greatest influence upon the prayer life of the primitive Christian community.[54] Strong and influential as this Judaic heritage seems to have been, however, the influence of Synagogue worship upon Christian worship is to be seen more in the type of worship and the times at which public prayer was held than in any verbatim borrowing of prayers.

Such early Christian prayers as have survived do not suggest any wholesale borrowing from the liturgy of the Synagogue. Individual phrases and occasionally whole sentences, are reminiscent of the wording of the Jewish prayers. But the Christians' debt to the past is revealed rather in the subjects of their prayers and the general framework of their services than in the phraseology employed in the petitions.[55]

Outside of this religious, institutional worship, the early Christians also seem to have observed the traditional hours of Jewish prayer which they customarily prayed thrice daily at the prescribed times.[56] These prayers comprised a fusion of the recitation of the *shema* twice a day, both in the morning and evening, with the praying of the *tefillah*, or Eighteen Benedictions, three times a day, in the morning, afternoon, and evening.[57] However, like Jesus, these early Christians did not merely confine themselves to all the traditional forms of Jewish cultic practice.[58] We are able to affirm the existence of a Christian cult which was independent of these traditional, religious institutions. Principally this revolved around the Eucharistic cult which, for the early Christians, constituted the culmination point of their life of prayer.[59] But it also involved other periods dedicated to continuous prayer which differed from the traditional Jewish patterns of prayer, not only in form but also in time and place.[60]

Therefore, it seems that aside from their regular Jewish cultic practices, it was a customary practice for these early Christian communities to continually come together and to hold informal, communal prayer services at various times in private homes during which they praised God for his marvelous works wrought on their behalf, as primarily exemplified in Christ's Paschal Mystery. It is striking to note that, similar to the characteristics of the ancient synagogal prayers, these cultic reunions of Christians also contained elements of praise and thanksgiving through the singing of psalms, hymns, and spiritual canticles,[61] as well as the teaching and preaching.[62]

Overall, although the New Testament evidence is certainly far from being extensive or conclusive, it seems that we do have good grounds for assuming that the early Christians, at least until the destruction of the Temple, continued to worship in both Temple and synagogue as well as privately in the traditonal Jewish manner. At the same time, they were also celebrating in their homes a very special form of worship, the Eucharist, as well as daily prayer gatherings marked by a certain degree of simplicity and spontaneity.[63]

After the destruction of the Temple in 70 A.D., and the growth in animosity between Jews and Jewish Christians which led to the eventual exclusion of Christians from the worship of the synagogue,[64] the early Church begins to take on more of a uniquely Christian character. Christ now becomes the new Temple,[65] and Christian prayer begins to take on a stronger Christocentric orientation. Throughout this period, the early Christians' conviction of the imminence of the parousia gave them added incentive to root their daily lives in prayer.[66] Eventually, as the imminence of the parousia wore off, and finding themselves increasingly cut off from their traditional Judaic ties, they were required to settle down realistically to the practical task of the daily living out of the Christian life. Perseverance in the observance of regular hours of prayer became normative and essential for these Christians.

Although praying three times a day was a custom which had precedence in their Judaic heritage, at this stage of development the early Christian communities are no longer bound to the fixed liturgical forms of Judaism as to the time and content of prayers. However, inescapably these new forms are always woven into and around the old forms of piety which comprised the traditonal, religious concepts of the Judaic people.[67]

In a very interesting and valuable document, the early Church Order entitled the *Didache*—The Teaching of the Twelve Apostles— Christians were specifically enjoined to recite the Lord's Prayer three times a day.[68] While this prayer which was given to the disciples by Jesus (Lk. 11:1-4) is seen by certain scholars as a substitute for the three daily Jewish prayers composed of the *shema,* the *Shemone Esreh* or Eighteen Benedictions, and the *Kaddish,* the ancient Aramaic doxology[69] to be prayed at the customary hours of morning, afternoon, and evening, the exact times and circumstances of its recital remain obscure for, "there is no consensus of scholarly opinion as to what the *Didache* means by the three hours and whether they are private or public prayers."[70] Although we may suffer from a lack of clear and sufficient textual evidence concerning the times and types of prayer practiced by the earliest Christian communities, the third century provides us with more numerous and precise texts concerning this matter.

The fiery Tertullian (c. 155-c. 220 A.D.), one of the most original and learned thinkers of the early Church, asserts that the principal prayer hours of morning and evening, which he seemed to simply take for granted, were to be considered obligatory for all Christians (*legitimae orationes*), while he considered the outward observance of the lesser hours of Terce, Sext, and None as profitable and consequently almost obligatory as well (*quasi lege*).

> With regard to the time, the outward observance of certain hours will not be without profit. I refer to those hours of community prayer which mark the main divisions of the day, namely, the third, sixth, and ninth, which you may find were in established use in the Scriptures. . . . Although these incidents simply happen without any precept for observing these hours, it would be good to establish some precedent which would make the admonition to pray a binding force to wrest us violently at times from our business, as by a law, to such an obligation, just as we read it was certainly also observed by Daniel according to the discipline of Israel (Dn. 6:11), that we pray no less than three times a day, as debtors to the Father, and to the Son, and to the Holy Spirit. Of course, we are expecting the appropriate prayers, which are due without any admonition at the approach of dawn and evening.[71]

The three common hours of Terce, Sext, and None referred to by Tertullian are to be found in Acts 2:15 (the third hour), Acts 10:9 (the sixth hour), and Acts 3:1 (the ninth hour). Although Tertullian affirms that these hours were "in established use" in the Sacred Scriptures, it seems that their eventual observance by the early Christian communities was based primarily on convenience rather than on any scriptural prescription.[72] Most likely a scriptural basis was sought for their observance only after they had already been adopted as regular Christian hours of prayer. This scriptural basis was provided by the three quotations from Acts cited above. This process of interpretation seems to be the one adopted by Tertullian.[73]

In addition to these three common hours and the two basic hours at the beginning of light and of the night, Tertullian mentions a sixth hour within the context of a question put to Christian women concerning their pagan husbands. "Will not your rising in the night to pray be interpreted to be some act of magic?"[74] This would, therefore, seem to constitute a midnight hour of prayer. Like Tertullian, Cyprian (d. 258) also asserts that the third, sixth, and ninth hours are hours which should be designated for prayer by all Christians. However, he strongly insists that they must also pray early in the morning (*mane*), "that the Lord's resurrection may be celebrated by morning (*matutina*) prayer."[75] He likewise declares that, "also at the sunsetting and at the decline of day of necessity we must pray again."[76]

In a work contemporaneous with that of Tertullian, the *Apostolic Tradition* of Hippolytus (c. 215 A.D.),[77] the author not only indicates the observance of seven hours of prayer, but also attaches to most of the hours specific Christian associations. Concerning morning prayer we are told:

> And let every faithful man and woman when they rise from sleep at dawn, before they undertake any work, wash their hands and pray to God, and so let them go to their work. But if there should be an instruction in the word, let each one prefer to go there, considering that it is God whom he hears speaking by the mouth of him who instructs.
>
> For he who prays with the Church will be able to avoid all the evils of that day. The God-fearing man should consider it a great loss if he does not go to the place in which they give instruction, and especially if he knows how to read. . . .
>
> And if there is a day on which there is no instruction let each one at home take a holy book and read in it sufficiently what seems profitable.[78]

Thus it seems quite clear that before beginning their daily work the faithful were encouraged, if at all possible, to attend the public reading and instruction as well as to join in public prayer. If there was no instruction available, then they were instructed to pray and read the Scriptures privately. This absence of instruction, however, seems to have been the exception which simply testifies to the proof of the rule, since the deacons and presbyters were directed to assemble daily unless prevented from doing so by illness.

> And let the deacons and presbyters assemble daily at the place which the bishop shall appoint for them. And let not the deacons especially neglect to assemble every day unless sickness prevents them. When all have assembled, they shall instruct those who are in the church, and after having also prayed, let each one go about his own business.[79]

It seems to become quite clear from these statements, therefore, that a congregation was most likely present for their instruction.[80] These gatherings, however, should not be confused with those for the purpose of celebrating the Eucharist, for the *Apostolic Tradition* speaks elsewhere about the reserved sacrament and the daily communion of the faithful.[81] For the third hour the faithful are advised: "If you are in your own home, pray at the third hour and praise God. If you are elsewhere at that moment, pray in your own heart. Because at this hour Christ was seen nailed upon the tree."[82] The distinction made between praising God in prayer in the privacy of one's home, and when elsewhere in the privacy of one's heart, seems to indicate that the former was understood to be vocal prayer.[83]

They are also asked to pray at the sixth hour. "Pray as well on the sixth hour. Because when Christ was nailed to the wood of the cross, the daylight was suspended and a great darkness came upon the land."[84] And on the ninth hour. . . . "Let there also be full prayer and praise at the ninth hour. . . . At that hour, therefore, Christ was pierced in his side and shed forth both water and blood."[85]

For nighttime prayer the *Apostolic Tradition* recommends prayer before retiring,[86] and thereafter two times during the night, once at midnight and again at cockcrow:

> Pray also before retiring for the night. But at about midnight rise and wash your hands with water and pray. And if you have a wife, both of you pray together; but if she is not yet baptized, go apart into another room and pray and return again to your bed. And be not slothful to pray. . . . It is necessary for the following reason to pray at this hour.
>
> Because the ancients who handed on the tradition to us have taught us that in this hour all creation pauses for a brief moment to praise the Lord. . . . [87]
>
> And at cockcrow, likewise rise (and pray). Because at that hour of cockcrow, the children of Israel denied Christ, who we have known by faith. . . . [88]

In all of the above statements, it appears that Hippolytus is professing to give the reader an accurate and authoritative account of the rites and organization of the Church in the sub-apostolic age relative to the obligation of all the faithful to prayers and the reading of Sacred Scripture. Therefore, praying at specific times of the day, seven according to Hippolytus, seems to be a well-established custom with the early Christians and reflects the original tradition of the Church.

While the Christian observance of the daily morning and evening hours of prayer seems to be generally recognized as a direct derivation through the hours of prayer in the synagogue, from the hours of the daily holocausts in the Jerusalem Temple, it is not very likely that the Christian hours of Terce, Sext, and None were based on any corresponding times of prayer in Judaism.[89] Thus it would not be a reliable approach to simply identify these hours with the Old Testament references in Daniel 6:10 and Psalms 4:13. It seems that the most likely theory is that terce, sext, and none simply formed the normal divisions of the day in the Roman world.[90] In addition, "if special times were to be allocated to prayer, it was natural to fix upon them, hallowed as they were for the Christian by the events connected with the Crucifixion."[91]

Concerning the private or public nature of these early prayers, there are some scholars who claim that all of these prayers of the early Church, including morning and evening prayers, were for the most part purely private devotions.[92] However, there is no evidence clear enough to completely dismiss the possibility of the daily public and communal dimension of at least morning and evening prayer.[93] Although Tertullian recommends the observance of the lesser hours, and simply takes for granted morning and evening prayer as an established part of every Christian's daily prayer life,[94] he does not reveal to us whether he is speaking about private or public prayer. However, while recommending the same hours of prayer, Cyprian asserts that prayer is public and common.[95] In the same vein, Origen affirms that daily prayer services were held in the Church of Alexandria characterized by the reading of Sacred Scripture, instruction and prayer.[96] Combined with the testimony of Hippolytus already cited above,[97] all of these references contribute to the stronger assumption that most likely by the end of the second century and in the early third century there were daily prayer services in both North Africa and Rome which the faithful were expected to attend.[98] But as open as this entire question may be to discussion up to the third century, we do know that through gradual stages of development, by the fourth century Christians did regularly gather publicly for these prayer services.

The Development of Public Prayer: Fourth to Sixth Centuries

The arrival of the fourth century witnessed to an era of significant development and formation for the Church. In the year 313 the Emperor Constantine issued the so-called Edict of Toleration which granted Christians full freedom of religion and worship. This new-found freedom and imperial favor had a profound effect upon the life of the Church particularly in her corporate, liturgical worship. Although Christians had gathered publicly in their own homes and churches in earlier times,[99] they had been considerably restricted both socially and culturally due to the tensions existing between themselves and a predominately pagan world in which they lived, a world which frequently expressed its hostility through open persecution.[100] Now with the official patronage of the Emperor Constantine, coupled with the endowment of numerous basilicas throughout the empire, the Church's life and worship experienced a new period of growth and development.[101] "From being the jealously, secluded action of an exclusive association, it was little by little transformed, as large and influential sections of society received baptism in increasing numbers, into a public activity of the population at large."[102]

Because of this new-found favor and freedom, Christians were now able to assemble publicly more frequently than for the celebration of the Eucharist alone. Since there already existed a well-developed Christian order of prayer outside of the Eucharistic celebration, it would only seem natural for the faithful to celebrate at least the principal hours of prayer in this manner.[103] One of the earliest witnesses to this practice, Eusebius of Caesarea (c. 263-339 A.D.), testifies that, in all the churches throughout the Christian world, at both sunrise and sunset, hymns and praises were raised to the Lord.

> The very fact that in God's churches throughout the world hymns, praises, and truly divine delights are arranged in his honor at the morning sunrise and in the evening is surely no small sign of God's power. These "delights of God" are the hymns sent up in his Church throughout the world both morning and evening.[104]

Epiphanius, Bishop of Salamis (c. 315-403), refers as well to these two prime times of prayer. "In addition morning praises and prayers are continuously celebrated in the universal Church as well as evening psalms and prayers."[105] And another early witness to the communal, public character of these times of prayer is St. John Chrysostom (c. 347-407), who in his commentary on 1 Tm. 2, wrote the following:

> What is the meaning of "first of all" in daily worship? Those soon to be baptized know that every day there are prayers both in the evening and the morning, and that we make supplication for the whole world, for rulers and all those of official dignity.[106]

Consequently, it seems quite clear that the popular, ecclesial character of both morning and evening prayer is not simply a gratuitous assumption, for at least from the beginning of the fourth century these two hours seem to have been normally celebrated with the people in the parochial churches.[107]

These liturgies were, under the new circumstances, appropriately solemn and impressive liturgies in which the fervent groups of laity were joined by their bishop and clergy in offering praise and thanksgiving to God. We get a taste of this in the *Apostolic Constitutions*, an ancient Church Order written about the year 380 as a manual of disciplinary and liturgical regulations for the Christian community. In this document the bishops are strongly urged to exhort all the faithful of their local communities to assemble daily for communal prayer.

> When you instruct the people, O Bishop, command and exhort them to make it a practice to come daily to the church in the morning and in the evening, and on no account to cease doing so, but to assemble together continually; neither to diminish the Church by withdrawing themselves, and causing the body of Christ to be without its member. For it is not only spoken concerning the priests; but let everyone of the laity hearken to it as concerning himself, esteeming that which was spoken by the Lord: "He who is not with me is against me and he who does not gather with me, scatters." Do not therefore scatter yourselves abroad, who are members of Christ, by not uniting the assemblies of the brethren. You who have Christ the head, according to his promise present and associated with us faithful, should not neglect your own care, nor should you deprive the Savior of his members, nor should you divide his body, nor should you disperse his members, neither should you give preference to the necessities of this life

over the word of God; but assemble yourselves everyday, morning and evening, singing psalms and praying in the Lord's house, in the morning saying the sixty-second psalm, and in the evening the one-hundred and fortieth psalm. Hasten to the church, therefore, with great desire and alacrity on the day of the Sabbath, and also on the day of the resurrection of the Lord, that is Sunday—the Day of the Lord, so that you may honor God with praises, who has built up all things through Jesus Christ, and who has sent him for us, permitted him to suffer, and has raised him from the dead.[108]

Therefore, in its early form this cult of prayer developed into the cathedral or parochial "Office," an official public prayer of the Church which involved the clergy and the entire community of the faithful,[109] and from which the present day Lauds and Vespers of the Divine Office were to ultimately evolve.[110] However, although the evidence seems to support the existence of an official custom of public, communal prayer in the Church of the fourth century, it does not provide us with absolute proof that this prayer was as yet fully organized. The first reliable evidence which we possess concerning the existence of a regular Office is provided by the pilgrim Egeria as recorded in the diary of her travels. In her fairly explicit and detailed description of the Jerusalem liturgy she recounts for us the existence of a well organized local liturgy of prayer wherein the faithful gathered daily for an established program of prayer together with their bishop and clergy. This program included the practice of *monazontes, parthenae* and dedicated laity coming day after day before dawn, to the Church of the Holy Sepulchre in Jerusalem to begin their prayers.[111] These prayers were continued throughout the day, at dawn, at midday, at three o'clock, at four o'clock and on till dusk. Most conspicuous in these daily offices were the morning and evening prayers since they were celebrated with greater solemnity and since more people were accustomed to participate, namely, the bishop, his clergy and the community of the faithful. In her *Diary of a Journey* (c. 381-384), Egeria recounts that:

All the doors of the Anastasis are opened before cock-crow each day, and the "monazontes and parthenae" as they call them here, come in, and also some lay men and women, at least those who are willing to wake at such an early hour. From then until daybreak they join in singing the refrains to the hymns, psalms, and antiphons. There is a prayer between each of the hymns, since there are two or three presbyters and deacons each day by rota, who are there with the monazontes and say the prayers between all the hymns and antiphons.

As soon as dawn comes, they start the Morning Hymns, and the Bishop with his clergy comes and joins them. He goes straight into the cave, and inside the screen he first says the Prayer of All (mentioning any names he wishes) and blesses the catechumens, and then another prayer and blesses the faithful. . . .

Again at midday everyone comes into the Anastasis and says psalms and antiphons until a message is sent to the Bishop. Again he enters. . . .

At three o'clock they do once more what they did at midday, but at four o'clock they have Lychnicon, as they call it, or in our language, Lucernare.[112]

From an examination of Egeria's diary we are able to determine some of the principal elements of this "cathedral" Office. The Christians gathered together in a public place to celebrate morning and evening prayers. While the bishop and his clergy did not initially participate in the service, they did enter in procession sometime during the liturgy to perform a specific function, namely, to officiate at the prayers and blessings. During the morning prayer service the people gathered to offer praise and thanksgiving to God for his mercy, while in the evening prayer service they assumed a penitential spirit asking God's forgiveness for the failings of the day. Psalms were not selected numerically but according to the spirit and purpose of the particular hour. For morning prayer the community usually recited Psalm 62 (63) and Psalms 148-150, and in the evening service Psalms 116 (117), 129 (130) and 141 (142). It is also evident that other antiphons and hymns were chanted but unfortunately we have no record of these. Both hours were then concluded with a litany of the catechumens, other prayers and a dismissal.[113] Out of all this historical evidence it seems clear that this cathedral or ecclesial tradition of the Office was the principal means used by the early Church to assemble publicly in order to give communal praise and thanksgiving to God especially at these principal hours of morning and evening.

The special importance attached to these times of prayer is best explained on the hypothesis that they represent the tradition of the primitive Church at Jerusalem, derived directly from synagogue practice and continued throughout that obscure period of which we have few, if any, records, until they became incorporated in the monastic Hours of Prayer sometime in the fourth century.[114]

Apart from her detailed and exceptionally valuable account of the program of prayer at the local Church of Jerusalem in the latter part of the fourth century, Egeria also makes us aware of the presence of the *monazontes* and *parthenae* at the daily liturgical offices conducted at the Anastasis. While these "monks" and "virgins" or "nuns" were most likely ascetics or *ferventes*,[115] Egeria's testimony to the fact of their constant presence at the daily prayer services, as well as her description of the well organized, ample and fairly formal liturgical celebrations conducted daily throughout the week is very significant. The inclusion of such daily, public prayer services as those in the early morning, at cock-crow, attended by the ascetics and *ferventes* with some dedicated secular lay men and women; the weekday nighttime vigils attended by the *monazontes* alone, outside of the solemn Sunday vigil which was attended by the entire Christian community; and the services at the third, sixth, and ninth hours,[116] alert us to the existence of a new "monastic" type current of prayer and spirituality which was making itself felt within the Church and which in turn would exert its own particular influence upon the cathedral Office.[117] We are in effect witnessing a formative period in the history of the Church's liturgical worship when the relatively simple pattern of worship previously celebrated by the ordinary clergy and laity was now being strongly influenced into a more expansive and formalized structure due to the particular needs of the growing number of ascetics and *ferventes* who apparently used the same parochial church edifices for their own daily worship.[118]

The entire phenomenon of monasticism involves an extremely complex and rich history. At this point we would be sorely tempted to examine this phenomenon in detail and to investigate such spiritual giants as Basil the Great (c. 330-379) in the East, John Cassian (c. 360-435) who spanned both East and West, and Benedict (c. 480-550) in the West, as well as their great influence upon the structure and use of the Liturgy of the Hours. However tempting and rewarding this would be, it would, nevertheless, be outside the scope of this study.

Since our primary concern is with the role of the laity in the celebration of the Hours and the consequent pastoral implications for our own day and age, such an investigation would simply take us unnecessarily afield. Therefore, my comments upon the phenomenon of monasticism will simply involve those aspects which have in some way influenced the degree of the participation of the laity in the Divine Office as it evolved over the centuries. There is an immense literature available on the subject of monasticism far too extensive to cite here.[119]

Therefore, in continuation of our development, we find a great phenomenon developing within the Church in these early centuries. More and more disillusioned people fled the world in order to live lives of greater isolation and of almost exclusive dedication to prayer. Throughout the fourth century this movement grew steadily and eventually gave rise to the formation of communities of like-minded individuals. Thus through their renunciation of the world, family and possessions, these communities could then devote their entire lives to the pursuit of spiritual perfection and to prayer in a way which was impossible for Christians still living in the world, including the clergy.[120] Although both the ordinary faithful and the ascetics prayed the Office together, freely and willingly, the ordinary faithful did so only to the degree that it was possible for them to do so in view of the everyday demands of their personal and family responsibilities, while the communities of ascetics were able to dedicate themselves to prayer with greater frequence and regularity.[121] Certainly, the fact that these "monks" had more or less totally abandoned the secular world and its particular responsibilities gave them the time and opportunity to dedicate themselves so willingly and freely to prayer in such a complete way for "prayer itself now became the sole undertaking replacing all other tasks."[122] Generally characteristic of these early "monastic" communities was the praying of the entire psalter "in course" over a prescribed period of time, and nocturnal prayer composed of fixed psalms, hymns, and various prayers, which were initiated at cockcrow, and which were terminated in the early hours of the morning when the traditional morning prayers began.[123]

Concurrent with the emergence and spread of monasticism, there occurred a gradual, almost universal growth within the Church of a twofold rhythm of liturgical prayer.

> The whole Christian community was called together for the morning and evening offices, for the vigils of great feasts and sometimes for the Sunday vigil. The monasteries kept a daily vigil and in the course of the day performed liturgical prayer at Terce, Sext, and None, adding almost everywhere a short prayer on rising and lying down—Prime and Compline.[124]

Throughout the fourth and fifth centuries, these two rhythms of prayer began to come together and intermingle. While this phenomenon certainly did not take place overnight, nor did it take effect throughout the Christian world to the same degree or at the same rate of speed, nevertheless, it did eventually lead to the merger of the cathedral and monastic rites into a twofold rite of public prayer within the Church.[125]

While the privileged site of Jerusalem seems to have been an ideal milieu for the introduction of the early monastic influence into the life of the local church, a similar type phenomenon was developing in other local churches as well. In Rome, for instance, by as early as the mid-fifth century, "monasticism" was already exerting a powerful influence upon local worship through the building of basilica convents, the duty of whose resident "monks" was to sing the Office in its full monastic cycle in the neighboring basilica.[126]

With this process now well under way, there would eventually rise in the West a single, mixed tradition which would come to be known as the urban-monastic tradition. In order to more clearly understand this situation we should first briefly examine the state of the secular clergy at the time, for any influence exerted by the "monastics" on the development of the Office was abetted by the conditions prevalent in the life of the secular clergy.

At the beginning of the fifth century, the clerics belonged to the clergy of a definite church presided over by a resident bishop. They would take part in the liturgical services of this church participating in the daily public prayers and sharing in its pastoral ministry.[127] Thus the liturgical life of the community was very centralized and localized in the cathedral church. Inevitably, however, beginning with the sixth century, some decentralization began to take place as secondary churches began to spring up around the cathedral church in order to meet the pastoral needs of a growing Christian community. This development initially took place only in a relatively few city centers, principal among which was Rome, since at this time Christianity remained essentially urban with only a very gradual spreading into the countryside. However, despite this development these secondary churches continued to be dependent upon the principal church and their clergy maintained their relationship to the bishop forming his presbyterum. This dependence was emphasized at the time by the fact that these churches were not permitted to celebrate the Sacrament of Baptism or to celebrate the Office on feast days.[128]

> Thanks to the grouping of all its clergy under the direction of the bishop, each church thus realized to a certain extent the life of the first Christian community, the "apostolic life." And the local church, the church wherein the celebration of the Divine Office was carried out each day and the sacraments were administered, was the title by which the cleric was ordained.
>
> The spread of Christianity, by bringing about the establishment of urban parishes around the *ecclesia senior*, afterwards the creation of rural parishes, and the construction of basilicas over the tombs of martyrs produced no essential change in this state of affairs. In each of these churches a clergy took shape, composed of the different orders—to which even *cantores* and *psalmistae* were frequently added—having at its head a priest, an archpriest or an abbot, living in common, praying in common, and recruiting for itself by means of its school-seminary. . . .
>
> The liturgy of the fifth to the eighth century must be seen in this ecclesiastical environment: the office was then the prayer of each local church, celebrated by the clerics who were in its service. This celebration could not be the same everywhere; above all, it could not everywhere be invested with the same solemnity: everything depended on the number and rank of the clergy of each church.[129]

Of particular interest in this entire development is the role of the laity in these church Offices. Egeria has already left us a memorable account of the Jerusalem liturgy of the late fourth century in which the participation of the clergy and at least the devout laity, in both morning and evening prayer, was a customary practice.[130] And despite the scarcity of sources we are able to conclude with reasonable certitude that in the fifth and sixth centuries this practice had also been customary in the West, at least within the regions of Italy, North Africa, Spain, and Southern Gaul.[131] In Milan the participation of the people in these prayer services is clearly referred to by St. Ambrose (c. 339-397), when he exhorts his people to faithfully attend these liturgical celebrations since they have been apparently negligent in doing so.

> . . . early in the morning hasten to church offering your first pious prayers, and afterwards if material necessities call you, do not forget to say: "Early in the morning my eyes reminded me to meditate upon your words," and then you can start your work. How joyful it is to start the day with hymns and songs from the beatitudes which you read in the Gospel![132]

Another early witness to this same liturgical practice was St. Augustine of Hippo (354-430) when he attested to the devotion of his mother, Monica, describing her going to church daily both in the morning and in the evening that she might hear God in his word and he might hear her in her prayers.[133] He also refers to the devotion of the entire community as daily they recite prayers and sing hymns and psalms in common,[134] as well as to the individual, zealous Christian who like an ant "runs daily to the church of God, to pray, to listen to the lesson, to sing the hymn and to ruminate on what he had heard."[135] This testifies clearly to the use of readings as well as psalms as was also evident in the Office at Milan in the time of Ambrose.[136] These liturgical hours affirmed above by both Augustine and Ambrose were obviously not Eucharistic celebrations but were most certainly daily hours of prayer, in the morning and evening, in which both clergy and laity participated. Therefore, it seems justifiable to conclude that within the Latin Church at the close of the early Christian times both clergy and laity celebrated in common a daily Office consisting of a Morning Hour and an Evening Vespers.[137]

While these Offices seemed to assume the presence of the clergy they were, nevertheless, geared primarily for the people's participation and were consequently comparatively short consisting of psalms, reading (homily), hymns, intercessions, and concluding prayers. By the end of the fifth century, morning and evening prayer emerged as the two focal points of this daily church Office in which both clergy and laity actively participated.[138] At this time it seems that the church leaders began to consider the celebration of the Office as an obligation incumbent upon themselves and their clergy. For instance in Rome itself, in a document dating from the end of the sixth or the beginning of the seventh century, we learn of an oath taken by suburbicarian bishops on the occasion of their consecration promising the Pope that together with their clergy they would be faithful to the celebration of the daily vigil.[139] The necessity for such an oath seems to indicate the presence of some problems with the constancy of the Roman clergy in the celebration of the Vigils. Apparently the same problem existed in Spain and Gaul and consequently throughout the sixth century the church authorities in all these territories were obliged to issue a number of canons wherein they insisted that the clergy participate in the recitation of the Office as in the past. This insistence was enforced through the provision of sanctions against those clerics who absented themselves from the public recitation of the Office.[140] In the year 528 the Emperor Justinian issued a decree in which he commanded the local clergy to participate in the Vigils as well as in Lauds and Vespers under pain of expulsion from the clerical ranks.[141] Unfortunately, however, despite these strong directives the negligence of the bishops and the clergy toward the liturgical life of their churches gradually became more prevalent as the bishops became increasingly involved in politics and the administration of their extensive domains.[142]

In the meantime, a class of faithful, who in principle embodied a life of perfection somewhat similar to that of the desert monks except without such a radical withdrawal from the world, began to make their influence felt in the sacramental and euchological institutions of the existing Christian communities. These were the type of monks such as the *monazontes* and *ascetae* of Jerusalem as we have already noted, the monks who were serving the Roman basilicas, or the *ferventes* or *devoti* of those monasteries of the Frankish kingdom.[143] This type of monk, contrary to the desert monks yet no less fervent, made liturgical prayer rather than asceticism the basis of their particular devotion and consequently exerted a strong influence upon the formation of the Divine Office in the parish churches.[144] It is to these monks, and more particularly to those of the Roman basilicas, that we can credit the establishment of the complete framework of the daily Hours and the assignment of particular psalms to certain Offices.[145] This, however, does not affirm the existence of a general uniformity in the celebration of the Hours. In fact, in the West, there was no such uniformity at least down to the ninth century.[146] Initially, each monastery basilica or group of monks continued to celebrate their own particular cursus of prayer. Eventually, however, because of certain similarities between them and because of the stronger influence of some dominant groups, there would evolve a greater uniformity of observance, as for instance in the Roman basilica monasteries.[147]

Within this period the people continued to come to church to pray the morning and evening Offices as often as they could with their bishops and clergy,[148] but because of practical limitations on their time and in the face of a general liturgical decline, the continuous and more comprehensive recitation of the Office was ensured in the cathedrals and greater churches by these various groups of monks.[149] However, while the stability and content of prayer was undoubtedly improved in many regards, a certain trend began to develop which would eventually cause a decided shift from the parishes to the monasteries as the centers of liturgical celebration.

Developments in the Middle Ages

It is an extremely difficult undertaking to be able to accurately trace the history of the Office in the city churches from the fourth century when the monastic movement began to flourish, and through the sixth, seventh, or eighth centuries when it gradually exerted a greater influence upon the singing of the Divine Office in the cathedrals and greater churches. From all the scattered and often confusing references that we do have, it appears that the local clergy attached to the cathedrals and other prominent churches, continued the traditional practice of the daily recitation of morning and evening prayers together with the people, and on certain occasions the observance of the nocturnal Vigils.[150] These Hours were very much part of the public prayer services of the church and not private devotions. On the other hand, within this period there still was no uniform Office celebrated throughout the Church of the West, for the great church centers in Italy, Gaul, and Spain continued to retain their own essential traditions, books, and ordering of the Office.[151] However, throughout the course of the fifth to the ninth centuries, the daily chanting of the Office in the Roman basilicas, as well as in many of the great churches outside of Rome, became more and more shaped by the monastic tradition.

As the monastic presence grew with the increased number of monasteries and monks, in and around Rome for instance, their influence upon the parish Office became more and more pronounced. While initially participating along with the clergy and laity in the celebration of the morning and evening Hours in the parish church, they continued to recite their expanded monastic cursus of prayer within their own oratories.[152] But this situation eventually helped to influence the local church communities to incorporate a program of prayer which more closely approached the more elaborate and fully developed monastic cursus. Although the fervor and magnificence of the monastic Offices contributed much toward attracting the faithful and causing the clergy to imitate the monks, to the degree that this was practical and possible, this process did not take place without protest. The clerics of Rome, for instance, resisted the imposition of the obligation to celebrate Vigils.[153] However, as an increasing number of monks were elected bishops, they tended to introduce monastic usages into their dioceses such as the inclusion of the Hours of Terce, Sext, and None each day in the Cathedral Office.[154] While this phenomenon was sporadic and uneven in its development, it nevertheless continued to progress inexorably toward a monasticisation of the prayer of the Church.

The Benedictines in particular exerted a singular influence toward this monasticisation of the Office. Initially affected by the liturgical practice of the Roman church, their own prayer order now found its way back into the monasteries of Rome and in turn effected its own unique influence.[155] Eventually this new order of prayer was adopted by the Roman basilicas and even the Vatican basilica itself,[156] and through the testimony of the many pilgrims and monks who came through Rome, it gradually spread itself throughout the West.[157] Notably, this Office reflected the responsibility of a particular community for the praying of all the Hours, from Vigils to evening

Compline, within the course of a single day. This was not a new idea in itself since as early as the mid-fifth century, long before Benedict's time, there were already existing in Rome convents staffed by "monks" whose principal duty was to sing the Office in its full monastic cycle within the basilicas to which they were attached, thereby ensuring the celebration of a full monastic Office within these churches.[158] However, the Benedictine Office did exert a very definite and unique influence of its own, part of which was the introduction of several new monastic elements into the Office such as the opening versicles, responses and hymns.[159] But the decisive influence the Benedictine reform had upon the Office was in eventually effecting the imposition of the solemn and daily celebration of the full monastic Office upon the resident clergy of all churches and parishes.[160] Consequently, wherever the Benedictine Rule became established it exerted a very powerful influence upon single communities thereby eventually affecting the general celebration of the Office throughout the West.[161]

Pope Gregory the Great (590-604) played a singularly important role in this entire process. As an ardent promoter of Benedictine monasticism, he employed the Benedictine monks as his principal emissaries in the evangelization of the rest of Europe, and thereby helped to spread the Roman liturgy throughout the Western world. In 596, he sent Augustine (of Canterbury) along with forty monks to evangelize England.[162] This mission proved to be singularly decisive for, through the example and leadership of Augustine and his band of monks, and that of his successors, the Roman liturgy, and the Office in particular, became firmly established in England.[163] In the late seventh and early eighth centuries a similar mission sent back to the continent from England proved to be equally influential in establishing the same Roman Office throughout the continent. St. Boniface (680-754), an English Benedictine monk, known as the Apostle of Germany, was especially effective in helping to spread the Roman liturgy and Office in all the countries north of the Alps.[164] Consequently, both in England and throughout those regions of Gaul which had come under the influence of this Anglo-Saxon mission, the Roman Office recited by the monks and the Roman basilicas gradually began to spread to all the churches.[165] This movement, known on the continent as the "reform" of St. Boniface, served as a prelude to the Carolingian "renaissance."[166] In the mid-eighth century it was the Frankish king Pepin III, son of Charles Martel, who together with his brothers and most likely under the influence of the Anglo-Saxon monks, sought to effectively establish the Roman rite in all of Gaul.[167] This same goal was shared and carried to fulfillment by his son, the Emperor Charlemagne. Concerning the Roman Office, it was he who was responsible for the issuance of many decrees which sought to ensure its daily celebration in all the churches of the empire.[168] Throughout this period of liturgical reform, therefore, thanks to the Benedictine influence, it became the general practice to celebrate daily the Roman Office in all the collegiate churches and chapels of the empire, just as it was celebrated in the imperial chapel at Aix-la-Chapelle.[169] Simultaneously, while the obligation for all monks to the choral recitation of the entire Office already had been forcefully and precisely laid down by rule and sanction,[170] the same obligation became gradually imposed upon the secular clergy as well.[171]

With the flowering of the Carolingian renaissance through the ninth century, the Romanization of the liturgy and Benedictine reform arrived at their logical climax with the high standard of monastic observance exemplified in the congregation at Cluny, whose decisive influence upon the liturgical worship of the Church would be felt throughout the tenth, eleventh, and twelfth centuries.[172] However, despite the introduction of the Roman liturgy into the Frankish kingdom, this liturgy soon became encumbered with supplemental practices and local customs eventually representing a heterogeneous mixture with little conformity to the original liturgy of Rome.[173] The work of Amalar of Metz (c. 780-850/1) is especially indicative of this trend.[174] It is this "Gallicanized" liturgy with its reshaped, mixed Frankish-Roman Office which in the tenth century makes its way back to Rome and influences the liturgical practices of the Eternal City itself.[175] At this time the Church at Rome was experiencing a general liturgical decline which adversely affected the celebration of the Divine Office as it continued to grow in volume and complexity becoming more and more of a burden to the secular clergy.[176] Despite the efforts of Pope Gregory VII (1073-1085) to initiate reforms, his efforts did little to rectify the situation,[177] and because of the frequent political problems which kept the papacy in a constant state of turmoil, the sad condition of the Roman liturgy persisted throughout the following century.[178]

In the course of the eleventh and twelfth centuries, the Office continued to grow when several new Offices were added to the full monastic cursus, such as the Office of the Dead and that of the Blessed Virgin Mary, as well as the seven penitential psalms, the fifteen gradual psalms, the Litany of the Saints, and a host of other prayers and rubrical elements.[179] It followed that, as a result of all these developments, the distinction between the ecclesial and monastic Offices now was no longer apparent. This did not mean, however, that absolute uniformity had been achieved in the celebration of the Office. Despite essential uniformity, there continued to exist certain divergences among many of the chuches in the West which had adopted the Roman rite, although they were relatively peripheral differences at best.[180] All of these events would gradually but radically change the role of the laity in the public, communal celebration of the Divine Office. In this entire development a certain pattern becomes increasingly clear. With the advent of the urban-monastic Office, and with the imposed obligation not only upon monks but upon the secular clergy as well, the choral recitation of the Office becomes essentially a matter for monks and clerics with the laity becoming less and less involved.

Throughout this period of history there was a growing separation occurring between the official liturgical activities of the Church and the worshiping community of the faithful. While the reasons for this general alienation are many and complex, as far as the Divine Office was concerned, certainly one of the principal reasons was this monasticisation of the Office and its continued development through the many accretions already cited into an elaborate and complicated prayer of excessive length. While this trend toward growth and elaboration had been initiated as early as the eighth century, in a very gradual and inconsistent manner it continued up into the eleventh century as exemplified in the community at Cluny. Under the definitive influence of Cluny, not only did the Office grow to excessive length, but the splendor and solemnity of its celebration was greatly increased as well.[181] Thus the Office had now become a prayer whose celebration was more suited to a community of monks who not only possessed the proper training but who also had the time available to pray the full cursus of the Hours in the magnificent and solemn manner which was required. While as an obligation this proved to be a tremendous burden for the secular clergy, for a predominately unlettered laity, who in general possessed neither the proper training nor the available time, their free participation proved to be all the more curtailed and difficult.

With the papacy of Innocent III (1198-1216), the Church experienced a new period of liturgical renaissance, witnessed in part by the compilation of the Office of the Papal Curia.[182] Substantially retaining the characteristics of the old Roman monastic Office, this "new" Office was marked by a much greater simplicity and austerity of style than the Romano-Frankish Office now firmly established in the Roman basilicas and was therefore much better suited to the needs of the times.[183] Eventually, since most likely it had become part of the liturgy of the cathedral of Assisi, and also because of very practical considerations, the Franciscan Order adopted this convenient and relatively easy-to-carry liturgical book, or breviary, which was in use at the papal court. Carrying their breviaries with them wherever they traveled, these itinerant preachers were instrumental in spreading this Office throughout Europe, the East, and Africa as well.[184] While initially this Papal Office was an improvement over the complex and disproportionately lengthy Romano-Frankish Office and consequently was well received everywhere, eventually it too, in its own turn proved to be unsatisfactory in properly meeting the contemporary spiritual needs of both clergy and laity.[185]

The Formation of the Breviary

Throughout these centuries, although the laity was being increasingly alienated from the public, liturgical worship of the Church, the Divine Office was still, at least in principle, considered to be a community prayer. However, as the concept of the corporateness of the Church and its public worship continued to break down, the practice of the public, communal recitation of the Office continued to diminish.

With the advent of the Breviary in the twelfth century,[186] this situation was further aggravated, for now the personal obligation of the private recitation of the Office facilitated the eventual transformation of this one-time communal act of worship into a private prayer book for the clergy.[187] With the continued spread of private recitation, the choral, communal celebration of the Office, although still practiced, became less and less a reality for the clergy, a practice which unfortunately had ramifications for the laity and which was far removed from the traditional concept.[188]

By the latter part of the Middle Ages the Divine Office had grown into so elaborate a prayer that from the close of the fifteenth century up to the Council of Trent (1545-1563), it became the object of almost continual reform. As the Middle Ages drew to a close, the cry for reform became more and more manifest. Before the Council of Trent, the Spanish Cardinal Francisco de Quinonez (d. 1540) was commissioned by Pope Clement VII (1523-1534) to restore the Office as far as possible to its ancient form, said restoration to be characterized by a simplification of the Office, a return to the Fathers of the Church, and a greater degree of historical accuracy.[189] In undertaking this reform the principal intention of Cardinal Quinonez was to revise the Hours so that they could more easily be recited privately by those clerics who were very involved in the pastoral ministry. In essence this revision "treated the Office, at least in practice, as a private prayer; in contrast to the Catholic idea of worship, it stressed the doctrinal end of the Office at the expense of that of divine praise. . . ."[190] Hence the view of the Office as primarily a personal obligation for religious and secular clergy is now given even further impetus. While initially the breviary of Cardinal Quinonez enjoyed great success, eventually the radical nature of this reform began to attract increasing opposition from the clergy.[191] In answer to the growing criticism among churchmen over the structure of this revised breviary further reforms were initiated by the Council of Trent which would eventually culminate in the revised breviary of 1568.[192]

The object of a special commission appointed by Pope Paul IV (1555-1565), was not to compose a new breviary, but to restore the old breviary of the Roman Curia, which was then still in use, to its original form, always keeping in mind the contemporary needs of the Church.[193] In the resultant reformed *Breviarium Romanum* promulgated by Pope Pius V (1566-1572) in 1568, "the fact that the breviary is a public prayer is heavily stressed, and the difference between public (choral) and private recitation almost entirely eliminated."[194] While in itself this reaffirmation of the Divine Office as a public prayer of the Church seems to be a very encouraging development, on the other hand the Council Fathers outrightly rejected the petition of certain reformers requesting that for doctrinal reasons the Church abandon further use of the Latin language in public worship and resort to the vernacular languages.[195] Therefore, despite some encouraging attempts by the Council of Trent to reform liturgical worship, the common Christian worshiper was still to be denied his rightful role of full, active participation in the liturgical prayer life of the Church.

From the Council of Trent to the Modern Liturgical Movement

Throughout the Middle Ages these developments had continued to contribute to the growing alienation between the laity and the public, communal celebration of the Divine Office. In spite of this trend, however, the parochial celebration of the Office managed to survive in varying degrees throughout Europe. People continued to participate as best they could under the circumstances and these services were generally well attended, especially for Matins sung before Mass and for Vespers on Sundays and Holy Days.[196] Such prominent churchmen of the period as St. Ignatius Loyola (1491/5-1556) and St. Francis de Sales (1567-1622) recommended the Office highly as a very special form of prayer. In his *Spiritual Exercises,* St. Ignatius affirmed the following:

> We ought to praise the frequent hearing of Mass, the singing of hymns, psalmody, the long prayers whether in the church or outside; likewise, the Hours arranged at fixed times for the whole Divine Office, for every kind of prayer, and for the canonical Hours.[197]

Yet when founded in 1540 the Society of Jesus did not have the obligation of communal recitation of the Divine Office, a fact which would have been unthinkable at an earlier period of time such as at the foundation of the Franciscans or Dominicans.[198] Likewise St. Francis de Sales in *The Introduction to the Devout Life* urged Philothea:

> Besides this (meditation and Mass) Philothea, you should assist at the Office of the Hours and of Vespers on feast days and Sundays, as far as it is convenient for you to do so; because these days are dedicated to God, ...there is ever more good and consolation in the public offices of the Church than in what is done individually, God having so ordained that what is done in common should be preferred to every kind of individual action.[199]

Originating in the fourteenth century and continuing to proliferate until the mid-twentieth century were a variety of Books of Hours for the laity and for lay religious.[200] Essentially these books contained such prayers as the Little Office of the Blessed Virgin Mary, the Office of the Dead, the Gradual and the Seven Penitential Psalms, the Litany of the Saints, and other such popular devotional prayers. Though in their own right these prayers were certainly praiseworthy, they were not really the canonical Office but simply votive derivatives from it. However, since the laity were being more and more effectively cut off from active and communal participation in the official prayer of the Church, these devotions did serve to bridge the gap which had developed between the prayer life of the faithful and the official prayer life of the Church. While the canonical Office was subject to certain variances, these devotions offered the people a relatively stable, and simpler form of prayer which enabled them to participate in spirit and at least to some degree, in form, in the canonical prayer of the Church.[201]

While the seventeenth century witnessed reforms of the Roman Breviary by Popes Clement VIII (1592-1605), Urban VIII (1623-1644), and Clement X (1669-1676), these reforms were not of great consequence and did nothing to restore the laity to full, active participation in the Office.[202] In the last analysis, however, the Latin liturgy proved to be a most formidable obstacle to this type of participation by the laity, a large portion of whom were uneducated. Those who were better educated were able to continue to participate but only to a degree. This alienation of language had long been a major problem which had contributed greatly to the estrangement of the laity from the public, communal celebration of the Office. Through the ages, because the Church had for the most part failed to make the liturgy linguistically adapted to the national languages which were emerging, the liturgy had become something increasingly foreign and almost completely incomprehensible to the Christian communities in general. Although our remarks are restricted to these developments in the West, the East had essentially undergone a like process of alienation albeit to a lesser degree.

While there were movements within the Church concerned with the correction of this problem, they were not successful in reversing this trend, for the Church authorities continually saw fit to reject their efforts. We have already noted such efforts rejected by the Council Fathers during the Council of Trent.[203] This attitude of the official Church authorities continued to persist as witnessed by the papal bull *Unigenitus*, issued by Pope Clement XI (1700-1721) on 8 September 1713. This papal bull rejected the eighty-sixth proposition of Quesnel (Quesnel: "To deprive the common people of the consolation of combining their own prayers with those of the whole Church is a usage repugnant to the practice of the Apostles and to the designs of God"), and on 28 August 1794, Pope Pius VI (1775-1799) condemned article sixty-six of the Synod of Pistoia (Pius VI: "The use of the vernacular in liturgical prayers is false and foolhardy...").[204] Thus, not only was the Divine Office becoming dominated by the monks and clergy through Church legislation, but it was also being celebrated in a language, namely Latin, which was essentially foreign and incomprehensible to the majority of the members of the Christian community.

From the time of the promulgation of the renewed *Breviarium Romanum* by Pope Pius V in 1568, to the time of Pope Pius X (1903-1914) no significant change was effected in the breviary despite various efforts at its reform.[205] It was only with the advent of the modern liturgical movement, and the first initiatives of Pope Pius X, with their eventual culmination in the convocation of the Second Vatican Council in 1964, that truly significant reform, related to the Divine Office as a prayer for all the People of God, was effected.

As we have attempted to demonstrate through this brief historical development, the Divine Office has undergone some dramatic changes from the age of the Early Church to this our own day. While this prayer originated as a hope-filled public expression of the communal worship of the early Christian community, it eventually evolved into an almost exclusive prayer of religious and clergy with little or no regard for the role of the faithful. That which had originated as a public liturgical expression of the faith of the Christian community gradually became the "official prayer" of the Church imposed by law upon the clergy. In effect, the prayer of the Divine Office had become essentially lost to the laity. It is only with the present-day reform of the Office that a serious attempt has been made to restore this treasured prayer to its rightful place as a public act of worship involving all the members of the Christian community.

It now devolves upon priests and religious to be conscious and appreciative of this restoration of the Divine Office and to promote it as a prayer of the whole Church, rather than have it remain as the official prayer of a select few. It is the hope of this study, from this point on, to examine this reform and its implications for the Church and to suggest ways and means by which this renewal could be effectively incorporated into the liturgical life of the Church today.

II

The Reform of the Liturgy of the Hours
From the Modern Liturgical Movement
to the Second Vatican Council

In the previous chapter we were presented with a brief historical survey of the Liturgy of the Hours as the communal prayer of the Church. Beginning with its Judaic heritage and its subsequent development in the early Christian Church, the evolution of this prayer was traced down through the ages to the modern liturgical movement. Throughout, we sought to highlight those major trends which initially made the Office a prayer for the whole Church and which eventually caused it to become the exclusive prayer of religious and clergy to the exclusion of the community of the faithful. The present century has borne witness to two trends evolving in Catholic thought concerning the Liturgy of the Hours. The first and by far the most prevalent trend has been that which has sought to improve this prayer making it a more accessible and rewarding experience for the clergy, many of whom had great difficulties with the obligation of its private recitation. The second trend, initially more subtle but in relatively recent times most clearly enunciated, seeks to reestablish the Liturgy of the Hours as the public, communal prayer for all the People of God. It is this second trend which most directly concerns us in the following phase of this study.

The Modern Liturgical Movement

When we speak of the modern liturgical movement, we refer to a phenomenon which did not simply have a spontaneous birth, but one which had been gradually growing through the influencing factors of certain important events as well as the pioneering work of many great scholars.[1] Consequently, it is very difficult to pinpoint a precise starting point for this liturgical period. However, as far as the Liturgy of the Hours is concerned, our interest is focused primarily upon that period of time beginning with the liturgical reforms of Pope St. Pius X (1903-1914) up to and including the reforms of the Second Vatican Council.

As we have previously noted, from the pontificate of Pope Pius V and the promulgation of the renewed *Breviarium Romanum* in 1568 to the pontificate of Pope Pius X, no significant changes were effected in the Liturgy of the Hours despite many attempts at reform.[2] With his ascendancy to the papacy in 1903, Pope Pius X chose as his guiding principle "to restore all things in Christ," (Eph. 1:10). Animated by an astute and sensitive pastoral judgment, as well as by a great love and respect for the Church's most authentic traditions, he sought to meet the needs of the times by giving a new impetus to the reform of the liturgy, a reform which had been so often asked for in the past and which unfortunately had been so long neglected. In 1903, in an attempt to reawaken the true Christian spirit of worship in which all the faithful would be actively involved, the Pope issued his famous motu proprio, *Tra le sollecitudini*, on *The Restoration of Church Music*.[3] Within this document he firmly delineated the rules for the use of chant and sacred music but at the same time pleaded for the restoration of the true role of the faithful in the liturgical worship of the Church. In the introduction to this important motu proprio we are told:

> It being our ardent desire to see the true Christian spirit restored in every respect and be preserved by all the faithful, we deem it necessary to provide before everything else for the sanctity and dignity of the temple, in which the faithful assemble for the object of acquiring this spirit from its foremost and indispensable fount, which is the active participation in the holy mysteries and in the public and solemn prayer of the Church.[4]

Whether totally aware of the full implications of this statement or not, the Holy Father seemed to be making a rather explicit plea that the faithful once again be allowed to participate actively and fully in all the public and solemn liturgies of the Church.

On December 22, 1905, inspired by the words and wishes of Pope Pius X, the Sacred Conciliar Congregation sought to further implement the restoration of the liturgy as the center of the Christian life by issuing the important decree on the daily reception of the Eucharist, *Sacra Tridentina Synodus*.[5] While the wide-ranging implications of this important document would not be fully realized for many years to come, it did represent a further meaningful step in the right direction. Six years later, on July 2, 1911, moving swiftly in his program of liturgical reform, the Pope established a commission for the purpose of attempting to restore some order once again to the Breviary.

> The two major disorders caused by the many feasts with special Offices were that the Psalter was seldom recited in its entirety and the Scriptural readings, too, were often excluded. And so the same old problem of reconciling the rights of temporal and sanctoral cycles had to be faced. The commission set two objectives before itself: (a) to make the ferial Office once again functional, and (b) to maintain the feasts of the saints.[6]

Despite many difficulties the commission was somewhat successful in its reform through the establishment of a mixed Office which comprised both temporal and sanctoral cycles. This was achieved principally through a redistribution of the Psalms throughout the Hours with a greater preservation of the dignity of Sunday and the Sacred Scriptures. However, there seemed to be no awareness on the part of the commission concerning the question of the active participation of the laity in this prayer according to the principles so beautifully expressed by Pope Pius X only eight years previously. While this reform of the Breviary proved to be quite successful to a certain degree, it still fell far short of its potential in many respects.

> However, the rubrics still remained too numerous and complicated. They continued the heavy rubrical tradition and the mentality that all ought to be meticulously predisposed and everything tacitly fixed. There was no indication at all of the atmosphere of freedom and variety which marked the ancient liturgy. The reformers seemed to see no need to adapt the Breviary to diverse persons, places, and situations.[7]

When this reformed Breviary was officially promulgated with the issuance of the Apostolic Constitution *Divino afflatu, The New Arrangement of the Psalter in the Roman Breviary*,[8] on November 1, 1911, Pope Pius X, seemingly aware of its shortcomings, also announced future plans for a more ample revision of the Office. This ambitious and promising amplification was unfortunately left unrealized due to the death of the Pontiff in 1914.

At first sight, it would seem somewhat incredible that these wonderful liturgical incentives, initiated during the Pontificate of Pope Pius X, did not have a more immediate, practical and pastoral effect upon the Church's liturgical life. However, when examined in the full light of the times and circumstances into which these new directives were proclaimed this fact does not seem so strange at all. This is so because while the principles in themselves were certainly praiseworthy, they remained nevertheless as relatively isolated statements conditioned by a particular view which the Church had of itself and of the People of God.

> . . . they did not have any practical follow-up in the other documents of Pope Pius X and of the Roman Curia. In other words, they were propositions which were not properly explained or propagated and consequently were not adaptable for translation into practical use from a theology which had revealed to the faithful the wonderful mystery and the dynamic context of the Church at prayer.[9]

However, while the reforms of Pope Pius X may seem to have had certain limitations, no one can deny that they did represent a very important step and a springboard toward the eventual reestablishment of that vital union between the faithful and the liturgy which had been lost so many years before. Thus, the powerful pastoral incentives of the Holy Father, characterized by the motu proprio, *Tra le sollecitudini,* by his reform of the Roman Breviary and by his reestablishment of frequent reception of the Eucharist as a normal aspect of the Christian life, helped to lead the way toward an eventual rediscovery of the liturgy as true prayer.

> And he had, by the same means, led the way toward a new realization of the fundamental principle that the liturgy is something which we are not meant merely to see or to hear, but which we are, above all, to take part, as in the traditional and collective glorification of God, bringing before Him the whole individual man in the whole Christian community.[10]

In the meantime, inspired by the liturgical incentives of Pope Pius X's pastoral concerns, a powerful new voice now began to be heard on their behalf. Dom Lambert Beauduin, a Benedictine monk of Mont-Cesar, seemingly grasped the full import of the Holy Father's exhortations on the sacred liturgy and church music and gave them the strong pastoral application they called for. For eight years he had been a diocesan priest in the Belgian diocese of Liege dedicated to the social ministry of the working class, providing material and spiritual help to the indigent population. In 1906, at the age of thirty-three, Dom Beauduin entered the Benedictine monastery of Mont-Cesar at Louvain and was soon assigned as Professor of Theology to the young student monks. He brought to this new vocation not only his extensive pastoral experience as a diocesan priest, but also a great zeal for souls as well as a deep personal piety and a profound interest and knowledge in the Christian dogmas which he had been assigned to teach. It is in the rich context of this pastoral heritage, coupled with his teaching and studying of dogma that Dom Beauduin was able to come to a true realization and profound appreciation of the incalculable power of the liturgy in the life of the People of God as previously envisioned by Pope St. Pius X. For this dedicated priest the liturgy was meant to be at the heart of the Christian life of all God's people and not simply to be a reserve for a select few. "He himself, led by the teaching of the Pope and by his own Christian and priestly experience, had come to rediscover the liturgy as the prayer and worship of the Christian people."[11]

In 1909, at the Catholic Conference of Malines, Belgium, given the opportunity to openly express his convictions, Dom Beauduin proposed a practical program for a liturgical renewal which would reiterate and promote the pastoral concerns of Pope Pius X and carry them a step further. The central idea of this program was to have all the faithful live a common spiritual life nourished by the official worship of Holy Mother Church. This was to be effected through a translation of the Roman Missal and its promotion among the faithful as their principal prayer book, as well as the promotion of Gregorian chant, with an attendant spiritual and liturgical formation of choirs, through retreats in liturgical centers such as Benedictine monasteries. Also included in this program was a special place afforded to the role of the Divine Office. "Seconding all efforts to preserve or to reestablish the

Vespers and Compline of Sunday, and to give to these services a place second only to that of the Holy Sacrifice of the Mass."[12]

That the Divine Office was to play such a vital role in this entire movement was not surprising, for Dom Lambert attached great importance to its place in the liturgical renewal of the Christian life. He felt very strongly that through the recitation of Compline as evening prayer, and through attendance at the parochial recitation of Vespers the piety of the faithful could be more fully and actively integrated into the Christian mysteries. Toward this end he very strongly advocated the restoration of earlier liturgical traditions in Christian homes.

> Centering around this hearth of the divine life (the Eucharistic Sacrifice) is the Divine Office, which establishes an uninterrupted exchange of praises and benedictions between heaven and earth, associates the Christian people, through their priests, with the liturgy of eternity and diffuses the blessings of the morning sacrifice over all the hours of the day and night.[13]

Acutely aware of the needs of both the faithful and the clergy he very wisely realized that unless the clergy was first convinced of the spiritual power of the liturgy, any hopes of applying these principles to the lives of the faithful would inevitably end in failure. Fortunately, Dom Beauduin's inspired views did not remain merely in the realm of theory but were soon translated into a practical program of pastoral action. With the monastery of Mont-Cesar established as the center for carrying out this program, these ideas became disseminated principally through the publication of a small people's missal published in fascicles, followed by a review entitled *La Vie liturgique,* published at Mont-Cesar, Louvain in 1910. Still in existence today and still highly respected, it is now entitled *Les Questions liturgiques et paroissiales.*[14] These wonderful publications, while extremely popular and influential in themselves, were also actively supported by the establishment at Mont-Cesar of the conferences of the *Semaines liturgiques.* With the words of Pope Pius X as their constant source of inspiration, Dom Lambert and his followers were always mindful of the pastoral needs of the Church. Consequently, they did everything in their power not only to reawaken the interest of both clergy and laity in the exciting and challenging mysteries of the liturgy but also to make them aware, by means of a clear, prudent and progressive presentation, that the active participation of all the faithful in the liturgical life of the Church is at the heart of the supernatural life of the Christian.[15] There is no question that the inspired work of Dom Lambert Beauduin and his followers had a lasting pastoral effect upon the Church through the launching of the highly influential Belgian liturgical movement.[16] Anything that followed of any consequence concerning the liturgy was primarily due to these providential initiatives.

Momentarily halted by the outbreak of the First World War, the liturgical movement once again began to grow and develop when hostilities had ceased, spreading its influence throughout Europe. In Germany, where just prior to the war, liturgical initiatives had already begun, the liturgical movement at first centered upon the monasteries of Beuron and Maria-Laach. While initially the German liturgical movement may have lacked the strong pastoral thrust which was so characteristic of the Belgian liturgical movement, it soon began to balance the great degree of scientific knowledge which it possessed with a deep pastoral concern. Under the inspired leadership and profound historical insights of such outstanding men as Abbot Ildephonse Herwegen (1874-1946), Dom Odo Casel (1886-1948), and Romano Guardini (1885-1968), to mention but a few, the movement was given great substance and impetus. Their balanced views of the liturgy helped to establish it at the heart of the entire life of the Church. Eventually, complemented by the predominantly pastoral characteristics of the school of Klosterneuberg in Austria, under the very able direction of Pius Parsch (1884-1954), the German movement tended to more closely identify with that of Belgium.

> Thus a movement sprang up in Germany which closely resembled that of Belgium in its practical inspiration and undertakings, while being able to make full use of the vast stores of scholarship and speculative thought, as well as the intense and magnificent piety of Maria-Laach.[17]

These powerful initiatives for liturgical renewal, with their strong thrust along pastoral lines, soon spread from Belgium and Germany and throughout the rest of Europe. In this brief review we cannot even begin to include all the multi-faceted dimensions of this phenomenon, embracing the many great scholars, pastors, and dedicated laymen who gave substance and meaning to this entire movement. However, we need simply affirm that the program proposed by Dom Lambert Beauduin initiated strong, irreversible movements for liturgical renewal within the Church prior to the First World War whose influence was to be felt even up to our own day and age. That this movement had awakened popular interest in the newly rediscovered view of the liturgy was clearly attested to by the increased demand on the part of the faithful for greater knowledge and involvement in liturgical matters. It was providential for the Church that many great men, some of whom have already been mentioned, were able to rise to the occasion and to meet the challenge of the times—a challenge not only for greater research into the history and theology of liturgy but also for the greater instruction of the faithful.

On December 20, 1928, recalling once again the prophetic words of Pope St. Pius X, Pope Pius XI and his Apostolic Constitution *Divini Cultus* on *The Liturgy and Gregorian Chant,* reaffirmed the true role of the faithful in the liturgical worship of the Church.

> It is most important that when the faithful assist at the sacred ceremonies, or when pious sodalities take part with the clergy in a procession, they should not be merely detached and silent spectators, but, filled with a deep sense of the beauty of the liturgy, should sing alternately with the clergy or the choir, as it is prescribed. If this is done, then it will no longer happen that the people either make no answer at all to the public prayers—whether in the language of the liturgy or in the vernacular—or at best utter the responses in a low and subdued murmur.
>
> Let the clergy, both secular and regular, under the lead of their bishops and ordinaries, devote their energies, either directly or through other trained teachers, to instructing the people in the liturgy and in music, as being matters closely associated with Christian doctrine.[18]

Here we have another important and clear statement of awareness, from the highest level of church authority, concerning the very basic need within the Church for a liturgical renewal along strong pastoral lines.

With the outbreak of the Second World War, the international liturgical movement, while momentarily reduced to inactivity, was not destroyed or weakened in any way. On the contrary, the terrible destruction, pain, and sorrow left in the wake of the war caused the

Church to meditatively reexamine and reevaluate its role in the world. Convinced of the need to renew itself, especially in terms of its relationship to the People of God, it saw this goal as being able to be accomplished primarily through the liturgy. Hence the liturgical movement was once again viewed as a most powerful and fundamental instrument for this vitally needed renewal. The earlier incentives of the liturgical movement now reawakened help to pave the way for the necessary reforms. "After the Second World War the fact could no longer be overlooked that a world-wide, comprehensive movement of ecclesiastical reform had been set in motion by these reforms of the liturgy."[19]

Pastoral-Liturgical Initiatives of Pope Pius XII

While the liturgical movement, still relatively independent and far from unified, may not have enjoyed complete serenity and acceptance everywhere within the Church, nevertheless, it continued to gain worldwide attention and momentum until it gradually began to attract the official recognition and support of the Holy See itself. Aware and wary of the many diversified aspects of this movement, Pope Pius XII sought to give it a more unified and positive direction. On June 29, 1943 he issued his encyclical letter *Mystici Corporis—The Mystical Body of Christ*,[20] which represented an important moment for the liturgical movement for, although speaking in relatively broad terms, the Pontiff did significantly affirm that the liturgy was both expressive and constitutive of the Church itself.

> But this noble title of the Church must not be so taken, as if that ineffable bond by which the Son of God assumed a definite human nature belongs to the universal Church; but it means that our Savior shares His most personal prerogatives with the Church in such a way that she may portray in her whole life, both external and interior, a most faithful image of Christ. For in virtue of the juridical mission by which our divine Redeemer sent His apostles into the world, as He had been sent by the Father, it is He who through the Church baptizes, teaches, rules, looses, binds, offers sacrifice.[21]

Two years later, on March 24, 1945 he published his motu proprio *In cotidianis precibus* on *The Use of the New Latin Version of the Psalms in the Divine Office*.[22] In this document he sought to explain that through the use of this new Latin version of the Psalms he wished to render the official recitation of the Divine Office a more perfect and intelligent act for all those involved.

> In our paternal solicitude and paternal affection for the men and women who are devoted to God, we trust that henceforth all may derive from the performance of the Divine Office ever greater light, grace and consolation, and that thus enlightened and encouraged they may, even in these most trying times of the Church, be more and more disposed to imitate the examples of sanctity which appear so resplendently in the psalms, and may be moved to cultivate and cherish those sentiments of divine love, strenuous courage and loving contrition to which, in the reading of the psalms, the Holy Spirit invites us.[23]

While there is no specific reference here to any participation by the faithful in the recitation of the Divine Office, nevertheless, it does underscore the Holy Father's concern in transforming this prayer into a much more rewarding experience for all those involved in its participation. At the same time, it illustrates the Pope's growing awareness of the powerful force he saw the liturgical movement to be as well as the wonderful contribution it could make in enriching and strengthening the prayer life of the Church.

Continuing along the lines of this realization and wishing to transform the liturgical movement into an officially recognized movement of the Church, on November 20, 1947 Pope Pius XII issued his famous encyclical on the liturgy entitled *Mediator Dei*.[24] Generally positive in tone, it does, however, contain many negative elements as well, no doubt reflecting some of the unrest caused by the liturgical movement in various areas of the Church's life. Being the first encyclical completely devoted to the liturgy, it provided the liturgical movement with a new and decisive impetus, representing "the first official recognition of the value of the liturgical movement on the level of the universal Church, becoming in fact, in this way, the 'magna carta' of the renewal which it intended to effect."[25]

Reemphasizing the strong pastoral initiatives of Pope Pius X, Dom Lambert Beauduin and so many others, this document displayed a keen awareness of the need for a responsible liturgical renewal in the Church. Flowing out of the theology of *Mystici Corporis, Mediator Dei* provides us with an excellent working definition of the liturgy which strongly underscores the vital role of the entire Christian community in the liturgical life of the Church. Rooted in the indissoluble union of its Head, Christ, and his members, the People of God, this permanent unity is that which constitutes for the Holy Father, the Mystical Body of Christ.

> In every liturgical action, therefore, the Church has her divine Founder present with her: Christ is present in the august Sacrifice of the altar both in the person of His minister and above all under the Eucharistic species. He is present in the Sacraments, infusing into them the power which makes them ready instruments of sanctification. He is present finally in the prayer of praise and petition we direct to God, as it is written: "Where there are two or three gathered together in My Name, there am I in the midst of them" (Mt. 18:20). The sacred liturgy is consequently the public worship which our Redeemer as Head of the Church renders to the Father as well as the worship which the community of the faithful renders to its Founder, and through Him to the Heavenly Father. It is, in short, the integral public worship rendered by the Mystical Body of Christ in the entirety of its Head and members.[26]

Within this definition, the constant union of Christ and his members in the liturgical mysteries is fundamental.

> And if one desires to interpret in this sense the adjective "integral" modifying "public worship," we must recognize in the authentic definition of the liturgy a doctrinal significance of singular vigor. The Pope does not cease to insist on this permanent unity of the Head and the members.[27]

Throughout the encyclical this salient point is underscored repeatedly. In paragraph eighty for instance, the Holy Father emphasizes the active participation of the faithful in the Eucharistic Sacrifice with these words:

> It is therefore desirable, Venerable Brethren, that all the faithful should be aware that to participate in the Eucharistic Sacrifice is their chief duty and supreme dignity, and that not in an inert and negligent fashion, giving way to distractions and daydreaming, but with such earnestness and concentra- tion that they may be united as closely as possible with the High Priest, according to the Apostle: "Let this mind be in you which was also in Christ Jesus" (Phil. 11:5). And together with Him and through Him let them make their oblation, and in union with Him let them offer up themselves.[28]

In Chapter III of this same document the Pope speaks specifically about the Divine Office as the prayer of the Mystical Body of Christ but seemingly only when recited by the official ministers of the Church on behalf of all the faithful.

> The Divine Office is the prayer of the Mystical Body of Jesus Christ, offered to God in the name and on behalf of all Christians, when recited by priests and other ministers of the Church and by religious who are deputed by the Church for this.[29]

There is no acknowledgment made here to any actual participation in this prayer by the laity. Further along, however, the Holy Father does address himself to the question of the active participation of the faithful at least in Vespers sung on feast-days.

> In an earlier age, these canonical prayers were attended by many of the faithful: but this gradually ceased, and, as we have already said, their recitation at present is the duty only of the clergy and of religious. The laity have no obligation in this matter. Still, it is greatly to be desired that they participate in reciting or chanting Vespers sung in their own parish on feast days. We earnestly exhort you, Venerable Brethren, to see that this pious practice is kept up, and that wherever it has ceased you restore it if possible.
> ...Sundays and Holydays, then, must be made holy by divine worship, which gives homage to God and heavenly food to the soul. Although the Church only commands the faithful to abstain from servile work and attend Mass and does not make it obligatory to attend evening devotions, still she desires this and recommends it repeatedly: moreover, the needs of each one demand it, seeing that all are bound to win the favor of God if they are to obtain His benefits.[30]

While the Holy Father enthusiastically recommended this praiseworthy practice, though limited in its scope, the Office would continue to be prayed in a language, namely Latin, which would effectively prevent any widespread and meaningful participation on the part of the faithful. Furthermore, there is no recommendation made in this encyclical to correct this language barrier. Despite these shortcomings, however, this document does demonstrate Pope Pius XII's general awareness of the great need for liturgical reform in the Church especially along pastoral lines.

Try in every way, with the means and helps that your prudence deems best, that the clergy and people become one in mind and heart, and that the Christian people take such an active part in the liturgy that it becomes a truly sacred action of due worship to the Eternal Lord in which the priest, chiefly responsible for the souls of his parish, and the ordinary faithful are united together.[31]

Throughout his pontificate Pope Pius XII consistently demonstrated an active and vital interest in the progress of the liturgical movement and particularly in its strong pastoral application. The sincerity of his concerns expressed itself in his valuable and timely pronouncements on behalf of a fuller understanding of the liturgical mysteries as well as by a more active participation in them by the faithful. Such documents as the Apostolic Constitution of January 6, 1953 on *The New Discipline for the Eucharistic Feast,*[32] and the decree and instruction of the Sacred Congregation of Rites of November 16, 1955 on *The Restoration of the Holy Week Order,*[33] demonstrate the Church's deep pastoral concern for the faithful. The decree of the Sacred Congregation of Rites of March 23, 1955 on *The Reduction of the Rubrics to a Simpler Form,*[34] was also inspired by the pastoral motive of simplifying the recitation of the Divine Office for the priest overly burdened with the many and varied duties of his parish ministry. In these documents and in many other instances as well, the Holy Father continued to emphasize his constant and deep concern that the faithful truly live the liturgical life of the Church. These concerns seem to be most admirably summed up in his *Allocution to the First International Congress of Pastoral Liturgy at Assisi-Rome,* delivered on September 22, 1956. Although containing many elements of critical reserve, this allocution is not devoid of both positive and constructive elements as is evidenced by the following statements.

If the hierarchy communicates by the liturgy the truth and the grace of Christ, it is for the faithful, on their part, to accept these wholeheartedly, and to translate them into living realities. Everything which is offered to them, the graces of the sacrifice of the altar, the sacraments and sacramentals, they receive not in a passive manner in allowing them simply to flow into them, but in collaborating in them with their whole will and all their powers, and especially in participating in the liturgical offices or at least in following their unfolding with fervor. They have contributed by a constant effort to add to the external things of worship, to construct churches and chapels, to decorate them and to enrich the beauty of the liturgical ceremonies by all the splendors of sacred art.

The contributions which the hierarchy and the faithful bring to the liturgy are not added as two separate entities, but represent the collaboration of members of the same organism which acts as a single living unit. The pastors and the flock, the teaching Church and the Church which is taught, form but one and the same Body of Christ. Thus there is no reason for maintaining a lack of confidence, rivalries, oppositions open or hidden whether in thought, in manner of speaking or in acts.

Among the members of one body, there ought to reign before everything else concord, unity and collaboration. . . . It is in this unity that the Church prays, offers sacrifice, sanctifies itself, so that it can be asserted with good reason that the liturgy is the work of the whole Church.[35]

With the convocation of this significant congress the modern liturgical movement seemed to have achieved its greatest degree of official recognition and approbation within the Church. Throughout the development of this movement great advances were made in the formation of a vital liturgical renewal along strong theological and pastoral lines. Emerging from the very complex social fabric of the times, which had been traumatically affected by two disastrous world wars, a new dynamic force gradually made itself felt within the Church. This force led the Church to realize most profoundly, not only its own great need for an interior, spiritual renewal and the ability to adapt to a radically changing world, but also the need to meet these challenges through a definite, coordinated plan of action. The modern liturgical movement pointed to the liturgy as the principal means by which these needs could be effectively met. Urged on by this irrepressible need for reform, the Church, nevertheless, demonstrated great reluctance in actually implementing many of these important theological and pastoral initiatives.

As far as the celebration of the Liturgy of the Hours was concerned, little was actually accomplished in promoting the idea of once again restoring this prayer to the faithful. Despite the pastoral principles so beautifully and consistently promoted by the popes most closely identified with the modern liturgical movement, Pope Pius X and Pope Pius XII, the communal recitation of the Divine Office on the parish level became more and more a very rare exception rather than the rule.

It continued to remain primarily a prayer for the clergy and religious alone. This is essentially where the matter of the active participation of the laity in the celebration of the Liturgy of the Hours rested up to the event of the Second Vatican Council. But the stage had been set and well prepared for the coming great liturgical reform which would bring to fruition the work of so many dedicated men who had so richly contributed in giving shape and substance to the modern liturgical movement.

Vatican II and the Reform of the Divine Office

Alert to the growing demands of all mankind for true justice and peace with a recognition of the rights and dignity of all, and seeking to impart a new and ever-increasing vigor to the Church and to the Christian life, on January 25, 1959 Pope John XXIII announced the convocation of the Second Vatican Council.[36] According to the directives of Pope John, this council was to clarify and renew the mission of the Church in the modern world and was to be predominantly pastoral in character. Conscious of the vital role which would be played by the sacred liturgy in this entire process, on June 5, 1960 the Holy Father appointed among others a new Pontifical Liturgical Commission to prepare the ground for the coming council. In contrast to the other commissions established by the Pope, the Liturgical Commission dealt with questions which had already been much discussed and clearly formulated years before the convocation of the Council.[37] Consequently, it was not surprising that the liturgical schema became the first document to be discussed at the general congregations of the council and after much heated debate and a certain degree of compromise, it was finally approved in principle by the council fathers.[38] Having undergone some final refinements according to the written suggestions of the fathers, the final draft of the Constitution was approved by the council fathers and promulgated by Pope Paul VI on December 4, 1963. *The Constitution on the Sacred Liturgy* therefore represented the first such document to be issued as an opening document by any other ecumenical council in history.

Beginning with the motu proprio of Pope Pius X, *Tra le sollecitudini,* of November 1903, and with the Congress of Malines of 1909, the achievements of the modern liturgical movement reached a climactic point of development in the official promulgation of this deeply theological yet promisingly practical document. Aside from the very striking reforms actually effected, such as the granting of permission for the reception of communion under both species, concelebration, and the liturgical use of the vernacular language, the Constitution above all reveals a profound vision, as well as a firm grasp, of what the liturgy is and what it should be as it seeks to arrive at a greater degree of adaptation to the needs of the modern world. It was within this unprecedented document that the reform of the Divine Office would be centered.

At this point, it would seem to be advantageous for our present line of study to examine *The Constitution on the Sacred Liturgy* in regard to its recommendations for the reform of the Divine Office as well as its entire approach to the question of the role of the laity in the celebration of the public prayer of the Church. However, although the Constitution does represent the first document to be promulgated by the Council, in the interests of methodology and clear development, it would appear that a brief comment on three other documents later promulgated by the Council would be in order since they all contain important pastoral and theological principles which bear directly upon our present area of concern.[39]

The Dogmatic Constitution on the Church-Lumen Gentium

It does not seem to be an exaggeration to assert that this most significant document, because of its wealth of doctrine, is central to the work of the entire Council. Officially promulgated on November 21, 1964 it brought to completion the labors of Vatican I (1869-1870) which had been prematurely interrupted by the outbreak of the Franco-Prussian War of 1870.[40] Of fundamental importance to this study, it established the integral connection between the Church and liturgy in a most profound manner. This relationship was certainly not a startlingly new discovery for it had always existed. However, it is only in the twentieth century that both ecclesiological and liturgical studies have advanced in such significant fashion, theologically and pastorally, that this vital union has been made progressively clearer.

Pope Pius XII underscored this relationship in his encyclical on the sacred liturgy, *Mediator Dei*,[41] by basing his definition of the liturgy upon the concept of the Church as developed in his earlier encyclical, *Mystici Corporis*.[42] It can be further affirmed that the modern liturgical movement, and the subsequent growth of liturgical consciousness it brought to our modern era, would have been impossible had it not been for the previously rediscovered reality of the Church which had provided the springboard for its origin and development. Concomitantly, the liturgy provided the means by which the true nature of this new vision of the Church as the Mystical Body of Christ would be given vital, concrete expression as sacrament in the action of the worshiping community of faith.[43] This entire relationship has been brought to a significant degree of development in this Constitution.

Being very pastorally oriented, the Constitution begins with the notion of the Church, not in juridical terms of structure and government, but as a community of believers to whom God gratuitously communicates himself in love. It is this type of inciteful initiative which provides the excellent groundwork from which to approach the entire question of the role of the laity in the Church and most particularly in worship. Although Chapter IV of this document is expressly devoted to the laity, this notion is dealt with in other areas as well, notably Chapters II and V. The entire document highlights in very strong terms the innate dignity and responsibility of the lay-Christian in the modern day Church as he shares with all clergy and religious in the overall task of witness, ministry, and fellowship.

It is significant that the chapter entitled *The People of God* (Chapter II) precedes the chapter on *The Hierarchical Structure of the Church* (Chapter III) since it reflects a particular understanding of the Church by the council fathers. Couched in strong biblical terms, the concept of the Church as the People of God[44] stresses the Council's wish to emphasize the human and communal side of the Church at the expense of the institutional and hierarchical aspect so strongly overstressed in the past. In using this terminology the Council asserts that everyone is in principle equal, seeing both clergy and laity as comprising the total community which is the Church. Fundamentally, the Church is being viewed as the new people established in history through the saving intervention of God. "You, however, are a chosen race, a royal priesthood, a holy nation, a people he claims for his own to proclaim the glorious works of the One who called you from darkness into his own marvelous light" (1 Pt. 2:9).[45]

Within this framework it becomes easier to understand that the task of the hierarchy is designated to be one of service to the laity who in turn have a particular responsibility of their own to fulfill within the life of the Church. Clericalism in the old sense, with its accompanying notion that all initiatives and activities in the Church must begin with and be the ultimate responsibility of the clergy, is no longer acceptable. The entire People of God is seen as a messianic people "in whose hearts the Holy Spirit dwells as in His temple" (1 Cor. 3:16; 6:19).[47] It is by the action of the Spirit that the Church is unified in love through a sacramental communion into an eschatological fellowship of life, love, and truth. This sacramental fellowship in the Spirit expresses itself most concretely and most efficaciously in cult especially in the Eucharistic celebration.[48]

> Through the celebration of the Eucharist God lays hold of His People and makes them more completely His own. The Christian at worship is called to acknowledge Christ in his brethren and to cherish the whole community as the sign of Christ's presence to the world.[49]

The New Testament description of the Church in Acts 2:42 is in terms of fellowship, a common sharing of faith expressed in prayer, Eucharist, and fellowship with the hierarchy (1 Jn. 1:3; Gal. 2:9), as well as the service rendered to the poor (2 Cor. 9:13).

> So the Church can be described as the fellowship in the Spirit which is manifested sacramentally. It is the temple of the Spirit, an organic whole constituted by spiritual bonds (faith, hope, charity) and the bonds of visible structures (profession of faith, the sacramental economy, the pastoral ministry) and which is continually developing and moving towards its eschatological completion.[50]

Christ's office as High-Priest is to offer sacrifice, worship, and praise to the Father. Through their regeneration in baptism and through their anointing in the Holy Spirit the People of God are consecrated into the messianic mission of Christ, therefore into his

priesthood.[51] As such, they consequently share, to a degree, in Christ's mission as High-Priest and also must offer, in their own way, praise, worship, and adoration to the Father. Thus the laity, together with the ministerial priesthood, and under its presidency, each in their own unique way, offer up this priestly work most clearly and efficaciously in liturgy, and especially in Eucharistic worship where the Church is most visibly herself.[52]

> Though they differ essentially and not only in degree, the common priesthood of the faithful and the ministerial or hierarchical priesthood are nonetheless ordered one to another; each in its own proper way shares in the one priesthood of Christ.[53]

Once this profound concept is fully understood and accepted it would perforce rule out any view of the laity possessing second class citizenship in the life of the Church and relegated to a purely passive role in the sacred commission of liturgical worship.

However, the laity, through their reception of the sacraments and through lives lived in witness to their commitment to Christ, must now translate this "life in Christ" into action. They must openly exercise and bear witness to their faith.

> Incorporated into the Church by Baptism, the faithful are appointed by their baptismal character to Christian religious worship; reborn as sons of God, they must profess before men the faith they have received from God through the Church. By the sacrament of Confirmation they are more perfectly bound to the Church and are endowed with the special strength of the Holy Spirit. Hence they are, as true witnesses of Christ, more strictly obliged to spread the faith by word and deed.[54]
>
> The holy People of God share also in Christ's prophetic office: it spreads abroad a living witness to him, especially by a life of faith and love and by offering to God a sacrifice of praise, the fruit of lips praising his name.[55]

It is primarily through the Eucharistic sacrifice, the sacrament of unity, that they must clearly demonstrate the unity of the People of God. Therefore, the Christian's participation in the liturgy is not merely a concession on the part of the clergy but it is a sacred right invested on them through their baptism and consequent sharing in the priesthood of Christ. It is in this liturgical attitude that their communal priesthood becomes clearly manifested.[56]

Taking part in the Eucharistic sacrifice, the source and summit of the Christian life, they offer the Divine Victim to God and themselves along with it. And so it is that, both in the offering and in Holy Communion, each in his own way, though not of course indiscriminately, has his own part to play in the liturgical action. Then, strengthened by the body of Christ in the Eucharistic communion, they manifest in a concrete way that unity of the People of God which this holy sacrament aptly signifies and admirably realizes.[57]

Following Chapter III on the hierarchical structure of the Church, the Constitution turns its attention in Chapter IV specifically to the laity. Acknowledging all that had been previously stated concerning the People of God in Chapter II and applying it equally to the laity, religious, and clergy, the Constitution goes on to stress that there are particular functions within the Church which pertain specifically to the laity according to their situation and mission. They are to contribute to the overall welfare of the entire Church through the proper exercise of their particular roles.[58]

Attempting to define the term "laity" the Constitution does so not merely in negative terms as all those who are not ordained or not in the religious state, but in positive terms as well as baptized Christians with an active role to play in the Church.

That is, the faithful who by Baptism are incorporated into Christ, are placed in the People of God, and in their own way share the priestly, prophetic and kingly office of Christ, and to the best of their ability carry on the mission of the whole Christian people in the Church and in the world.[59]

Because of their particular status in life the laity is seen as especially qualified to deal with temporal affairs of all types, but this by no means limits them merely to this area of activity.

Although by Christ's will some are established as teachers, dispensers of the mysteries and pastors for the others, there remains, nevertheless, a true equality between all with regard to the dignity and to the activity which is common to all the faithful in the building up of the Body of Christ.[60]

To speak of the Church as the People of God is to speak paradoxically of two seemingly contradictory notions, that of unity and that of diversity. This is so because while the phrase itself certainly implies unity it by no means implies flat uniformity. Despite the very real differences that do exist between clergy, religious, and laity and their particular charisms and missions in the Church, the Constitution stresses that there also exists a very real relationship between them rooted in mutual respect, support, and dependence. All the People of God are one in Christ Jesus but the Church would not be a people at all in any real sense unless it were to some degree a well-ordered and structured people.[61] Yet this diversity, this order and structure, must never be allowed to interfere with the rightful role of the lay-Christian to participate as fully as possible in the life of the Church and especially in her worship.

> All the laity, then, have the exalted duty of working for the greater spread of the divine plan of salvation to all men, of every epoch and all over the earth. Therefore may the way be clear for them to share diligently in the salvific work of the Church according to their ability and the needs of the times.[62]

The Constitution stresses the need for constant cooperation and mutual respect which must take place between the laity and the clergy. While the lay-Christian is urged to obey the pastors which the Church has designated as their teachers and guides, the clergy for its part must also respect the lay-Christian as a person and must in turn encourage his active participation in the life of the Church.

> The pastors, indeed, should recognize and promote the dignity and responsiblity of the laity in the Church. They should willingly use their prudent advice and confidently assign duties to them in the service of the Church, leaving them freedom and scope for acting.[63]

Having considered the various classes of members in the Church in light of their innate dignity, special charisms, and unique responsibilities, the Constitution goes on in Chapter V to emphasize the fact that all the People of God are called to holiness and therefore to Christian witness and service. All Christians without exception, regardless of position or rank, are called to bring to perfection "those fruits of grace that the Holy Spirit produces in each and every one of them."[64] In stressing the holiness which must be the goal of all Christians the

Council also stresses that no particular group within the Church has a monopoly on holiness; all are in need of it; all must seek it together in mutual support and love. Therefore, this universal call to holiness helps to eliminate any false or distorted distinctions differentiating between higher and lower levels of Christian faithfulness, on the strength of that holiness which is affirmed as not only a possibility but also as an imperative for all Christians.

> It is therefore quite clear that all Christians in any state or walk of life are called to the fullness of Christian life and to the perfection of love, and by this holiness a more human manner of life is fostered also in earthly society. In order to reach this perfection the faithful should use the strength dealt out to them by Christ's gift, so that, following in his footsteps and conformed to his image, doing the will of God in everything, they may wholeheartedly devote themselves to the glory of God and to the service of their neighbor.[65]

Thus, in its dedication to holiness the Church as the People of God is consecrated to the offering of a true and worthy act of worship to God, and the Church as the Body of Christ expresses itself in the clearest possible fashion that very moment in which the People of God assembles as a community of faith in an attitude of offering worship to God.[66]

The Decree on the Apostolate of the Laity—
Apostolicam Actuositatem

It is notable that this particular document, officially promulgated by the Council on November 18, 1965, marked the very first time in the history of the Church that a theme expressly dealing with the laity became the subject of conciliar deliberations. Papal pronouncements from the turn of the century to the eve of the Second Vatican Council had shown increasing interest and concern for the laity,[67] but officially no complete and coherent doctrine of the rights and duties of the laity in the Church had previously existed. While other documents of Vatican II also deal with the status and mission of the laity in the Church,[68] none of them are as totally devoted to this topic as is this *Decree on the Apostolate of the Laity*. However, it cannot be considered in isolation, since most of its principles are already contained in one way or another in these other documents and, more importantly, it is essentially based upon the theology of the Church as developed in *The Dogmatic Constitution on the Church,* primarily in Chapter II on the People of God and Chapter IV on the laity.[69]

In the very first chapter entitled *The Layman's Call to the Apostolate* the decree unequivocally affirms that the Church and the People of God are one.[70] Within the Church there exists a multiplicity of roles but one common goal toward which all the People of God must strive together.[71] That the laity has a vital role to fulfill in the mission of the Church is rooted in the principle that they also share in the messianic mission of Christ. "But the laity are made to share in the priestly, prophetical, and kingly office of Christ; they have therefore, in the Church and in the world, their own assignment in the mission of the whole People of God."[72] These rights and duties of the laity flow from their incorporation into the Body of Christ, the Church, through Baptism and are given the strength of commitment through the outpouring of the Holy Spirit in the sacrament of Confirmation.[73] "If they are consecrated a kingly priesthood and holy nation (1 Pt. 2:4-10), it is in order that they may in their actions offer spiritual sacrifices and bear witness to Christ all the world over."[74]

Love of God and neighbor, which lies at the very heart of the entire apostolate, is communicated and nourished through the sacraments of the Church and most especially through the Holy Eucharist.[75] Infused with the Holy Spirit all Christians must become actively involved in the apostolate of the Church. Endowed with the special charisms of the Holy Spirit (1 Cor. 12:7; 11) through ministry and sacrament, each Christian has the right and duty to use these gifts for the building up of the whole body in charity (Eph. 4:16).[76]

In a very significant way the decree stresses that the success of the entire apostolate of the Church depends upon the union of the People of God with Christ their Head. This vital union can be most efficaciously achieved through the active participation of the laity in the liturgical life of the Church.

> This life of intimate union with Christ in the Church is maintained by the spiritual helps common to all the faithful, chiefly by active participation in the liturgy. Laymen should make such a use of these helps that, while

meeting their human obligations in the ordinary conditions of life, they do not separate their union with Christ from their ordinary life; but through the very performance of their tasks, which are God's will for them, actually promote the growth of their union with him.[77]

In Chapter III the laity are reminded that their apostolic activities should not merely be directed to the world but must also be exercised within the Church itself.[78] Drawing strength from their active participation in the liturgical life of the Church they will be better able to contribute to the building up of the Body of Christ in the world.[79] Close cooperation between clergy and laity, in matters spiritual and temporal, is seen as essential to this entire process.[80] Certainly this reiterates what has already been said in *Lumen Gentium* concerning the necessity for cooperation at all levels of the Church's life and the co-responsibility of bishops, priests, and laity for the total life of the Church.[81]

Overall, this document is a very important one for the Council to have issued because the laity are the People of God and they are the Church sharing with the clergy and religious in the saving mission Christ has entrusted to his Church. The emphasis placed upon the co-responsibility of the laity and clergy as well as upon the essential cooperation and respect which must exist between them both is vital to the Church's mission to a world that is constantly becoming more and more alienated from the truth of the Gospel. And fundamental to the Church's apostolate is that it be rooted in the liturgical life of the Church, from which she must draw all of her nourishment and meaning.

> For it is the liturgy through which, especially in the divine sacrifice of the Eucharist, the work of our redemption is accomplished, and it is through the liturgy, especially, that the faithful are enabled to express in their lives and manifest to others the mystery of Christ and the real nature of the true Church.[82]

The Pastoral Constitution on the Church in the Modern World—Gaudium et Spes

While this lengthy document seems to consist essentially of a synthesis of Catholic thought on social teaching, especially as reflected in the social encyclicals promulgated from the pontificates of Pope Leo XIII (*Rerum Novarum*, 1891), to that of Pope Paul VI (*Populorum Progressio*, 1967), it does contain significant areas of emphasis as well as certain important shifts in thought and attitude which bear directly upon our topic. Most of these ideas, we will find, have already been touched upon in one way or another in the two documents we have previously reviewed.[83] Promulgated by Pope Paul VI on December 7, 1965 it is most likely the outstanding pastoral achievement of a Council whose orientation was essentially pastoral. This is so because while resting on sound doctrinal principles, thus making a valuable contribution to the doctrinal developments of *Lumen Gentium*, it also seeks to express the relationship of the Church in the modern world to every person and his needs. In this manner the *Decree on the Apostolate of the Laity* finds its primary fulfillment in this *Pastoral Constitution*.

Being principally centered on contemporary man, the Church consciously places itself at the service of the entire human family.[84] In order to respond to the restlessness and the yearnings of modern persons, the Church has an obligation to read the signs of the times and to interpret them for all mankind within the light of the Gospel. This is especially important today, for mankind is experiencing a new and traumatic evolution in history involving a cultural and social revolution which affects it profoundly on all levels of life, secular and religious as well.[85] Caught in the vortex of such rapid change, modern man has shifted from a rather static concept of reality to a more dynamic, evolutionary one which has created a series of crises totally new to his experience.[86] The Church must encounter modern man in this climate of flux and must help him to find the truth, the peace, and the order which he seeks.[87]

In the very first chapter great stress is placed once again upon the innate dignity of man rooted in his invitation to union with God.[88] Keenly aware of the existence of deep conflict within the historical dimension of the human condition, this Constitution nevertheless approaches the question of human worth positively and optimistically emphasizing creation in God's image as the basis of the dignity of humanity.[89] Consequently, in the deepest recesses of his being, man is endowed with true freedom of conscience, the exercise of which is fully authentic only when fully responsible.[90] Not only does this freedom guarantee the individual immunity from coercion, but it also guarantees him the inviolable right to share in those meaningful decisions which most affect his life.[91]

Fundamental to this entire theme is the gradual emergence of the laity, not as individuals who develop into social beings; but as beings whose individuality achieves credibility only in relationship with others.[92] There is great stress placed upon the promotion of the common good,[93] the dignity of man,[94] and the need for corporate action in order to truly promote the fellowship of service and to restore all things in Christ.[95] If, therefore, such great stress is placed upon the corporate responsibility of man in the ministry of service to the world and to his fellow man, it stands to reason that it must be applied as well to the need for corporate responsibility in the specific ministry of service to God through the communal offering of praise and worship. For, while the liturgy may not exhaust all the Church's activity, nevertheless, it is the fountain from which all the Church's life draws its power and nourishment.[96] This is in no way suggesting the abrogation of the principle of specific roles within the service of worship based upon distinct ministries in the Church which are essentially different, but it does suggest the abrogation of separations where none should exist, with the relegation of the laity to simple passivity in the Church's life.

Addressed to the entire family of mankind, the Church's mission is therefore universal.[97] *The Dogmatic Constitution on the Church* described the role of the Church in the world as that of a sacrament, or efficacious sign of union with God and the union of all; and, through the power of Christ who is present in his Church, she also becomes the means by which this union and unity is effected.[98] Concealing and yet revealing, the Church is an indissoluble complex of visible and invisible elements.

> The one mediator Christ, established and ever sustains here on earth his holy Church, the community of faith, hope, and charity, as a visible organization through which he communicates truth and grace to all men. But, the society structured with hierarchical organs and the mystical body

of Christ, the visible society and the spiritual community, the earthly Church and the Church endowed with heavenly riches, are not to be thought of as two realities. On the contrary, they form one complex reality which comes together from a human and divine element.[99]

Thus Christ becomes both the content of salvation as he reveals the Father to us in the fullest sense possible; and at the same time he is also the only means by which we have access to the Father. Through his resurrection and glorification Christ as risen Lord continually pours down the Spirit upon his Church, and thus it is that the Church is identified with both the historical Christ and the glorified Christ. Therefore, the Church, as sacrament of Christ, as the community of faith, hope, and charity, must now serve as the means by which God the Father and his incarnate Son are made present and in a sense visible to all.

For it is the function of the Church to render God the Father and his incarnate Son present and as it were visible, while ceaselessly renewing and purifying herself under the guidance of the Holy Spirit. This is brought about chiefly by the witness of a living and mature faith. . . . This faith should show its fruitfulness by penetrating the whole life, even the worldly activities, of those who believe, and by urging them to be loving and just especially towards those in need. Lastly, what does most to show God's presence clearly is the brotherly love of the faithful who, being all of one mind and spirit, work together for the faith of the Gospel and present themselves as a sign of unity.[100]

The Church as sign of unity exists as a community of believers, the People of God. It is, therefore, encumbent upon all the People of God to manifest the presence of God the Father and Christ his incarnate Son to all mankind in the clearest, most efficacious terms possible. The Constitution tells us that this is accomplished chiefly through the witness of a mature faith, expressed in love and unity.[101] The most concrete and efficacious means by which the Church can express itself in this manner is when she is gathered together as a community of believers in an attitude of worship, most especially in Eucharistic worship, the sacrament of unity.[102]

Precisely because it is an essential obligation of the Church as such, as the mystical community in Christ, the liturgy calls for the involvement of the community in the celebration. . . . "Church" is not an abstract concept, but a concrete reality; where several are assembled in hierarchical order in Christ's name, there is the Church. Every local Church community (diocese, parish, monastic community, etc.) is the Church, the universal Church community as a concrete phenomenon. It is the becoming visible, the epiphany of the universal Church. In it the universal Church becomes apparent, steps into the light of day. Every local Christian community is the Church of Christ in this place. And because the liturgy is the chief and highest life-function of the Church, this fact also must attain expression in the liturgical celebration, in which the whole local community ought to be actively involved as the Church of Christ.[103]

While the *Pastoral Constitution* certainly has much more to say concerning the communitarian nature of man's vocation in the world according to God's salvific plan, nevertheless, because of obvious limitations we must now return from our brief but important digression to the consideration of *The Constitution on the Sacred Liturgy.* Within the three documents we have just examined we will find a strong theological and pastoral basis upon which to organize our present investigation, for most of the ideas discussed in the first part of this chapter will find their terminus in this fundamental document. It is here that we will discover a more specific application of these principles to the rightful role of the laity in the liturgical life of the Church.

The Constitution on the Sacred Liturgy—
Sacrosanctum Concilium

This remarkable document, promulgated by Pope Paul VI on December 4, 1963, had as its principal purpose the reformation and promotion of the Roman liturgy. The professed goals of the Council—to strive to impart an ever-increasing vigor to the Christian life, to adapt changeable institutions more suitably to contemporary human needs, to foster unity among all Christians and to work tirelessly for the spread of the Gospel[104]—all attest not only to the theological and evangelical thrust of the Constitution, but to its eminently pastoral concerns as well. Upon examination it becomes abundantly clear that the Council Fathers' chief concern was the prayer of the People of God.

All the principles we have sought to review in *Lumen Gentium,* *Apostolicam Actuositatem* and *Gaudium et Spes* on this particular concept are admirably embodied within this document as it seeks to establish the essential relationship between life and prayer, between service to man and the worship of God.

As we review this Constitution we are not only struck by what is so admirably declared but also by what is left undeclared, for the Council realized that while many specific problems and complex questions concerning the liturgical life of the People of God needed to be solved, its obvious limitations prohibited it from doing so at this time. At best it could demonstrate an awareness of these problems, discuss them, suggest avenues of action, and most importantly provide the means and the initiative for further study, development and renewal. Its primary purpose was to delineate the basic principles which would be used as the guidelines for the specific changes which would eventually come in a meaningful way only through further research, consultation and experimentation. Let us now examine this document more closely in order to determine with greater specificity those singular areas which apply themselves most clearly to the particular focus of this study.

Drawing upon the same theological foundations as those found in the *Dogmatic Constitution on the Church,*[105] *Sacrosanctum Concilium* states in a most meaningful way that in the liturgy the praise and adoration rendered to God the Father by the People of God in, with, and through Christ, as a community of faith, becomes the most sacred action which the Mystical Body of Christ, the Church, can possibly perform.[106] Thus the liturgy is always viewed as an action involving the entire Church.

While the sacred liturgy does not encompass all of the activities of the Church,[107] nevertheless, at the very heart of the Church's teaching on the liturgy, it is seen as "the summit toward which the activity of the Church is directed; and the fount from which all her power flows."[108] Within this solemn pronouncement the Council affirms that the goal of apostolic works is to bring the entire community of faith to the praise and worship of God. In turn it is the liturgy, and especially the Eucharist, which will forge them into a community of love, sanctified by the Spirit and committed to the service of mankind and the glorification of God.[109]

Proclaiming a theological concept of the utmost importance, the Constitution stresses that the objective gift of grace will prove to be unfruitful if it is not received by the faithful with the proper dispositions and with a mature faith. However, at the core of this profound operation, the Council professes its awareness of the absolute need for the full and active participation of the faithful in the liturgical life of the Church. The members of the clergy are especially reminded of their solemn obligations in this matter.

> But in order that the liturgy may be able to produce its full effects it is necessary that the faithful come to it with proper dispositions, that their minds be attuned to their voices, and that they cooperate with heavenly grace lest they receive it in vain. Pastors of souls must, therefore, realize that, when the liturgy is celebrated, something more is required than the laws governing valid and lawful celebration. It is their duty also to ensure that the faithful take part fully aware of what they are doing, actively engaged in the rite and enriched by it.[110]

Underscoring the pastoral obligation of the clergy in regards to the promotion of the laity's full and active participation in the worship of the Church, the Council reemphasizes this most fundamental principle, namely, that not merely the clergy but the entire People of God must be the subject of the liturgy, ". . . in other words, the entire body of the faithful has been summoned to participation in it as the priestly People of God. . . by reason of their baptism."[111]

> Mother Church earnestly desires that all the faithful should be led to that full, conscious, and active participation in liturgical celebrations which is demanded by the very nature of the liturgy, and to which the Christian people, "a chosen race, a royal priesthood, a holy nation, a redeemed people" (1 Pt. 2:9, 4-5) have a right and obligation by reason of their baptism.
>
> In the restoration and promotion of the sacred liturgy the full and active participation by all the people is the aim to be considered before all else, for it is the primary and indispensable source from which the faithful are to derive the true Christian spirit. Therefore, in all their apostolic activity, pastors of souls should energetically set about achieving it through the requisite pedagogy.[112]

The reference to the full participation of the faithful in the liturgy as the primary and indispensable source from which they are to derive the true Christian spirit is a phrase which the Council has borrowed directly from Pope Pius X's famous motu proprio *Tra le sollecitudini*[113] which Dom Lambert Beauduin had adopted as the watchword of the Belgian liturgical movement. "Now while he had been repeatedly accused of inflating and perverting the meaning of that sentence, the Council makes his interpretation its own in the most uncompromising way."[114]

In order that the liturgical reform enjoy any success at all it is essential that pastors engaged in the parochial apostolate receive every possible aid to grasp the full import of the sacred rites which they perform, and then to share this knowledge with the faithful committed to their care.[115] Aware of this sacred duty entrusted to them, pastors must strive to see that the faithful are well instructed in the liturgy so that their active participation is ensured, not only in external observation, but primarily in an interior commitment which will lead to a truly fruitful experience. A most important part of this instruction is the additional admonition placed upon the clergy to provide the indispensable element of good example for the faithful, whereby, they must ensure they embody in practice that which they teach in word.

> With zeal and patience pastors of souls must promote the liturgical instruction of the faithful and also their active participation, both internal and external, taking into account their age, condition, way of life and standard of religious culture. By so doing pastors will be fulfilling one of the chief duties of a faithful dispenser of the Mysteries of God, and in this matter they must lead their flock not only by word but also by example.[116]

Seeking to guarantee "that the forms of the liturgy should be understood and participated in by the Christian people as expression of its own prayer and sacrifice,"[117] the Council declares in bold and decisive terms that both texts and rites should be adapted to the times whenever possible in order to facilitate both understanding and participation in the liturgy. This vital liturgical principle will be discussed in more specific terms in other parts of this Constitution but it is important to note the presence of the strongest pastoral concern that the liturgy be adapted whenever possible to the needs of the people, even to the point of making changes in an area of the liturgical life of the Church which had heretofore remained essentially inviolable for many centuries.

In order that the Christian people may more certainly derive an abundance of graces from the sacred liturgy, Holy Mother Church desires to undertake with great care a general restoration of the liturgy itself. For the liturgy is made up of unchangeable elements divinely instituted, and of elements subject to change. These latter not only may be changed but ought to be changed with the passage of time, if they have suffered from the intrusion of anything out of harmony with the inner nature of the liturgy or have become less suitable. In this restoration both texts and rites should be drawn up so as to express more clearly the holy things which they signify. The Christian people, as far as is possible, should be able to understand them with ease and take part in them fully, actively, and as a community.[118]

Emphasizing the need to be open to the movement of legitimate progress, the Constitution also calls for the retention of sound tradition. In order that this delicate yet essential balance be maintained it is recommended that the revision of any part of the liturgy be preceded first by sound, scholarly investigation, not only along theological and historical lines, but along pastoral lines as well.[119] The effect of these changes upon the laity is to be of prime concern. Drawing once again upon the vision of the Church as later developed in *Lumen Gentium*,[120] the Constitution affirms that the liturgy must no longer be merely an isolated act of the clergy which the faithful attend passively. The rapport between the liturgy and the Church seen as the entire People of God, must now be affirmed as an act of total fellowship, which, however, continues to be hierarchically ordered. The Council underscores its intention that the Church does not expect merely to enact reforms which remain purely on a theoretical level but reforms which have a genuine application in practical action on the pastoral level. Therefore, the liturgy must be seen as the action of the entire Church in which all its members, united as a community of faith, have to fulfill their specific functions if the Church is to be truly manifested as the Body of Christ, the sacrament of unity.

Liturgical services are not private functions but are celebrations of the

Church which is the "sacrament of unity," namely, "the holy people united and arranged under their bishops."[121]

Therefore, liturgical services pertain to the whole Body of the Church. They manifest it, and have effects upon it. But they also touch individual members of the Church in different ways, depending on their orders, their role in the liturgical services, and their actual participation in them.[122]

Following through on this particular concept, the Constitution continues to accentuate the communal nature of the liturgy by recommending community oriented services in preference over those that are performed privately and individually when the very nature of the service does not preclude communal participation.

It must be emphasized that rites which are meant to be celebrated in common, with the faithful present and actively participating, should as far as possible be celebrated in that way rather than by an individual and quasi-privately.[123]

While continually repeating its conviction of the communal aspect of the liturgy, the Council, nevertheless, also emphasizes that within the liturgical celebrations of the Church there continue to exist distinctions of roles and functions. Each person or group participating in a particular liturgical service is required to perform a certain function which must not be usurped by others, and he should perform that function alone. "In liturgical celebrations each person, minister, or layman who has an office to perform, should carry out all and only those parts which pertain to his office by the nature of the rite and the norms of the liturgy."[124] This particular recommendation indicates the Council's reaction against...

...that leveling of liturgical communal forms, as a result of which, since the Middle Ages, among other things, all partial functions of individual office-bearers, even at High Mass, had to be performed or co-performed by the celebrant priest as if they only thus received their validity.[125]

Viewing the liturgy as the action of Christ the High Priest within his Church, the Council now reaffirms the theology of the priesthood of the laity in very practical terms. The lay person, though not a cleric, shares in the priesthood of Christ.[126] This sharing encompasses the very specific functions which the lay person has a right to perform within the liturgical celebration and this function he must be permitted and encouraged to exercise. Thus the laity discharge a genuine liturgical function when participating in the divine liturgy. Whether they act as servers, lectors, commentators or members of the choir, they are exercising a real liturgical ministry to which they are entitled through the Church's commission. The right and duty to perform this genuine liturgical service must be exercised as authentically as possible with the proper degree of piety and decorum demanded by such an exalted ministry. Consequently, all the ministers involved in the liturgical celebration must be thoroughly imbued with the spirit of the liturgy and properly trained to discharge their duties in the most efficient way possible.[127]

Reaffirming the Church's wish to promote the proper celebration of the liturgy the faithful are encouraged to participate fully and actively, not only by such positive means as acclamations and responses, singing psalms, antiphons and hymns, and by the proper actions, gestures and bodily attitudes, but also by the proper use of such a so-called negative element as silence. Far from being negative, however, these periods of silence can be used most positively and effectively for reflection as well as for the enhancement of those more active moments of song and prayer. The faithful must be helped by the clergy in the proper use of silence within the liturgical services and all must work together to use these periods of silence properly and profitably in the liturgy.[128]

In establishing this priority of involvement, the people are being encouraged once again to participate in those parts of the liturgy which have been traditionally regarded as the people's prayer, at least in word if not in fact. Accompanying this recommendation is the Council's firm belief that the people will now indeed perform these actions and it would appear to be implicitly understood as well that they will do so in their own language. To expect this extensive, active participation on the part of the laity to be carried out in Latin, especially when many of the texts will be changing constantly throughout the liturgical year, would seem to be highly unrealistic and impractical. In order to facilitate the laity's involvement, the liturgical books are not only to be revised in order to be able to express with the utmost clarity the profound realities which they are meant to convey,[129] but they are to provide the rubrics as well for the people's parts.[130] Of course, the rubrics involved are not concerned with the faithful's bodily movements alone, but with their responses as well, and more importantly with "their active roles in general and roles of special service during the liturgy in particular."[131] Thus the faithful are now to receive their proper place in the liturgical books thereby reversing "a tendency to treat the liturgy as a clerical affair that goes back over a thousand years."[132]

While the Constitution has repeatedly underscored the communal and hierarchical aspects of the liturgy properly understood, it likewise affirms that it possesses a didactic and pastoral role as well. Being primarily dedicated to the Church's worship of the Divine Majesty, the liturgy is also a school of faith for the People of God wherein God speaks to his people and they respond to him in word and prayer. Together with these visible elements the Church through signs also seeks to convey the teaching of the invisible things of God.

> Thus not only when things are read "which were written for our instruction" (Rom. 15:4), but also when the Church prays or sings or acts, the faith of those taking part is nourished and their minds are raised to God, so that they may offer him their rational service and more abundantly receive his grace.[133]

Considering the faithful's capacity for comprehension, the sacred rites should be characterized by their brevity, clarity, and simplicity so that they may be more readily understood, and in order that the faithful may participate in them as easily and as fully as possible.[134]

Having first established the communal, hierarchical, and didactic nature of the liturgy, as well as the necessity for simplicity and clarity in the visible signs of the sacred rites in order to ensure greater and freer participation by the people, the Constitution now quite logically moves on to the very vital and controversial area of language. Initially reaffirming that "the use of the Latin language, with due respect to particular law, is to be preserved in the Latin rites,"[135] the Constitution then goes on to open the door to the use of the vernacular languages in the liturgy.

But since the use of the vernacular, whether in the Mass, the administration of the sacraments or in other parts of the liturgy, may frequently be of great advantage to the people, a wider use may be made of it, especially in readings, directives and in some prayers and chants.[136]

Interestingly enough, this concept had previously appeared, to a certain degree, in the encyclical of Pope Pius XII, *Mediator Dei*.[137] In this encyclical, permission for the use of the vernacular was extended to certain areas of the liturgy which were left unspecified. Expanding upon this point and being much more specific, the Constitution now declares that the vernacular may be more widely used in such areas of the liturgy as the Mass and the sacraments and in other parts of the liturgy as well. Significant enough as the use of the mother tongue in the Mass and sacraments may be, of much greater importance seems to be the implicit admittance by the Constitution of the principle that in reality the vernacular is not excluded from any part of the liturgy. Although, besides the Mass and the sacraments, the statement specifies the possible use of the vernacular for readings, directives and in certain prayers and chants, in effect, the Council has opened the way to further extension of the use of the vernacular in every part of the liturgy also.

As liberal as this view may seem, however, the Council goes on to urge that this question be left up to the competent territorial ecclesiastical authority.

To decide whether, and to what extent, the vernacular language is to be used, its decrees have to be approved, that is confirmed, by the Apostolic See. Where circumstances warrant it, it is to consult with the bishops of neighboring regions which have the same language.[138]

Having opened the door to the use of the vernacular, the Council now seeks to ensure a very prudent use of this privilege. In turn, it recommends caution in the acceptance of any translations of Latin liturgical texts into the vernacular language reserving the approval of any such translations to the competency of the territorial ecclesiastical authority previously mentioned.[139]

All things considered, the Constitution seems to envision a much wider use of the vernacular than had heretofore ever been permitted or even contemplated. This entire recommendation admits to the acceptance of a principle which had been the center of many discussions and often bitter debates of the past and which will prove to be of enormous significance in promoting the full, active, and intelligent participation of the laity in the liturgical life of the Church.

Continuing along this strong pastoral vein, the Constitution makes further recommendations that in contrast to rigid uniformity the liturgy will always respect and seek to foster the genius and talents of the entire community of faith regardless of race or nationality, admitting into the liturgy such particular cultural elements which prove to "harmonize with its true and authentic spirit."[140] Seeking always to preserve "the substantial unity of the Roman rite," the revision of the liturgical books should always take into consideration "legitimate variations and adaptations to different groups, regions, and peoples, especially in mission countries."[141] All of this should be undertaken according to the fundamental norms laid down by the Constitution and according to the approval of the competent territorial ecclesiastical authority in consultation with the Holy See.[142]

Following these meaningful outlines for reform, the Constitution now turns to a fundamental consideration of the liturgy viewed as the assembly of the faithful gathered around the bishop its shepherd, fully and actively participating in the liturgical celebration. It is in such an assembly, and especially in the celebration of the Eucharist, that the Church is most perfectly realized and most clearly manifested to all people of faith.[143]

> Therefore, all should hold in the greatest esteem the liturgical life of the diocese centered around the bishop, especially in his cathedral church. They must be convinced that the principal manifestation of the Church consists in the full, active participation of all God's holy people in the same liturgical celebrations, especially in the same Eucharist, in one prayer, at one altar, at which the bishop presides, surrounded by his college of priests and by his ministers.[144]

Viewing parishes as localizations of the diocese and of the entire Church, the Constitution urges the promotion of "the liturgical life of the parish and its relation to the bishop," fostering a deep sense of community primarily through the liturgical interaction between clergy and laity.[145]

Summing up all the soundest principles of the Church's teaching, the Constitution, in a series of profoundly theological passages, views the most sacred mystery of the Eucharist as the paschal mystery of Christ personally consummated on the cross and perpetuated as memorial in the liturgical life of the Church.[146] Seen as the "source and summit of the Christian life,"[147] the faithful are invited to participate in the Eucharistic celebration knowledgeably, fully and actively, offering thanksgiving to God not only through the ministry of the priest but also in collaboration with him as they offer themselves to God along with the Divine Victim.[148] It is primarily through the power of Christ the High Priest in the liturgical celebration of the Eucharistic sacrifice that the faithful "should be drawn day by day into ever more perfect union with God and with each other, so that finally God may be all in all."[149] Therefore, in order to ensure the fullest pastoral efficacy of the Eucharistic celebration in the devout and active participation of the laity, the Council seeks to revise the rites of the Mass to the degree that their intrinsic nature and purpose, as well as their interconnection, may be manifested in the clearest possible manner.[150] That the Constitution specifically singled out Sundays and feast day Masses for this revision was done so only to remind the faithful of those days of obligatory worship for the entire Church and was in no way meant to restrict the revisions of those particular days.

Continuing to display a deep consciousness of the legitimate liturgical role of the laity, the Constitution recommends a greater and wider use of the Sacred Scriptures[151] as well as the proper utilization of such effective pastoral tools as the homily,[152] the prayer of the faithful,[153] the freer use of the vernacular in the Eucharistic celebration,[154] and the reception of the Eucharist by the faithful within the Mass and from the same elements consecrated during that Mass.[155] Underscoring once again the necessary role of the clergy in this entire process, "this sacred Synod strongly urges pastors of souls that, when instructing the faithful, they insistently teach them to take part in the entire Mass, especially on Sundays and holy days of obligation."[156]

Throughout Chapter III the Constitution calls for an adaptation of sacraments and sacramentals to the unique pastoral needs of the faithful. Viewing the sacraments as real encounters with the redeeming Christ, to whom man is drawn into a special conformation according to the specific significance of each sacrament experienced, the Church calls for their effective accommodation to the faithful. The sacramentals are also seen as further aids which the Church offers to the faithful as sacred signs by which people are more fully disposed to the fruitful reception of the sacraments. "It is therefore of the greatest importance that the faithful should easily understand the sacramental signs, and should eagerly frequent those sacraments which were instituted to nourish the Christian life."[157] Working from this principle the Constitution calls for such adaptation to be effected in each of the sacraments outside of the Eucharist itself which has already been covered. Again, the Church's motivation is pastoral in calling for the revision of the sacraments and sacramentals reiterating that because of their indispensable importance for the faithful they must be made as intelligible, as effective and as fruitful as possible.[158]

Up to this point we have attempted to explore those particular articles of the Constitution which represented the prominently pastoral areas involving in one way or another the legitimate role of the laity in the celebration of the liturgy. It seemed especially advantageous for us to do so before moving into Chapter IV which deals specifically with the Divine Office since these concepts are essential for a fuller theological and pastoral understanding and appreciation of the revised Liturgy of the Hours, most particularly in it communal dimensions.

In the very opening paragraph of Chapter IV on the Divine Office it is affirmed that the priestly work of Jesus Christ, carried on through the Church, is by no means restricted to the sacraments. For while the Eucharist is rightfully maintained as the core of the liturgical and sacramental life of the Church, the Divine Office is seen as sharing eminently in the continuous offering of praise and worship to God, and in effecting the salvation of all mankind.[159] Quoting in essence from the encyclical *Mediator Dei*,[160] the Constitution thus affirms that the Divine Office is of paramount importance for the prayer life of the Church. Speaking in profound theological terms, the Council sees the

Divine Office as the on-going dialogue carried on between Christ and his Body the Church, and ultimately directed to the Father. By means of this continuous song of praise the course of the entire day and night is consecrated for the participating Christian. As to the question of those who should be reciting this prayer, the Constitution responds that this is to be done "by priests and others deputed to it by the Church, or by the faithful praying together with a priest in the approved form, then it is truly the voice of the Bride herself addressed to the Bridegroom."[161] While admitting to the possibility of lay participation in this prayer, the Constitution, however, stresses the conditions of proper deputation and approved form as well as the presence and leadership of the clergy for the office to enjoy official status. Whether or not this prayer would be considered an official prayer of the Church when engaged in by the laity alone, is not specifically answered in these particular articles.[162] When the Church is thus engaged in praying the Divine Office under these prescribed conditions, she is not only being faithful to a sacred obligation but she is performing one of its most essential and prestigious functions as well.[163]

Exhorting the clergy to a greater dedication to prayer in general, and to the Divine Office in particular,[164] the Constitution proposes that the latter be reformed in order that it "may be better and more perfectly prayed, whether by priests or by other members of the Church."[165] Once again the Constitution speaks about other members of the Church who are not specifically clergy participating in this prayer.

In order to eradicate certain long-standing abuses, and to conform more faithfully to the exigencies and demands of modern life, the Constitution calls for a restoration of the traditional sequence of the Hours so that "as far as possible, they may again become also in fact what they have been in name."[166] Seeking to have the Divine Office truly fulfill its purpose of sanctifying the entire day, the Constitution insists upon a general revision of the Office with "Lauds as morning prayer, and Vespers as evening prayer,"[167] viewed as axial to the entire celebration of the Hours. While the Hours of Compline, Matins, Terce, Sext, and None are to be retained, but revised, the Hour of Prime is to be suppressed.[168]

As the official public prayer of the Church, the Office is seen to be a source of piety and nourishment for the personal prayer life of priests and others who take part in its celebration. Consequently, all are urged to pray the Office with greater devotion abetted through an improved understanding "of the liturgy and of the Bible, especially of the psalms."[169] Therefore, any revision of the Office must be concerned with rendering the Hours more intelligible and efficacious for those who are participating in them.

In a series of propositions the Council called for: a revision of the psalter with the psalms distributed over a longer period of time than one week and with both psalms and hymns being rendered linguistically capable of being sung; the availability of a richer selection of readings from the Sacred Scriptures, from the Fathers, Doctors, and ecclesiastical writers; and strong consideration given to the preservation of historical authenticity in all biographical material dealing with the saints.[170] The treasury of hymns used in the Office is to be revised and expanded in order to guarantee a more intelligent, facile, and varied participation on the part of all those involved.[171]

With Lauds and Vespers seen as the two anchor points of the Office, each Hour is to be prayed at the canonical time with which it is specifically associated thus helping to truly sanctify the day. This practice, if faithfully adhered to, will not only provide spiritual advantages but will also help to avoid such abuses of the past wherein all too often the Hours would be entirely recited in a block, at a particularly convenient time of the day, often in a mechanical rather than in a prayerful manner.[172]

Without providing a precise juridical definition in theological or moralistic terms, the Constitution does emphasize the choral and/or private obligations for the recitation of the Divine Office by "orders of canons, monks, and nuns, and of other regulars bound by law or constitutions to choral office"; by "cathedral or collegiate chapters bound to recite those parts of the Office imposed on them by general or particular law"; by "all members of the above communities who are in major orders or who are solemnly professed, except for lay brothers";[173] and by all clerics not bound to the choral recitation of the Office but who are in major orders.[174] Any of the nonmonastic groups of religious who have been enjoined by their constitutions to a partial recitation of the Divine Office are declared to be also sharing in the public prayer of the Church. This would include as well all those groups who recite any approved form of the Little Office by virtue of their constitutions.[175]

Insisting upon the dignity and importance of the public recitation and singing of the Divine Office as the voice of the Church, that is, of the whole Mystical Body publicly praising God,[176] the Constitution also urges that those clerics not obliged to the choral celebration of the Office, such as parish priests, when they live together, or come together for some specific purpose, should see to it that they pray "at least some part of the Divine Office in common."[177]

Manifesting an appreciation of the ancient cathedral Office, the Constitution recommends that pastors of souls be conscientious in promoting the chief Hours of prayer, and to see to it that especially Vespers be communally celebrated in church on Sundays and on the more solemn feasts of the liturgical year.[178] That the laity are encouraged as well to recite the Divine Office, not only with the priests, but also among themselves, or even individually, shows a marked advance in thought from the encyclical *Mediator Dei* which, while recommending lay participation in the recitation of the Office with the clergy in church, said nothing about recitation among the laity alone either in groups or individually.[179] This additional recommendation of the Liturgical Constitution "conforms to the high degree of the tradition of prayer accumulated in it, and finally, also to the ecclesial nature of the Hours which are not confined to certain ranks."[180]

Dealing once again with the vital and perennially troublesome question of language, it is stressed that the Latin language is to be preserved in the recitation of the Divine Office. However, in a magnanimous concession, and implicitly reaffirming that the Office is to provide the clergy with a rich source of nourishment for their personal piety and prayer, the Constitution declares that the local ordinary has the power to grant the use of an approved vernacular translation to those clerics who would find the use of Latin a grave obstacle to their praying the Office as it should be prayed, that is, with dignity, attention, and devotion.[181] It would seem to be most reasonable and appropriate that for the same reason this permission be extended to the laity as well. In a certain broadening of this permission, competent local superiors are granted the power to permit the use of the vernacular, even in choral recitation, to religious as well as to men who are not religious.[182] If any cleric obligated to the recitation of the Office should recite the Office in an approved form of the vernacular "with a group of the faithful or with those mentioned above," his obligation is to be considered fulfilled.[183] It would seem that the nature of these permissions, by the terms of the Constitution itself, go far beyond merely a question of material difficulty with the Latin language.

> Priests are exhorted to make their office above all things prayer. The mere saying of words, even with a broad intention of union with Christ, does not constitute real prayer and there are great numbers who have an adequate knowledge of Latin for reading purposes but who find it difficult if not impossible to pray at length in Latin. For these reasons it is held that the regulation of the Constitution should be interpreted with magnanimity.[184]

Concerning the role of sacred music in the liturgy, the Constitution declares that liturgical worship is ennobled whenever it is celebrated in song by the sacred ministers accompanied by the active participation of the people.[185] It is in such circumstances that the music helps to establish a certain unity of minds, hearts, and voices within the liturgical assembly as it offers praise and glory to God. Displaying a truly pastoral attitude, it is insisted upon that the bishops and other pastors of souls be extremely conscientious in ensuring that "whenever the sacred action is to be accompanied by chant, the whole body of the faithful may be able to contribute that active participation which is rightly theirs."[186] This active participation is to be encouraged as well through the careful design of any newly constructed church building, assuring the suitability of the edifice for the proper celebration of the liturgy and the unhindered liturgical activity of the faithful.[187]

In a general assessment of the recommendations of *The Constitution on the Sacred Liturgy* concerning the active, conscious and full participation of all the People of God in the liturgical celebrations of the Church, we find them to be quite emphatic, and stated repeatedly and urgently.[188] Article 26, establishes the Constitution's basic premise on this point by declaring that liturgical actions are not merely the private actions of persons duly delegated by the Church, nor are they actions which pertain to the clergy alone, but in effect. . .

> . . . they are the celebrations of all the holy People, reunited and organized under the authority of the bishops, not only in a juridical fashion but in a sacramental manner. In effect the delegation to liturgical action by virtue of baptism is ordered to the liturgical action by virtue of ordination from which it flows. At the same time, the right to liturgical action by virtue of ordination highlights, inspires, elevates, and presupposes the delegation by virtue of baptism of all the People of God. Liturgical actions, therefore, affect the entire Body of the Church: they manifest it, they make it accessible. All the members of the Church are influenced in different ways by these actions, following the diversity of orders, of functions, and of active participation.[189]

Nevertheless, despite the diversity of roles rising from the sacramental delegation of Baptism and Orders, in principle, all liturgical celebrations are seen as essentially celebrations of all the People of God.[190]

Upon our investigation of Chapter IV, however, which deals specifically with the question of the Divine Office, we are presented with what seems to be certain inconsistencies. The Constitution does rightly call for a complete reform of the Divine Office in order to correct many long-standing problems which had developed in this prayer effectively transforming it into a mere ritual obligation for many. This form of the Office could hardly be said to fulfill its enormously rich potential for the Church. However, upon consideration of all the specific recommendations proposed for the renewal of the Divine Office, it would seem that while the clergy had obviously benefitted greatly, the laity had not fared as well. The principal preoccupation of this Chapter seems to be with the celebration of the Office by clergy, religious, and other canonical groups.[191] As far as the laity's participation in the Office is concerned, it is almost always cited as being celebrated with the clergy present and deputized for this purpose on their behalf, echoing a similar recommendation made in *Mediator Dei.*[192]

Although there is a recommendation that the laity be encouraged to recite the Divine Office not only with the clergy, but also among themselves, or even individually,[193] it would seem, on the basis of what had been previously stated,[194] that without sacerdotal leadership, the authentic participation of the laity in the official prayer of the Church would at best be questionable. The Constitution does declare that when the faithful pray the Divine Office together with the priest, in the approved form, "then it is truly the voice of the Bride herself addressed to the Bridegroom. It is the very prayer which Christ himself together with his Body addresses to the Father."[195] And canons, monks, nuns, Christian brothers, and others are told that their Office is part of the official prayer of the Church because they have been deputed for its recitation.[196] Yet presumably, the prayer of a group of lay people who decide to recite some part of the Office, such as Compline, after a parochial or religious function, without the benefit of sacerdotal leadership, would seem to be considered as not being an authentic part of the official prayer of the Church. This seems to be foreign not only to so much that has been said in recent years concerning the dignity of the laity by virtue of their baptism, but also to much of what the Constitution itself has declared so forcefully.[197]

Nevertheless, despite these apparent inconsistencies, it must be admitted that the Constitution on the whole has provided the opening and the incentive by which the Church could once again rediscover and recover the essential role of the laity in the celebration of the Divine Office. The revisions called for in the structure of the Office, helping to make it more understandable, more spiritually rewarding and easier for participation;[198] the new, though cautious openings given to the use of the vernacular in the Divine Office;[199] the recommendation that parish priests join with the entire parish community for the common recitation of the Divine Office on Sundays and more solemn feasts;[200] the overall insistence upon the need for the full, active and conscious participation of the faithful in all liturgical celebrations;[201] the adaptation of rites and texts to the faithful as far as is possible;[202] and finally the encouragement given to the development of a true sense of community within the local Church;[203] all of these initiatives have been very positive steps taken toward the achievement of a fuller and more meaningful integration of the laity into the public prayer life of the Church. This will become even more apparent when we examine *The General Instruction on the Liturgy of the Hours* which obviously found in *The Constitution on the Sacred Liturgy* the springboard and inspiration from which it would launch its practical reform of the Divine Office.

All of this development now leads us quite naturally to the actual, present-day reform of the Office precipitated by the Second Vatican Council and actuated in the *Apostolic Constitution on the Breviary—Laudis Canticum* of 1970, and *The General Instruction on the Liturgy of the Hours* of 1971. The following chapter will be concerned with an analysis of these two key documents.

III

An Examination of Post-Conciliar Documents on the Reform of the Liturgy of the Hours

While history has shown us how the Divine Office had originally grown out of the daily prayer life of the early Christian communities, it has also demonstrated in what manner, step by step, through the centuries it evolved into a prayer which had become almost exclusively clerical in nature and from which the laity had become practically estranged. As we have already noted, the present-day reform of the Divine Office has been a phenomenon which was part of that greater phenomenon involving the contemporary renewal of the entire liturgical life of the Church. Beginning with the pastoral initiatives of Pope Pius X, and steadily developing through the modern liturgical movement, this reform reached its greatest degree of realization in the deliberations of the Second Vatican Council culminating in the promulgation of *The Constitution on the Sacred Liturgy.*

While this Constitution established a strong theological rationale for the Office as "the very prayer which Christ himself together with his Body addresses to the Father,"[1] it also proposed a series of recommendations for the renewal of the entire Divine Office for the specific purpose of transforming it into an occasion for better and more perfect prayer for "priests or by other members of the Church, in existing circumstances."[2] The entire reform embraced a restoration of the traditional hours of prayer as a sanctification of the entire day;[3] with Lauds and Vespers celebrated as the principal Hours around which the entire Office revolves.[4] Maintaining Compline as an ideal prayer to mark the close of the day,[5] the Council proposed that the Hour of Matins be composed of fewer psalms, longer readings and be so adapted that it may be celebrated at any hour of the day.[6] While suppressing the Hour of Prime,[7] the Hours of Terce, Sext, and None were adapted more equitably to the pastoral needs of the day.[8] As well as proposing a redistribution of the psalms over a longer period of time, namely over a four week cycle,[9] the Constitution also recommended the availability of a newer, more authentic and enriching form of lectionary for both biblical and nonbiblical readings.[10]

Consistent with the predominantly pastoral concern of the entire Second Vatican Council, the *Constitution on the Sacred Liturgy* sought to reform the Divine Office in order to adapt it more effectively to contemporary circumstances, and yet, at the same time, maintain its essential roots in tradition. While seeking to restore its choral and communal nature, and perfecting its manner of celebration, the principal pastoral accomplishment of this reform was the opening made once again toward restoring this prayer to all the People of God.[11]

Soon after the promulgation of the *Constitution on the Sacred Liturgy* on December 4, 1963, attempts were initiated to put its recommendations into effect. On January 25, 1964, Pope Paul VI issued a motu proprio on the Sacred Liturgy, *Sacram Liturgiam*,[12] in which he called for the establishment of a special commission to ensure the effective and efficient implementation of the proposed liturgical reforms. This commission was called the *Consilium ad exsequendam Constitutionem de sacra Liturgia,* and was placed under the very able direction of Cardinal G. Lercaro, and secretary of the commission, A. Bugnini.[13]

The reform of the Divine Office was to be one of the many specific projects undertaken by this commission and was entrusted to a special group of international liturgical experts under the title of *Coetus IX*.[14] The entire commission undertook its vast and difficult assignment with great dedication, and although often experiencing many painful and disappointing moments, brought the work forward in remarkable fashion. With the creation of the new *Congregatio pro cultu divino* on May 8, 1969,[15] their labors were substantially brought to completion.

As far as the reform of the Office was concerned, many fundamental and varied propositions were discussed and eventually presented to the Synod of Bishops in October 1967,[16] and in 1969 an experimental version of the proposed new Office was sent to all the bishops, prelates, and superiors general of the world for their perusal and evaluation.[17] In anticipation of the final approbation and publication of the renewed edition of the Divine Office, an approved experimental version made its appearance on the scene. Utilizing all those elements which had already been sanctioned for publication, it sought to placate the growing desire and need within the Church for a usable, interim version of the reformed Office. Originating in France,[18] it was soon translated into English[19] and enjoyed instant success as it served to prepare the way for the introduction of the final and definitive version of the reformed Divine Office. Finally, the entire reform arrived at its definitive stage with the publication of the *Apostolic Constitution on the Breviary—Laudis Canticum* on November 1, 1970,[20] which officially promulgated the final, reformed version of the Divine Office, followed by the publication of the *General Instruction on the Liturgy of the Hours* on February 2, 1971,[21] and of the four volume Latin edition of the *Liturgy of the Hours,* 1970-1971.[22] The various translations into the vernacular languages were to follow, and it was not until December 1973 that the first of the English translations finally made its appearance in England.[23] Thus the actual reform of the Divine Office of the Roman Church, which had been decided upon by the *Constitution on the Sacred Liturgy—Sacrosanctum Concilium,*[24] was, in effect, brought to its completion.

Because the liturgy is alive and must always be in a state of authentic adaptation and reformation, this new edition of the Office, the culmination of a long, very difficult and detailed preparation, represents but a new chapter in the history of the official prayer life of the Roman rite. While a detailed study will undoubtedly alert us to a greater understanding and appreciation of the many spiritual riches which it contains, because of the very complexity of the work we will also be made well aware of its inevitable limitations.

In the following pages we will seek to analyze those particular portions of the post-conciliar documents most closely related to the question of the role of the laity in the celebration of the reformed Liturgy of the Hours and, consequently, which most faithfully conform to our process of development. This examination will involve primarily the *Apostolic Constitution on the Breviary—Laudis Canticum,* and the *General Instruction on the Liturgy of the Hours.*

Motu Proprio on the Sacred Liturgy—Sacram Liturgiam, 25 January 1964 [25]

As we have already noted, it is this motu proprio which inaugurated the *Concilium for the Implementation of the Constitution on the Sacred Liturgy,* out of which the reform of the Divine Office was to be eventually realized. This was effected so that those prescriptions of the Constitution which needed study and time for implementation would be initiated and completed with the greatest possible haste, and yet with the requisite wisdom and prudence.[26]

Following closely upon the promulgation of the *Constitution on the Sacred Liturgy,* this document urges that both clergy and laity be inclined to assiduously study the Constitution and then "be prepared to put it wholeheartedly and loyally into execution."[27] Echoing once again the recommendation of the Constitution, it calls upon all bishops and priests to ensure that their people are properly educated concerning the value and power of the liturgy in their lives so that "their shared knowledge will enable the faithful to take part in the religious services together, devotedly and with body and soul."[28] Seeking to put into effect those areas of the Constitution which lent themselves to immediate implementation, the motu proprio recommended that under the direction of the bishop a liturgical commission be established in every diocese whose task would be to render more effective the pastoral objective of instilling a deeper understanding of the liturgy and of promoting the entire liturgical apostolate.[29]

Although the revision of the Divine Office had not as yet been effected, the motu proprio reaffirms the Constitution's declaration:

> . . . that members of any institute dedicated to acquiring perfection who, according to their constitutions, are to recite any parts of the Divine Office or any short office, provided this is drawn up after the pattern of the Divine Office and is duly approved, are to be considered performing the public prayer of the Church.[30]

While this statement could possibly include the laity in certain instances, such as members of secular institutes, there is no mention made, however, to the effect of attaching this same value to a similar recitation of this prayer by a group of the laity who are not members of any institute.

In view of the permission granted by the Constitution for the use of a vernacular translation of the Divine Office, under certain circumstances, to those obliged to the recitation of the Office, the motu proprio recommends that these translations be initiated at once. However, these vernacular versions must be approved by the competent territorial ecclesiastical authority before they are able to be used.[31]

Although this motu proprio has not contributed any new insight or interpretation to that of the *Constitution on the Sacred Liturgy* in relationship to the reform of the Divine Office, it has set up the machinery and initiated the process by which this reform would eventually become actualized.

Instruction on the Proper Implementation of the Constitution on the Sacred Liturgy—Inter Oecumenici, 26 September 1964 [32]

In the very opening remarks of this Instruction, the Sacred Congregation of Rites declares that the benefits derived from the *Constitution on the Sacred Liturgy* will only be experienced fruitfully in proportion to the efforts put forth by both clergy and laity in the assimilation and execution of its genuine spirit accompanied by the basic good will of all concerned.[33] Before the restoration of the liturgical books is effected, this Instruction seeks to clarify certain areas of the Constitution which need further amplification and elucidation as well as to guarantee its proper implementation.[34]

The primary purpose for putting forth these directives is to more effectively promote the active participation of the laity in the liturgy. Seeking to ensure the greatest possible degree of acceptance of the liturgical reforms on the part of the faithful, the Instruction calls for a prudent and gradual implementation of the reforms, accompanied by a thorough catechesis directed by the clergy.[35] It is necessary to convince all concerned that the specific objective of the *Constitution on the Sacred Liturgy* is "to foster the formation of the faithful and that pastoral activity of which the liturgy is the summit and source."[36]

Despite the fact that the liturgy does not exhaust the entire activity of the Church, the Instruction calls for the promotion of the greatest possible unity between the sacred liturgy and the Church's pastoral activity so that no false dichotomy is created between them. This relationship is especially stressed between the liturgy and catechesis, religious formation and preaching.[37] For this reason, the clergy is called upon to strive to promote, within their own ministries, the closest possible relationship between the liturgy and their entire pastoral apostolate. The ultimate purpose of this unity will be for the benefit of the faithful, in order that they "may derive the divine life in abundance from the perfect participation in the sacred celebrations and, made the ferment of Christ and the salt of the earth, will proclaim the divine life and communicate it to others."[38]

Stressing the absolute necessity for the provision of a thorough liturgical formation for all clerics and members of institutes dedicated to acquiring perfection,[39] the Instruction also emphasizes very strongly the necessity of providing a similar liturgical formation for the faithful.

> Pastors of souls shall strive diligently and patiently to carry out the command of the Constitution concerning the liturgical formation of the faithful and their active participation, both internal and external, "according to their age and condition, their way of life, and standard of religious culture." (SC 19) They should be especially concerned about the liturgical formation and the active participation of those who are engaged in religious associations of the laity, since it is the latter's duty to share more intimately in the life of the Church and also to assist the pastors of souls in properly promoting the liturgical life of the parish.[40]

In repeating once again the Constitution's declaration on the diversity of roles within the liturgy, the Instruction also reemphasizes that any liturgical roles assigned to the laity be viewed as the authentic exercise of a proper liturgical prerogative and that these functions are not to be duplicated privately or in any other way usurped by the clergy.[41]

Because of its great importance, the Instruction contains a further clarification of the question concerning the use of the vernacular in the liturgy as already presented in the *Constitution on the Sacred Liturgy*[42] and the motu proprio, *Sacram Liturgiam*.[43] Once again establishing Latin as the fundamental language of the liturgy, the Instruction urges that through the wise and competent collaboration of both clergy and laity, the very best possible vernacular translations be sought. The greatest care and prudence must go into these efforts "for the perfect translation of the liturgical text into the language of the people must necessarily and properly fulfill many conditions at the same time."[44]

Concerning the Divine Office, the Instruction merely seeks to amplify and clarify those areas of Chapter IV of the *Constitution on the Sacred Liturgy* which involve: the celebration of the Office by those bound to the obligation of choir;[45] the faculty of dispensing from or commuting the Divine Office;[46] the Short Offices and their celebration in common by members of institutes dedicated to acquiring perfection;[47] and the language to be used in the recitation of the Divine Office.[48] In this entire section there is no specific mention made of the general laity and of their relationship to the Divine Office. The principal concern of the Instruction seems to be in clarifying the Constitution's recommendations concerning the celebration of this prayer by those individuals bound to the obligation of choir or who are members of institutes dedicated to acquiring perfection. No further mention or clarification is given to those areas of the Constitution which do speak about the role of the laity, either directly or indirectly, in the celebration of the Divine Office, albeit in limited terms.[49]

Overall, this Instruction signals no radical departure from the *Constitution on the Sacred Liturgy,* but merely seeks to clarify and amplify those principles and reforms already declared and recommended. While there is no new element contributed to the specific question of the reform of the Divine Office as it affects the participation of the laity, it does demonstrate a further pastoral emphasis and concern for the promotion of the full, active and conscious participation of the faithful in the liturgical life of the Church.

The Instruction on Music in the Liturgy—Musicam Sacram, 5 March 1967[50]

Within this Instruction, the Sacred Congregation of Rites merely reiterates, in more specific terms, the general principle laid down by the *Constitution on the Sacred Liturgy* by which it declared that, "liturgical worship is given a more noble form when the Divine Offices are celebrated solemnly in song, with the assistance of sacred ministers and the active participation of the people."[51] Throughout this document there is a strong pastoral emphasis placed upon sacred music as a most effective vehicle for enlisting the active participation of the faithful in liturgical worship, wherein their communal worship is joined in an exemplary way with that of the clergy.

> Indeed through this form, prayer is expressed in a more attractive way, the mystery of the liturgy, with its hierarchical and community nature, is more openly shown, the unity of hearts is more profoundly achieved by the union of voices, minds are more easily raised to heavenly things by the beauty of the sacred rites, and the whole celebration more clearly prefigures that heavenly liturgy which is enacted in the holy city of Jerusalem.
>
> Pastors of souls will therefore do all they can to achieve this form of celebration; they will try to work out how that assignment of different parts to be performed and duties to be fulfilled, which characterizes sung celebrations, may be transferred even to celebrations which are not sung, but at which the people are present. Above all one must take particular care that the necessary ministers are obtained and that these are suitable, and that the active participation of the people is encouraged.[52]

Stressing once again *Sacrosanctum Concilium's* fundamental affirmation that all "liturgical services are celebrations of the Church, that is, of the holy people, united under and directed by the bishop or priest,"[53] the Instruction on music goes on to continually underscore the active role of the faithful in the liturgical worship of the Church, most exemplary when immersed in liturgical music. This liturgical role of the faithful "which is demanded by the nature of the liturgy itself and which is, by reason of baptism, the right and duty of the Christian people,"[54] can only be fulfilled through their full, active, and conscious participation, which must not only be expressed above all internally,[55] but externally as well, "by gestures and bodily attitudes, by the acclamations, responses, and singing."[56]

The importance that *Musicam Sacram* places upon this full participation of the faithful in the liturgy thus becomes quite obvious. However, it becomes even more emphatic in light of the following statements.

One cannot find anything more religious and more joyful in sacred celebrations than the whole congregation expressing its faith and devotion in song. Therefore, the active participation of the whole people, which is shown in singing, is to be carefully promoted as follows:
a) It should first of all include acclamations, responses to the greetings of the priest and ministers and to the prayers of litany form, and also antiphons and psalms, refrains or repeated responses, hymns and canticles.

b) Through suitable instruction and practices, the people should be gradually led to a fuller—indeed, to a complete—participation in those parts of the singing which pertain to them.[57]
The formation of the whole people in singing, should be seriously and patiently undertaken together with liturgical instruction, according to the age, status and way of life of the faithful, and the degree of their religious culture. . .[58]

Concerning the Divine Office, the Instruction advocates the sung form as that which more strongly accentuates the true nature of this prayer. "It expresses its solemnity in a fuller way and expresses a deeper union of hearts in performing the praises of God."[59] Since this same Instruction has previously advocated, consistently and emphatically, the absolute necessity of the full, active, and conscious participation of the faithful, "which is demanded by the very nature of the liturgy itself. . .,"[60] in sung celebrations, in effect, it would be now declaring that this very same participation would be essential to the celebration of the Divine Office as well. This assertion is even further amplified when the faithful, having been given the proper instruction, are enjoined to celebrate Vespers or other Hours, on Sundays and feast days, and to arrive at a deeper understanding and more fruitful use of the psalms in their own prayer lives. While this invitation is essentially repeating those previously extended in *Mediator Dei* and *Sacrosanctum Concilium*,[61] nevertheless, the concluding phrase seems to add a further pastoral dimension which heretofore had never been so explicitly stated proffering as a rationale for this encouragement, "so that they (the faithful) may gradually acquire a stronger taste for the use of the public prayer of the Church."[62]
Relative to the language to be used by clerics for the celebration of the Divine Office in choir, the Instruction, in accordance with the norm already established by the *Constitution on the Sacred Liturgy*,

retains Latin as the official linguistic form. However, admitting to the concession extended to nuns, members of institutes, and the faithful for the use of the vernacular by the same Liturgical Constitution, the Instruction recommends that proper vernacular hymns should be carefully prepared for their use in the celebration of the Hours in the native tongue.[63]

While this Instruction was meant to provide a further elaboration and clarification to the statements of the *Constitution on the Sacred Liturgy* concerning the use of sacred music in the liturgy, it has succeeded as well, in a pre-eminent manner, to add to the decisive incentives taken by the Constitution concerning the active participation of the faithful. "No previous Roman document has ever been so concerned with the people. None has so persistently taken into account what and how the people are thinking, their desires, or their capabilities."[64] Accordingly, we find this document to be certainly a strong contribution to the eventual restoration of the Divine Hours as a celebration for all the People of God.

Second Instruction on the Proper Implementation of the Constitution on the Sacred Liturgy—Tres Abhinc Annos, 4 May 1967[65]

This second post-conciliar Instruction proposes further changes in liturgy "designed to increase the faithful's participation and to make the rites, especially the rites of Mass, clearer and more intelligible."[66] In Section V, we have an interesting pastoral note concerning various ways by which the celebration of the Hours of Lauds and Vespers may be more suitably adapted to the participation of the people. In place of the short readings for instance, there may be substituted a more ample scriptural reading taken from either the Office of Readings, or from the Mass of the day, or even from the ferial lectionary. If deemed opportune, a brief homily may also be added, and if Mass does not immediately follow, a prayer of the faithful may be added just before the final oration.

Whenever this adaptation is employed, the number of psalms may be reduced to three. At Lauds one may recite or sing any one of the first three psalms, the canticle, and the last psalm, while at Vespers one may freely choose any three of the five psalms. Whenever Compline is celebrated with the people the psalms from Sunday may always be used.[67]

In a further elaboration of the use of the vernacular, as originally outlined by the *Constitution on the Sacred Liturgy*, the Instruction declares that in those liturgical celebrations involving the active participation of the faithful, the competent authority may also specifically extend the use of the vernacular in the Canon of the Mass, in the entire rite of Ordination, and in the lessons of the Divine Office, even for choral celebrations.[68] All of these post-conciliar documents thus far examined have this in common, namely, that all of their recommendations and clarifications are in effect a further concession and more specific invitation extended to the promotion of a fuller, more active and conscious participation by the faithful in the liturgical celebrations of the Church and more specifically in the celebration of the Divine Office.

The Apostolic Constitution on the Breviary—Laudis Canticum 1 November 1970[69]

Having opened with a very brief historical survey of the Divine Office, this Apostolic Constitution then proceeds to outline and discuss the new regulations of the Liturgy of the Hours and their motivations. At this point, a very positive note is sounded for the participation of the people in this newly reformed prayer.

> Since the Office is the prayer of the whole People of God, it has been drawn up and prepared in such a way that not only ecclesiastics but also religious and even lay-people can take part in it. By introducing various forms of celebration, the attempt has been made to meet the specific requirements of persons of different order and degree. The prayer can be adapted to the different communities that celebrate the Liturgy of the Hours, according to their condition and vocation.[70]

Thus, at the very outset, we have a very clear affirmation that the reformed Office has been developed not only with the clergy in mind, but with due consideration given to its use by the laity as well. In addition, there has been included within the reformed prayer a certain degree of elasticity and adaptability so that the specific needs and requirements of all the People of God in the modern world may be met. A very important aspect of this adaptation centers around the sanctification of time through an authentic application of this prayer to the various hours of the day.[71]

Through a considerable reduction of the daily portion of prayer, the introduction of a greater variety of texts, and the addition of such aids to meditation as the titles, antiphons, psalmodic prayers and recommended moments of silence, this Constitution also seeks to guarantee "that in the celebration of the Office the mind may more easily be attuned to the voice, and the Liturgy of the Hours may really be a source of piety and nourishment for personal prayer."[72]

Having abolished the former weekly cycle, the psalter is now to be distributed over a longer period of time, namely four weeks, excluding those few psalms and verses which are rather difficult to understand and to adapt to celebration in the vernacular. Moreover, in order to further enhance the spiritual richness of the two principal Hours, certain new canticles from the Old Testament have been introduced into Lauds, while other canticles from the New Testament have been introduced into Vespers.[73] Obviously these changes will not only prove to be a help to the clergy but will prove to be even more beneficial to the participation of the laity who, in general, are relatively uneducated in the theological and historical meanings of the psalms, and who would most certainly be praying the Office in the vernacular.

This Constitution further establishes a more generous distribution of the readings taken from Sacred Scripture throughout the Liturgy of the Hours. This has been accomplished in such a manner so as to add further cohesion between the Liturgy of the Hours and the Liturgy of the Word from the Mass of the day. In this fashion, a more effective exposition of the highlights of the history of salvation throughout the liturgical year is achieved.[74] For the community of the faithful and the clergy this part of the reform can only prove to augment their understanding and appreciation of this prayer, since it provides for a greater sense of continuity and unity between the Liturgy of the Hours and the Eucharist.

Providing a richer and better selection of texts, the new daily Office will offer readings not only from the Fathers of the Church, but from other ecclesiastical writers as well. These nonscriptural texts, presented in a modern and readable rendition, will seek to correspond more closely to present-day piety and thus will provide a more personal and meaningful point of contact between the Office and the problems and needs of contemporary man.[75] Furthermore, in all of these texts, especially those concerned with the accounts of martyrdom and the lives of the saints, a greater degree of reality and historical accuracy has been sought.[76] Perhaps in past ages various forms of exaggeration and fanciful embellishments were more readily accepted and appreciated, but in dealing with modern man and his innate demands for scientific facts and historical proof, many of these elements would prove to be a hindrance to his credibility and participation.

Certain new prayers have been added to Lauds to help consecrate the day and the beginning of our daily labors; while other prayers of supplication have been introduced into Vespers in the form of universal prayer. The Lord's Prayer has been reinserted at the end of these prayers in both Lauds and Vespers. Therefore, together with its recitation at Mass, the ancient Christian custom of reciting this prayer three times daily is restored.[77] This not only serves to establish a further link between these two axial Hours and their sanctification of the entire day, but also demonstrates an additional connection between the Divine Office and the Eucharistic Sacrifice. All of these elements provide a strong sense of continuity between the early Church community and the contemporary community of faith.

In concluding this particular section, the Apostolic Constitution expresses its great hope that the reformed Liturgy of the Hours will indeed fulfill all the purposes envisioned for it by the Church as a source of inestimable spiritual nourishment for all the People of God.

> The prayer of holy Church having, therefore, been renewed and completely restored according to her earliest tradition, and in consideration of the necessity of our time, it is highly desirable that it should deeply penetrate all Christian prayer, become its expression and effectively nourish the spiritual life of the People of God.

For this reason we hope and trust that there will be a new awareness of the prayer to be recited "without interruption" (Lk. 18:1; 21:36; 1 Th. 5:17; Eph. 6:18), which our Lord Jesus Christ laid upon his Church. In fact the book of the Liturgy of the Hours, distributed in the right time, is intended to sustain prayer continually and help it. The very celebration, particularly when a community meets for this reason, manifests the true nature of the Church in prayer, and appears as her marvelous sign.[78]

Acknowledging Christian prayer to be that of the entire human family united to Christ the Head, the Apostolic Constitution proceeds to affirm that it is through the prayer of this unified Mystical Body, which is the Church, that intercession is made to the Father on behalf of all the desires and needs of all mankind.[79] "It is necessary, therefore, that while we celebrate the Office we should recognize the echo of our voices in that of Christ and the voice of Christ in us."[80]

In order that these purposes may indeed be more fully realized by all the People of God within the celebration of the Liturgy of the Hours, a greater use and understanding of the Word of God, accompanied by a genuine love for that same Word must be encouraged. "This will happen more easily if a deeper knowledge of the psalms is more diligently promoted among the clergy, in the meaning understood by sacred liturgy, and if an opportune catechesis makes all the faithful participate in this study."[81]

United in the life of Christ in his Mystical Body, there can never be countenanced any opposition between the prayer of the Church and the personal prayer of its individual members. The intimate relationship between these two essential elements of the Christian life must be continually nourished and strengthened. This can be accomplished most effectively through the celebration of the Divine Office. Therefore, this prayer must always be made adaptable, as far as is possible, to the specific needs of modern life, in order that it may be able to properly fulfill its noble purpose of enriching the personal prayer life of all the faithful; who in turn may then offer their lives more effectively as a prayer of praise and thanksgiving to God.

When the prayer of the Office becomes real personal prayer, then the bonds that unite Liturgy and the whole life of the Christian are more clearly manifested. The whole life of the faithful, during the single hours of the day and night, constitutes a *leitourgia*, as it were, wherein they offer themselves to the ministry of the love of God and their fellowmen, and are joined to the actions of Christ who, by his life among men and by his sacrifice, sanctified the lives of all men.

The Liturgy of the Hours expresses clearly and confirms effectively this lofty truth inherent in Christian life.

For this reason the prayers of the Hours are proposed to all the faithful, also to those who are not obliged by law to recite them.[82]

On the other hand, all those who have received the obligation of praying the Liturgy of the Hours as a mandate from the Church, should do so faithfully, competently, and at the proper times. In sanctifying the entire day all clerics and religious should indeed experience the Office more as a celebration than as a mere legal obligation, and they should be prompted to do so by a "recognition of the intrinsic importance of prayer and by its pastoral and ascetic usefulness."[83] When these noble objectives are accomplished, then the Church as it reveals itself to all men, will do so in the clearest possible terms as truly a praying Church. The Constitution then officially proclaims the new book of the Liturgy of the Hours as duly established, approved, and promulgated through the Apostolic Authority of the Holy Father.[84]

In conclusion of this, our brief review, we find that although the *Apostolic Constitution on the Breviary* may be somewhat short in length, it is certainly very rich and profound in its depth of meaning. Viewing the Liturgy of the Hours as a "necessary completion, as it were, of the whole divine worship contained in the Eucharistic Sacrifice, to be poured forth and spread at every hour of man's life...,"[85] it then proceeds to comment on the ways and means by which these vital principles may be more fully realized in the lives of all the People of God.

Throughout this document the role of the laity is seen as part and parcel of the Church's participation in this sanctification of time through the prayer of the Hours. Declaring the Office to be a prayer of the whole People of God; revising the Office so that not only ecclesiastics may pray it but lay-people as well; expressing its desire that this prayer penetrate all Christian prayer and become not only a most wonderful expression of that same prayer but, outside of the Eucharist, its principal means of nourishment; all show, in its clearest statement yet, the Church's desire and recommendation that the Divine Office be once again restored to all the People of God.

We have therefore, in this Apostolic Constitution, a very strong and clear endorsement of the personal and communal participation of the laity in the Liturgy of the Hours. Furthermore, this involvement is seen not only as an authentic and meritorious expression of this wonderful work of the Church, but it is also seen as a vital and valid expression of the laity's right and duty to do so.[86]

While the *Constitution on the Sacred Liturgy* provided the opening as well as the incentive for the renewal and reformation of the Church's worship in 1963, and more specifically the renewal of the Divine Office, six years later the *Apostolic Constitution on the Breviary* summed up in a beautiful way the principles and key elements comprising the Church's accomplished reform of the Breviary.

Realizing that the final, full implementation of this renewal of the Office, in the form of publication of the actual volumes of the Liturgy of the Hours, would be a long and difficult task, due to the obvious magnitude of the work and its attendant difficulties, the Sacred Congregation, with the approbation of Pope Paul VI, sought to anticipate these volumes with the publication of the *General Instruction on the Liturgy of the Hours,* in February of 1971. The purpose for this particular move is given by Archbishop Anibale Bugnini, at that time the Secretary of the *Sacred Congregation of Divine Worship,* in a brief introduction to the General Instruction.

> Thus priests, religious and the faithful, whether individually or in groups gathered for study or prayer, may have the opportunity to familiarize themselves with the values of this new book of the Church, its special structure and the norms for celebrating the Liturgy of the Hours, as well as the spiritual benefits the People of God will gain from it.[87]

In effect this General Instruction is an elaboration of all the principles put forth by both the *Constitution on the Sacred Liturgy,* and the *Apostolic Constitution on the Breviary,* but often spelling out in very clear and positive terms what, in many instances, had previously only been intimated. Upon reading this Instruction, however, we can see that in reality it is much more than just a compendium of prescriptions for the purpose of providing guidelines for the proper celebration of the Office. In reality it invests the Liturgy of the Hours with a certain spirit which, if properly understood, will help promote a truly intelligent, pious, and fruitful participation of the Hours, and which will in turn cultivate a genuine opportunity for a deepening of personal prayer and spirituality.

Obviously then, the principal reason for the anticipated publication of this Instruction on the Hours was for catechetical purposes. In this manner priests, religious, and the faithful would be able to study the new reforms, to familiarize themselves with them, and be imbued with their true spirit. At the same time this study could be put to immediate, practical use through the utilization of the approved interim forms of the Breviary which were already in circulation. Thus the theory could begin to be put into actual practice and the People of God would begin to derive the spiritual benefits attached to the recitation of the Liturgy of the Hours. With the eventual full publication of the definitive volumes of the reformed Divine Office, the General Instruction would then take its place at the beginning of the first volume.

At this point, let us examine this General Instruction, once again with an eye specifically on those points most relevant to our particular study.

The General Instruction on the Liturgy of the Hours—Institutio Generalis De Liturgia Horarum, 2 February 1971[88]

To seek to define as concisely as possible the true nature of the Liturgy of the Hours we need to look no further than the very first sentence of this Instruction where its central theme and principal message are clearly stated. "The public and communal prayer of the People of God is rightly considered among the first duties of the Church."[89] While this may seem to be a rather general statement, nevertheless, it does indicate the very essence of this prayer of the Hours to be a public and communal celebration in the name of the Church by all the People of God. All of these elements make this prayer both unique and valuable for the life of the Church.

Drawing principally upon the Acts of the Apostles, the Instruction underscores the ancient Church's practice of private, public, and communal prayer wherein the early Christians sought to sanctify their entire day.[90] We have witnessed these very same elements being stressed often throughout the course of this study, as the Church has sought to restore those principles once again into Christian worship which had been previously weakened or almost lost over the ages. The Liturgy of the Hours is not a prayer solely for monks, religious, or clergy, but for all the People of God, and it is through this Instruction that the Church now seeks to restore a proper perspective to this entire question.

Throughout the first nineteen articles of this Instruction we are presented with a theological and spiritual elaboration of the principles governing the Liturgy of the Hours previously so beautifully expressed by both the *Constitution on the Sacred Liturgy* and the *Apostolic Constitution on the Breviary*. At the heart of this development is the Liturgy of the Hours seen as the prayer of the Church joined to the prayer of our perfect model Jesus Christ, and addressed to the Father.[91] United with Christ in baptism, and consequently sharing in his sacred priesthood,[92] the entire Body of the Church becomes "capable of taking part in the worship of the New Testament, not thanks to themselves, but to the gift and merits of Christ."[93] United in the Holy Spirit the entire praying Church is led through the Son to the Father.[94] Emulating Christ the exemplar, the Church must see the practice of continuous prayer as an authentic expression of its very essence as a community. The fundamental characteristic of the first Christian community was its unity of minds and hearts in steadfast prayer,[95] rooted in the Word of God and the "breaking of bread."[96] While private prayer is certainly always a most necessary and praiseworthy part of the Christian's life, community prayer possesses a very special dignity all its own.[97] Ultimately, however, both of these forms of prayer must be integrated in the Christian life, each drawing strength and inspiration from each other.

Consequently, Christ's injunction to pray always and not lose heart (Lk. 18:1), is not to be viewed merely as some unattainable ideal. While it is certainly an ideal, it is one that every Christian must strive to inculcate into his own life. Coupled with the necessary promotion of a strong personal prayer life, the faithful are actually able to sanctify each day of their lives in prayer principally through the communal celebration of the Eucharist and other devotions as well, among which the Liturgy of the Hours is pre-eminent.[98] It is for this very reason that the Church has seen fit to restore the authentic and traditional sequence of the Hours.[99] Celebrated in this manner, this prayer maintains a very special relationship with the Eucharist, the heart and soul of the whole Christian life. This is accomplished through the sanctification of the entire day of the community of faith through prayer; prayer which in effect duplicates by extension the sacrifical aspect of the Eucharist, as the faithful, in, with, and through Christ, lift up their hearts and gifts to God in praise, thanksgiving, supplication, and intercession, receiving grace and sanctification in return. In this way they are disposed to a more fruitful participation in the Eucharist as a loving dialogue takes place between God and man throughout the course of the day.[100]

Accentuating a very important and often neglected pastoral note, the Instruction stresses that through a conscious and devout active participation in the Liturgy of the Hours, and the consequent exposure of the beauty and richness of God's Word in such a salutary manner, the faithful, whether obliged to the recitation of the Office or not, "express in their lives and manifest to others the mystery of Christ and the real nature of the true Church."[101]

Declaring in much more specific terms what had been previously stated in the *Constitution on the Sacred Liturgy,* the Instruction reemphasizes and upholds the right and duty of the laity to full, active participation in this prayer. "The Liturgy of the Hours, like the other liturgical services, is not a private function, but pertains to the whole body of the Church. It manifests the Church and has an effect upon it."[102] Thus in very strong terms it insists that the Divine Office is a prayer for all the faithful, and that whenever it is celebrated by the bishop and the clergy and involves the participation of the laity, which should always be actively sought, the ecclesial dimension of the celebration is placed into the sharpest focus.[103]

Whenever possible, this participation of the laity is to be encouraged even on the parish level, as together with their pastor, who is the bishop's representative, they are invited to come to church in order to pray the more important Hours in common,[104] thereby making the universal Church more visible. Therefore, when the faithful do come together in this manner, uniting their hearts and voices in the celebration of the Hours, "they manifest the Church celebrating the mystery of Christ."[105]

In our previous analysis of the *Constitution on the Sacred Liturgy,* we noted what we felt to be certain deficiencies in regard to the question concerning the role of the laity in the celebration of the Hours. While the lay person was indeed encouraged to participate in the recitation of the Office,[106] the authenticity of this prayer as a true prayer of the Church always seemed to be dependent upon sacerdotal presence and leadership.[107] While this may not seem to be a bad notion in itself, it does seem to imply that a certain essential element is missing whenever a group of lay people come together to pray the Office in common without the benefit of priestly assistance.

Now, however, in the General Instruction, this notion seems to have been dispelled or perhaps clarified. There is no mention made here to the effect that the validity or full efficacy of this prayer as the official prayer of the Church, is contingent upon sacerdotal presence. On the contrary, it states quite clearly that whenever the faithful come together, and this could constitute the laity alone, to pray the Liturgy of the Hours together with one heart and mind in word and song, then it is the Church of Christ that is made manifest in this local community of believers and worshipers and their celebration is fully and authentically liturgical with everything that this implies.[108]

Therefore, while the value of this prayer celebrated by the laity may not depend necessarily upon priestly presence, as it would in the celebration of the Eucharist, nevertheless, the example, leadership, and instruction imparted by the clergy is highly recommended and represents an indispensable aid for its full and fruitful celebration by the People of God.

> Pastors of souls should see to it that the faithful are invited and helped by requisite instruction to celebrate the chief Hours in common, especially on Sundays and feasts. They should teach them to draw sincere prayer from their participation and so help them to understand the psalms in a Christian way that they may gradually come to use and appreciate the prayer of the Church more fully.[109]

Repeatedly the General Instruction emphasizes the importance of celebrating the Hours in common. All communities of canons, monks, nuns, and other religious are told that when praying the Liturgy of the Hours they show forth the Church in a special way, as in her name they offer up with one voice an unceasing hymn of praise to the Father.[110] The Instruction goes on to recommend that all sacred ministers, clerics, religious of both sexes, who are not obliged to the recitation of the Office in common, should try to celebrate at least some part of the Liturgy of the Hours in common or with the people, particularly the Hours of Lauds or Vespers.[111]

Many centuries have passed wherein the laity have been almost entirely excluded as full, normal participants in the celebration of the Divine Office. Now that the Church has restored this privilege to them, it will not be easy for them to once again naturally assume their rightful roles without proper help and guidance. They will need the example, leadership, and instruction of the religious and clergy from whom this initiative should come. Hence, every opportunity for catechesis and proper implementation must be patiently and prudently employed in order to encourage the People of God to once again seek a renewed knowledge, love, and appreciation of this beautiful and meaningful liturgical celebration. With this type of conscientious direction they will be enabled to more effectively participate in a fruitful way in the renewed Liturgy of the Hours as well as to integrate its use into their everyday lives.

> Whenever groups of laity are gathered and whatever the reason which has brought them together, such as prayer or the apostolate, they are encouraged to recite the Church's Office, by celebrating part of the Liturgy of the Hours. For they should learn to adore God the Father in spirit and in truth especially through liturgical worship; they must remember that by public worship and prayer they can have an impact on all men and contribute to the salvation of the whole world.[112]

Having thus encouraged the local Christian community, to make greater use of the Hours in their everyday lives, the General Instruction then proceeds to make a most important and fundamental suggestion.

> Finally, it is fitting that the family, as the domestic sanctuary of the

Church, should not only offer common prayer to God but also say certain parts of the Liturgy of the Hours, in this way uniting themselves more closely to the Church.[113]

By faithfully implementing this recommendation, every Christian will be able to experience in a singular way, the beauty and the salutary effects of this prayer, thereby exercising their participation in the priesthood of Christ as official ministers of the liturgy in a most personal manner.

As an assurance that each day be constantly and devoutly sanctified in prayer, and as an indispensable source of devotion and nourishment for personal prayer and pastoral ministry, bishops, priests and other sacred ministers and religious are mandated to pray the Hours even though the community of the faithful may not be present.[114] They are to recite the entire Office daily, with special attention given to Lauds and Vespers, maintaining as far as possible the proper time sequence for each hour.[115]

Recommending the recitation of the Office to permanent deacons,[116] and reminding cathedral and collegiate chapters, as well as designated religious communities and their individual members to the obligation of the Office in choir or individually,[117] the General Instruction goes on to encourage other religious communities who are not bound to the recitation of the Office to celebrate, whenever possible, at least some part of the Liturgy of the Hours. While no suggestion is proffered as to how this should be done, it would seem that, based upon the spirit of the entire reform, it would be ideal if it could be celebrated communally rather than just recited privately. The very same encouragement is to be extended to the laity as well.[118] Throughout this entire section of the Instruction concerning the mandate of celebrating the Liturgy of the Hours, there seems to be less emphasis upon obligation and more upon invitation to participate willingly and freely in this marvelous prayer of Jesus Christ and of his Church.[119]

In all of these articles we have examined thus far, the role of the laity in the public and communal recitation of the Hours has been strongly defended and encouraged. Continuing in this same vein, the General Instruction reveals how the very structure of the celebration itself also speaks very clearly on behalf of these very same truths.

Whether it is celebrated in common or in private, the essential structure of this Liturgy is a dialogue between God and man. Celebration in common shows more clearly the ecclesial nature of the Liturgy of the Hours. It fosters the active participation of all according to their individual circumstances through acclamations, dialogues, alternating psalmody and other things of this kind, and takes into account various forms of expression. As often as the communal celebration may take place with the presence and active participation of the faithful, it is to be preferred to individual and quasi-private celebration.[120]

At the beginning of Chapter II, the General Instruction describes Lauds and Vespers as the principal Hours of the day and consequently recommends that they be celebrated as such.[121] In article twenty-nine of this very same document we were made aware of a similar recommendation made to "bishops, priests, and other sacred ministers who had received from the Church the mandate of praying the Office." However, in this present reference, the General Instruction does not speak in terms of those mandated to the Office, but instead calls our attention to article one hundred of the *Constitution on the Sacred Liturgy* in which pastors are strongly urged to guarantee that these principal Hours, especially Vespers, are celebrated communally in church on Sundays and the more solemn feasts, and that the laity are to be encouraged to participate, either with the priests, among themselves, or even individually. Therefore, it would seem obvious that it is this particular element which the General Instruction now wishes to emphasize. Consequently, in the prayer life of the entire Christian community, outside of the Eucharist itself, these two Hours are to be given the highest priority, with a special recommendation for their celebration among those living a common life.[122]

As the General Instruction proceeds to discuss the overall structure of both Lauds and Vespers, it becomes quite clear that many elements which have been newly introduced or reformed, were effected with the express idea of making the Office more conducive to communal participation for both clergy and laity. Such elements as the opening hymn,[123] the disposition of the psalms,[124] the various scriptural readings,[125] the brief optional homily,[126] the silent pauses,[127] the responsorial song or other songs of the same type,[128] the Gospel canticle and antiphon,[129] the prayers of consecration and intercession,[130] the Pater

Noster,[131] as well as the wide variety of options made available, seem to have been selected not only for their suitability to the sequence of the Hours themselves and to the needs of the clergy, but for their adaptability to the communal, active participation of the laity as well.

While Lauds and Vespers are rightfully considered as the pre-eminent Hours in which the participation of the faithful is strongly encouraged, the entire sequence of the Hours is thereby open to the laity's active involvement. This will depend for the most part upon the varying social circumstances and conditions of the different parish communities as well as upon their willingness to pray some or all of the other Hours in common. According to the spirit of this document, they should certainly be encouraged to do so by the clergy whenever this may be feasible

Part III of Chapter II declares the express purpose of the Office of Readings, formerly known as Matins, to be that of making available "to the People of God, and particularly to those who are consecrated to God in a special way, a more extensive meditation on sacred scripture and on the best writings of spiritual authors."[132] This is to be accomplished in such a manner so that while maintaining its characteristic element of nocturnal praise for choral celebration, it will be so adapted so as to be able to be prayed at any other time of the day as well. Its celebration will also be simplified and enriched through a reduction of psalms and the introduction of longer, more varied readings.[133] By utilizing these recommendations effectively, the Office of Readings can be read by anyone at the most convenient time of the day, and the inestimable riches of the sacred scriptures, the Fathers and other sacred writings, would be made more readily available, not only to clergy, religious, and other sacred mininsters, but to the laity as well, to whom these writings are normally less accessible.

Sacrosanctum Concilium declares that in choir the celebration of the little Hours of Terce, Sext, and None are to be observed.[134] Now, the General Instruction essentially reiterates this very same recommendation with the added pastoral dimension that "this is also recommended for everyone, especially for those who take part in retreats and pastoral gatherings."[135] Thus, moving from an apparent affirmation of the obligation concerning clergy, religious, and other sacred ministers, the Instruction recommends the possible use of the little Hours by everyone, and this would certainly include the laity, for such varied occasions as participation in retreats and other pastoral gatherings. Outside of choir any one of these three Hours may be selected for recitation depending upon the hour of the day.[136]

Commenting upon the Hour of Compline the General Instruction views it as the ideal prayer for the Christian to recite before retiring for a night's rest.[137] This would seem to be most appropriate as a concluding bedtime prayer not only for the various groups of clergy, religious, or other sacred ministers but for the laity as well, especially as a family unit.[138] The option of being able to substitute the Sunday psalms for the other psalms on weekdays is a further incentive facilitating the use of this prayer, perhaps when traveling or whenever books may not be available, since it would permit the possibility of celebrating Compline by memory.[139]

While section VII of Chapter II deals with the manner in which a liturgical Hour may be joined to the celebration of the Mass on certain occasions, it becomes clear that this is a practice which the Church does not seem to actively encourage. In fact it urges that special care should be taken to ensure that this type of liturgical function does not prove to be pastorally harmful, especially if done on Sundays.[140] Celebrated in this fashion, the coupling of one of the Hours with the Eucharistic sacrifice would seem to rob or at least diminish each celebration of its own individual uniqueness and pastoral effectiveness. However, used prudently and only when warranted, according to the rubrics outlined by the General Instruction,[141] this type of liturgical celebration may be able on occasion to serve a particular pastoral need.

At the beginning of Chapter III, the General Instruction treats of the psalms and their close relationship to Christian prayer. There is no doubt that the psalms have always maintained a very prominent place within Christian prayer and this is most assuredly true of the Liturgy of the Hours, both in the past, and in the present reform as well. The Church has always viewed these inspired songs as especially conducive to fruitful prayer.[142] However, despite their obvious beauty and power, they are not easy for modern man to understand and translate into personal prayer.[143] This is most especially true for the average layperson who has not had the benefit of theological training. Therefore, despite the undeniable presence of the Holy Spirit in the hearts of those who choose to use these inspired songs sincerely as personal prayer, it would be extremely presumptuous to expect these psalms to truly become effective and fruitful means for personal prayer without at least the benefit of a thorough catechesis. Hence the Instruction recommends "more intensive biblical instruction" in the meaning and use of the psalms as personal prayer.[144] Since the psalms were originally composed as poetic songs of praise, they retain that essential quality despite their translation through the ages into various languages.[145] This fundamental musical quality inherent in the psalms should continue to determine the way in which they may be prayed properly, whether in choir or privately.

Although the text of a psalm may be praiseworthy in itself, certainly when sung it is far more inspirational and effective in moving the participants to a greater degree of contact with the original spirit of the composer as well as facilitating a fuller, more prayerful response to the movements of the Holy Spirit. Modern man certainly needs this type of assistance to foster a greater degree of devotion in his prayer life.[146]

There are times when, despite the best of intentions, the psalms will still present difficulties to those who seek to use them as prayer. Much will depend upon the degree of understanding which the reader possesses concerning the literary genre of the psalm, his awareness of the intentions of the sacred author and the meaning which he wished to impart to the psalm, as well as the circumstances under which the psalm was composed.[147] Obviously this presents a very real problem for the average layperson and reemphasizes the absolute need for a good, thorough catechesis on the psalms being made available to all the faithful.

The participant must learn to enter into the literal spirit of the psalm being prayed, joining his own sentiments to those of the psalmist, finding therein a bridge from the past to the present. Although divided by time and culture, there are certain invariables which proceed from the very nature of man and which therefore remain essentially unchanged down through the ages.[148] We must remember that when praying the psalms in the Liturgy of the Hours, we do not do so in a selfish, individualistic manner, even though we may be praying the Office privately, but we do so as a member of the entire praying Church, the Body of Christ and in the name of Christ himself. Therefore, in the celebration of the Liturgy of the Hours our own personal feelings and preferences should be sublimated to the particular emotion expressed by the psalmist, and which the Church wishes to convey at this particular time.[149]

However, as important as all of these aspects may be for the fruitful and meaningful praying of the psalms in the Liturgy of the Hours, above all we must learn to pray the psalms in light of the meaning which the Church has either discovered in them or which she has attached to them. Ultimately, we must learn to Christianize the psalms, to find Christ in them, and through them to pray with him, in him and to him.[150] To help the faithful accomplish this particular purpose, the Church offers three specific aids, "namely the headings, the short quotations from the New Testament or the Fathers, and especially the antiphons."[151]

While the headings are not actually recited as part of the Office, they do afford the reader with further assistance in arriving at an intelligent understanding of the importance and meaning of a particular psalm in the Christian life. However, even more valuable in this regard are the short quotations from the New Testament or the Fathers found before each psalm which help to "promote prayer in the light of the new revelation."[152] It is important therefore, that the heading and short quotation not be totally excluded in any recitation of the psalms, but be read and dwelt upon briefly before going on to the psalm proper. In fact, at certain times, these short quotations or phrases may even be used in place of the antiphon itself.[153] As the General Instruction explains, the antiphons are meant to underline the particular sense of the psalm, to help turn the psalm into personal prayer, and to give a special emphasis to a psalm under changing circumstances, especially for the great seasons and feasts.[154]

In discussing the means by which the psalms may be more efficaciously prayed by all the People of God,[155] the General Instruction makes clear that while a certain amount of rubrical directions are to be observed in order to insure a more dignified, prayerful experience, there is a great freedom of choice available in adapting the psalms more effectively to the particular group that is celebrating the Office. These options should be considered all the more carefully when the celebration involves the active participation of the people.

Giving specific shape to the general recommendation of the *Constitution on the Sacred Liturgy* concerning the redistribution of the psalms in the reformed Liturgy of the Hours,[156] the General Instruction has specified that the psalms will now be distributed over a four week cycle with the more important psalms being repeated more frequently. In turn, the Hours of Lauds, Vespers, and Compline will have psalms which will reflect more faithfully the spirit and tone of their respective hours.[157] Since both Lauds and Vespers have been designed for public celebration with the people, the psalms used for these Hours have been carefully selected because of their marked suitability for such a purpose.[158] Throughout the Hours, there has been an effort to have the psalms correspond as faithfully as possible with the spirit of the Office of the day, as well as with the particular liturgical season which they reflect.[159]

In a further effort at accommodation and adaptation, certain psalm verses have been passed over in silence, while three entire psalms have been omitted from the psalter. This was done because of their violent and deprecatory character.[160] Although this could be a point of discussion and disagreement among biblical scholars, it was judged to be necessary because of very valid pastoral reasons. While the present reform of the Office has attempted to remain as far as possible in harmony with tradition, it realizes that it must adapt itself to the needs of our own day and age, being always conscious to allow for the full, active participation of the faithful. Certainly this action becomes all the more valid when we consider the practical difficulties involved in the use of these psalms in the vernacular. Having come to praise God in the Hours, such verses and psalms proclaimed aloud during the communal celebration could prove to be offensive to many causing the possible alienation of the faithful from the Liturgy of the Hours.[161]

Rather than prolong the reading of the Divine Office unnecessarily, psalms of greater length have been divided and allocated to the same

Hour to be read over several days. In this manner, they may be recited in their entirety by those people, most likely lay people, who do not usually celebrate other Hours.[162] Upon reflection it becomes obvious that throughout this entire section not only are we made aware of the many real and formidable obstacles to the use of the psalms as fruitful personal prayer, but we are also made aware of the Church's constant belief in their validity as prayer and her concern that every effort be undertaken to make them as pastorally effective as possible. Therefore, the Church continues to use them as the inspired nucleus of her official prayer, the Liturgy of the Hours.[163]

> She recommends the psalms to her priests, her monks, her nuns, and even to her lay people, in order that they may have the mind of Christ, in order that they may develop an interior life which is truly the life of their Mother, the Church. It is by singing the psalms, by meditating on them, loving them, using them in all the incidents of our spiritual life, that we enable ourselves to enter more deeply into that active participation of the liturgy which is the key to the deepest and truest interior life. If we really come to know and love the psalms, we will enter into the Church's own experience in divine things. We will begin to know God as we ought. And that is why the Church believes the psalms are the best possible way of praising God.[164]

The addition of a great number of canticles both from the Old and New Testaments into the sequence of the psalms in the reformed Office should prove to be helpful as well in rendering the Office more pastorally effective. This is especially true concerning the New Testament Canticles included in the Hour of Vespers, for this should help the people to see more clearly the Christian message and spirit of the Hour, and also should facilitate transforming the Office into personal prayer. However, all of the canticles, both from the Old Testament, with their applied Christian understanding, and from the New Testament, are poems of spiritual value traditionally revered by the Church, and, consequently, should never be considered as merely supplementary to the course of the psalms,[165] but complementary to their appreciation and understanding.

Assuredly one of the greatest pastoral tools in the Divine Office is the expanded use of the readings from Sacred Scripture. That a very prominent place has been reserved for the Sacred Scriptures in the reformed Liturgy of the Hours is certainly not surprising for the Church has always realized their infinite spiritual value in the prayer lives of all the faithful.[166] The major selections are provided in the Office of Readings wherein they have been so arranged that the riches of God's word has been made more abundantly available as well as more easily accessible.[167] The rich variety of texts made available within the entire Office, the ability to adjust the length of readings according to the pastoral need,[168] the due harmony maintained between the readings, the particular liturgical season, and the Eucharistic Sacrifice,[169] all of these elements contribute to the unified view of salvation history,[170] and to the overall pastoral value which the Sacred Scriptures bring to the life of the faithful.

Traditionally in the Office of Readings, formerly known as Matins, the passages from Sacred Scripture were always followed by selections from the Fathers or ecclesiastical writers, or even a hagiographical reading when called for.[171] While essentially maintaining this tradition, the General Instruction, however, presents a vigorous new initiative in providing a greater collection of texts which have been more thoroughly screened, more carefuly selected, and of greater spiritual quality than in the past.[172] These writings also include the more pastoral documents of the Second Vatican Council.

All of these new initiatives were instituted in order to make these readings much more pastorally suited to our own day and age, taking into careful consideration the full, active involvement of the laity. The entire corpus of these patristic writings is meant to provide a deeper meditation on the word of God, rooted in the Church's tradition and inspirationally interpreted for the faithful by the great bishops, pastors and doctors of the Church.[173] Through this particular expression of the riches of our Christian heritage the Church offers all participants the means by which they may arrive at a greater awareness and deeper appreciation of the seasons and feasts of the liturgical year, as well as an indispensable guide for the promotion and nourishment of their personal prayer lives. By offering the clergy texts more readily adaptable to the task of preaching the word of God, the General Instruction underscores its concern for the promotion of the proper instruction of all the faithful in the spirit and meaning of that word, as well as in their full, active participation in its celebration.[174]

Another type of reading made available in the reformed Office involves those known as the hagiographical readings, namely those comprising various aspects of the lives of the saints.[175] Because of the many literary and historical problems concerning these readings in the past when they appeared in the second nocturn of the former breviary,[176] the General Instruction now recommends that these biographical accounts be considered primarily along the lines of historical authenticity and spiritual efficaciousness in order to prove more pastorally effective in the life and spirituality of the faithful.[177]

True to her tradition, the Church views the saints as most worthy of veneration and places great pastoral value upon these readings in the reformed Liturgy of the Hours.[178] Through the example of the saints the People of God are encouraged and inspired to imitate their virtues in their own lives and to find in them believable and powerful intercessors with God.[179] This is the reason why the Church, through the recommendations of the General Instruction, seeks historical authenticity in these readings of the Office; for she sees them not merely as statistical and historical accounts of the lives and deaths of the saints, but more importantly as inspirational instruments of prayer for all the People of God.[180]

The responsories following both the biblical and second readings in the Office of Readings fulfill a very definite function, not only adding beauty and variety to the texts but also properly orienting them within the entire scope of salvation history. Most importantly, they help to clarify and enliven the texts, transforming them more readily into true meditation and prayer as well as enabling the participating community to offer a proper response to the lesson which has been read. This would certainly be most apropos for the biblical lessons.[181] This applies as well to the brief responsories at Lauds, Vespers, and Compline, and the versicles used in the little Hours although in a simpler form.[182]

Having been constituted as part of the Divine Office for many centuries, the hymns continue to occupy an important position within the framework of the new Office. Located at the beginning of every

Hour, they possess a lyrical form especially adapted to the offering of praise to God, and not only are they able to quickly reveal the principal characteristic of each Hour or feast, but also through their literary beauty are able to effectively "move the people taking part and draw them into the celebration."[183]

When the Divine Office is celebrated in community, the hymn is one of the most popular and pastorally effective elements of the celebration, encouraging and supporting the full, active participation of all those taking part.[184] While many of the finest and most ancient hymns of the Office have been restored and preserved, many other hymns have been introduced, both old and new, offering variety and adaptability as well as an effective deterrent to monotony.[185] Despite the fact that now old familiar melodies may be adapted to new vernacular hymns, this must be undertaken with care and expertise provided that these hymns prove to be aesthetically, spiritually, and pastorally suited for use in the celebration of the Hours.[186]

In restoring the prayers or *preces* to Lauds and Vespers, the Church has introduced a valuable new element into the Liturgy of the Hours.[187] While on the whole the Divine Office represents a prayer of praise directed heavenward to God, these *preces* in turn represent petitions and invocations being drawn out of this praise expressing the community's constant need of God's help.[188] Somewhat similar to the general intercessions newly restored to the Mass,[189] these petitions, addressed directly to the Divinity, have been very carefully composed representing petitions for almost every conceivable human need "according to the different states, groups, persons, conditions, and times. . . for each day in the arrangement of the psalter and for the sacred seasons of the liturgical year, as also for certain festive celebrations."[190] The invocations addressed to God at the Hour of Lauds concern themselves more directly with the consecration of the various activities of man throughout this new day, while those at Vespers represent the various intercessions offered up for the world, the universal Church, and for the faithful departed.[191]

Despite the wide variety of invocations and intercessions already provided in the new Office, the formation of new prayers is also permitted provided that certain norms are observed.[192] This type of freedom and openness reveals the Church's deep pastoral concern to be responsive to the sensibilities and particular needs of the local Christian community, the universal Church, and indeed those of all mankind.[193] Although the form of these prayers may seem to be somewhat complicated in design, actually a great degree of flexibility has been provided for their use,[194] thereby offering a greater possibility for the active involvement and participation of the entire community. The practice of utilizing proper moments of silence between each prayer affords the participants the opportunity to personalize them in their lives. A proper amount of silence at the very end of the series of prayers offers a further possibilty for individuals to contribute their own personal petitions either in silence, within their own hearts or, if well thought out, proclaimed aloud as the other petitions. Thus these prayers can contribute greatly to the overall pastoral effectiveness of the Divine Office by convincing the faithful that not only are all of their activities, needs, and problems part and parcel of the Church's daily supplication to God, but above all that in the routine of their daily lives they may realize the actuation of their redemption and their incorporation into the flow and continuity of salvation history.[195]

After a prolonged absence, the Lord's Prayer has been reintroduced to the Divine Office as a fitting conclusion to the *preces* of Lauds and Vespers.[196] With its recitation at Mass, this prayer will now be solemnly recited three times a day during the Church's official worship, and will help establish a stronger sense of continuity between the Holy Eucharist and the Liturgy of the Hours.[197] Being a prayer with which all Christians are familiar, it will help to further the promotion of their active involvement in the celebration of the Hours.

Traditionally recited by the deacon or priest, the concluding prayer encapsulates the particular spirit of the feast or the Hour being celebrated and also serves as a means of summing up and concluding the prayer of the entire community. All the praise, aspirations, invocations, and intercessions are brought to a fitting climax within the contents of this concluding prayer. A very welcomed aspect of the reform is the addition of so many new and varied concluding orations ensuring a more sensitive accommodation to the individual characteristics of each Hour being prayed as well as to the spiritual sensibility of the celebrating community.[198]

Silence is a most precious commodity which seems to be disappearing more and more from the life of modern man. When engaged in prayer, specifically that of the Liturgy of the Hours in common, one is not merely offering praise to God, but is disposing himself as well to hear the voice of God in his own heart and to unite his own personal prayer with the word of God and with the public prayer of the entire Church. This is why the General Instruction, echoing the recommendation made by the *Constitution on the Sacred Liturgy,* exhorts a judicious use of silence within the communal recitation of the Hours in order to promote a more active and profound participation by the faithful. Properly used these precious moments of silence can spell the difference between what is genuine prayer and what becomes mere mechanical recitation.[199]

In Chapter IV we are dealing primarily with a rubrical view of the Divine Office which does not really concern us in our particular area of study. However, there is a reference which needs to be mentioned and to be commented upon. Considering the Sunday Office, the General Instruction repeats a recommendation which we have already discussed at greater length on a number of previous occasions, namely, that at the very least Sunday Vespers should be celebrated in common with the people.[200] We have seen this same recommendation made in the encyclical of Pope Pius XII, *Mediator Dei*,[201] as far back as 1947, and repeated in the *Constitution on the Sacred Liturgy* of Vatican II.[202] And yet despite these clear exhortations, the broad principle involved here, namely the full, active participation of the people in the Liturgy of the Hours has been one of the least considered areas of the entire reform of the Office. However, we shall be discussing this particular point at greater length in the following chapter.

In the first section of Chapter V the General Instruction concerns itself with the maintenance of the separation of roles in the celebration of the Liturgy of the Hours as well as in all liturgical services. Upon stressing the communal aspect of the Liturgy, the Church, at the same time, recognizes that within any authentic communal celebration there exists a harmonious blend of a multiplicity of diverse and unique roles and functions. Therefore, repeating the recommendation made by the *Constitution on the Sacred Liturgy*,[203] the General

Instruction declares that within the communal celebration of the Liturgy of the Hours the hierarchical character of the liturgy is to be maintained, wherein the particular charism and function of each individual participant is to be recognized, preserved and fully exercised.[204] While the General Instruction states that in every communal celebration of the Divine Office in which clergy and laity are present, a deacon or priest should normally preside; if they should be unavailable, one of the faithful may preside provided he or she does so as one among equals. Consequently, in preserving the hierarchical character of the liturgy, this person would not enter the sanctuary, nor greet or bless the assembly.[205]

The final section of the General Instruction deals with the very important question concerning the role which singing should occupy in the celebration of the Liturgy of the Hours. Throughout the ages singing has continued to exercise a very vital function in the liturgical worship of the Church. This is certainly true today for the public, communal celebration of the Divine Office. Beginning with the recommendation made by the *Constitution on the Sacred Liturgy*,[206] and its elaboration in the Instruction, *Musicam Sacram*,[207] the General Instruction now reiterates the fundamental principle previously established by these two documents, namely that singing the Hours is to be considered superior to and preferred over their simple recitation. This affirmation is motivated by the conviction that when the Liturgy of the Hours is celebrated in song, the true nature of this prayer is more fully realized, its solemnity is more effectively expressed, and the communal dimension of praise is enhanced and promoted.[208]

Proper instruction and practice are to be provided, not only to clerics and religious, but to the faithful as well, so that especially on Sundays and festive days, they may celebrate the Office together in a manner that is both efficient and enjoyable. No matter how difficult it may be to realize this type of celebration, the faithful are in no way to be excluded from full participation.[209] Therefore, their rightful role is not be be absorbed or usurped by either clerics, religious, professional singers or by a *scola cantorum* or choir.

While singing the entire Office is ideally the most solemn form of celebration, realistically speaking, in many instances it may not be very practical. However, to simplify liturgical music, or to perform it in a way which will reduce its artistic quality or its spiritual value, and which will prove to be both discouraging and distracting to the faithful, obviously does not provide a satisfactory solution. Therefore, aside from providing all the necessary pastoral preparations in which the faithful are encouraged and readied to be as fully involved as possible, the General Instruction speaks about the principle of progressive solemnity, wherein a choice is provided between the full singing and the full recitation of the Office. Since not every part of the Divine Office is of equal importance, it would be more apropos to sing certain parts rather than others. Whatever the choice may be as to which parts are to be sung and which are to be recited, it should be decided only after careful consideration of the unique circumstances surrounding the particular celebration as well as the character of the particular community celebrating.

Apart from the question of practicality, this type of flexibility offers the celebrating community a valuable opportunity to achieve a great degree of variety and adaptation. Once again, therefore, pastoral concerns override pure aesthetics and idealism in liturgical worship, for while the Church treasures and seeks to preserve the utmost beauty in her rites, she also realizes that the liturgy cannot be reduced to merely a beautiful and unrealistic monument oblivious to change and adaptability.[210]

In the same vein of thought, since it is now possible to sing the Liturgy of the Hours in the vernacular, even to the point of being able to use several languages within the same celebration, great care should be exercised in providing melodies that are properly adapted to the particular language being used and to the unique celebrating community.[211] Therefore, over and above the proper instruction and practice that should be provided, there must always be a certain degree of adaptability and flexibility employed in order to encourage the full, active participation of the faithful, by making the service as comfortable, and yet as moving and meaningful an experience as possible. It is in this spirit that the General Instruction tells us:

> The celebration should not be rigid or artificial, nor should we be merely concerned with formalities. Above all, the thing to be achieved is to instill

a desire for the authentic prayer of the Church and a delight in celebrating the praise of God.[212]

As we conclude our particular analysis of the *General Instruction on the Liturgy of the Hours,* we are struck by the beauty and depth of the theological, spiritual, and pastoral dimensions which this superb document possesses and which it so efficaciously shares with all the People of God. In our examination of the *Dogmatic Constitution on the Church—Lumen Gentium* in the previous chapter, we were made aware of an ecclesiology which did not view the Church exclusively in terms of an institutional hierarchy, but rather in terms which emphasized the human and communal aspects as well.[213] Aside from the necessary institutional and hierarchical elements, the Church was seen above all as a communion of all those baptized in the Lord.[214] It is for this reason that in the General Instruction the full, active participation of all the People of God is recommended for the public celebration of at least the principal Hours of the Divine Office.[215]

It is quite clear that the Church desires this participation of the faithful not as something to be merely tolerated, or as some peripheral, devotional support to the worship of the clergy, but quite to the contrary, their involvement is seen as an exercise of their rightful role in the official worship of the Body of Christ, the Church.[216] Therefore, pastors of souls, as well as other ministers of the Church, are urged to promote the full, conscious, active participation of the faithful through the proper instruction,[217] and through a common celebration of the Hours.[218] In the very same manner, the laity are encouraged to use the Divine Office as often as possible, when gathered together for whatever purpose, or most importantly within the family unit itself, as a vital part of their daily consecration in prayer.[219]

Just as all the faithful share in the celebration of the Eucharist through their baptism and insertion into the priesthood of Christ, for the very same reasons the Liturgy of the Hours, seen as an extension and, as it were, completion of the Eucharist, also includes the community of the faithful in its public and communal celebration. Consequently, the General Instruction views this promotion of the involvement of the laity as fundamental to the entire reform of the Divine Office and has made it one of its principal recommendations.

IV

Pastoral Considerations of the Reformed Liturgy of the Hours

Having examined the Church's gradual restoration of the Liturgy of the Hours to all the People of God, principally through an analysis of the recommendations of various Church documents of the Second Vatican Council and concluding with the *General Instruction on the Liturgy of the Hours,* we have been made aware that the Church has spoken clearly and forcefully on this matter. We have also been alerted to the fact that restoring this prayer once again to all the faithful was not simply a question of correcting a deficiency in the Church's liturgical life, but also a question of a necessary revitalization of the spiritual life of the entire Church.[1]

Today there has been a change in the Church's attitude concerning the Divine Office and the laity. This change involves a rediscovery of the true role of the laity, not only in praying the Hours, but in the entire liturgical life of the Church. While this development has been given definition by the Second Vatican Council and by the subsequent studies and research conducted by the various commissions created by the Pope, it is the present historical situation which has underscored the importance of this development for the Church and for the world, and which has added a sense of urgency to its effective implementation.

Why the Liturgy of the Hours?

We are presently living in very difficult times and there is a great need for a deep spiritual reawakening not only within the Church, but in the world as well.[2] In recent years, motivated by various movements and popular currents, many men and women have become increasingly aware of the social ills of our times and the need to do something about them. Great numbers of religious, clergy, and laity plunged completely and dedicatedly into the sphere of social action with, in many instances, an unfortunate neglect of many other important factors involving the spiritual life. When this type of one-sided dedication to action asserted itself more and more insistently, it resulted in a slow spiritual starvation for many. At this critical point many activists either drifted away from God and religion altogether,[3] or realizing the imbalance caused in their lives by this approach, began to reestablish the vital relationship with God in prayer that was necessary to give meaning and vitality to a life of service to their fellow man. The fallacy which was involved in the course of total social action was that many well-intentioned people felt that prayer was not the answer to solving social ills and that one could be a good Christian activist without having to take time out to pray. There seemed to be no necessity for discovering God in prayer before discovering him in our neighbor.

This type of Catholic, social, and apostolic activism, despite its admirable sincerity and generosity, continues to exert a strong and imbalanced influence on many people within the Church today, clergy and laity alike, causing a crisis of prayer and faith involving "a painstaking search for a better material world, without a parallel spiritual advancement."[4] It is in this context that the horizontal, social dimension of the Christian life is given full priority to the total, or near total, neglect of the vertical dimension, namely, man's relationship to God in prayer. In reality, these two dimensions involving man's relationship with God and neighbor should not be separated at all, but should be intimately integrated one with the other.

When undue stress is placed upon the horizontal dimension, the focal point of the Gospel seems to be changed from the cult of God to a very tangible law of universal brotherhood, and the Gospel message appears, in effect, to be primarily concerned with the process of reciprocal fraternal love rather than of a fraternal love which grows out of the love and worship of God. Therefore, placing a disproportionately greater value upon this particular perspective causes a diminution of, and at times total alienation from, that generous dedication to prayer, to the public praise and adoration of God, to the deepening of man's understanding of the mystery of God, which should be at the heart of every Christian life. "Prayer is therefore placed in question as the privileged place for the encounter with God, because it is judged to be an escape from the reality of life and from the encounter with God within my brother."[5]

On the other hand, there is no doubt that this particular approach is not without much merit since the social-horizontal dimension which it stresses is a vital part of the Gospel message which had been very much neglected in the past. Consequently, through this movement, attention has been once again refocused upon man and his everyday problems. However, it also creates a risk of reducing Christianity to a purely humanistic term, thereby depriving it of the unique originality which is hers through its vertical relationship with God.[6] The ideal would be the proper balance of both dimensions within the Christian life.

> What must be aimed at is complete humanism. And what is that if not the fully-rounded development of the whole man and of all men? A humanism closed in on itself, and not open to the values of the spirit and to God who is their source, could achieve apparent success. True, man can organize the world apart from God, but without God man can organize it only to man's detriment. An isolated humanism is an inhuman humanism. There is no true humanism but that which is open to the Absolute and is conscious of a vocation which gives human life its true meaning. Far from being the ultimate measure of all things, man can only realize himself by reaching beyond himself.[7]

This situation confronts Christianity with a very real and serious problem which demands the total attention of the Church as it seeks to find the ways and the means to resolve this very challenging and dangerous crisis of prayer and faith. It is within this context that the Church sees, as especially relevant and necessary for our times, the full and active reintegration of the community of the faithful into the prayer life of the Body of Christ. Aside from the fact that the celebration of the liturgy by its very nature assumes the gathering of the faithful,[8] and that all the People of God have a rightful role to play within the liturgical worship of the Church,[9] it seems especially provident for this day and age that this particular element of Christian worship be not only theoretically affirmed, but that it also be actually restored. Therefore, because of this urgent necessity to rediscover the power of prayer, for the glorification of God and the sanctification of man, the Church has seen fit to reform the Liturgy of the Hours and to consign it, not only to religious and clergy, but to all the People of God, as a prayer which, outside of the Eucharist itself, she views as pre-eminently qualified to accomplish this goal.[10]

While throughout the preceding chapters we have already discussed in principle the effectiveness of the Liturgy of the Hours as an instrument for promoting and strengthening the prayer life of the faithful, it seems advantageous for us at this moment to consolidate those thoughts once again to cover this particular aspect in our development. The rationale for the Church's conviction in this matter seems to be contained germinally and even prophetically within the very opening statements of the *Constitution on the Sacred Liturgy*.

> For the liturgy, through which the work of our redemption is accomplished, most of all in the divine sacrifice of the Eucharist, is the outstanding means whereby the faithful may express in their lives, and manifest to others, the mystery of Christ and the real nature of the true Church. It is of the essence of the Church that she be both human and divine, visible and yet invisibly equipped, eager to act and yet intent on contemplation, present in this world and yet not at home in it; and she is all these things in such wise that in her the human is directed and subordinated to the divine, the visible likewise to the invisible, action to contemplation, and this present world to that city yet to come, which we seek. While the liturgy daily builds up those who are within into a holy temple of God, into a dwelling place for God in the Spirit, to the mature measure of the fullness of Christ, at the same time it marvelously strengthens their power to teach Christ, and thus shows forth the Church to those who are outside as a sign lifted up among the nations under which the scattered children of God may be gathered together until there is one sheepfold and one shepherd.[11]

As complete as this magnificent statement may sound, nevertheless, experience tells us and the *Constitution on the Sacred Liturgy* affirms, that no matter how essential the liturgy is to the Christian life, it does not exhaust all the activity of the Church,[12] but is seen as the summit toward which all the activity of the Church is directed and the fount from which all her power flows.[13] The goal of all pastoral and apostolic work, therefore, is to bring the entire community of faith to the necessary praise and worship of God in prayer. In turn it is the liturgy, and especially the Eucharist, which will form them into a community of love, sanctified by the Spirit and committed to the service of mankind and the glorification of God.[14]

Specifically then, it is the Eucharist which is at the heart of the sacred liturgy and which is the source and summit of the entire liturgical life and the entire Christian life. Therefore, it represents the sanctification of the most precious moment within a Christian's day or week, a time of particular spiritual intensity and realism in his life. But the Eucharist is not an isolated reality, for Christ, while continuing his priestly work through the instrumentality of his Church, "which is ceaselessly engaged in praising the Lord and interceding for the salvation of the whole world," does so, "not only by celebrating the Eucharist, but also in other ways, especially in praying the Divine Office."[15] Thus, the Eucharist is complemented by, and in a sense brought to completion by, the Liturgy of the Hours, for the Hours serve not only as a proper preparation for the Eucharist, but also as a continuation of its sanctifying power throughout the day.[16] Consequently, the Liturgy of the Hours is that special prayer being proclaimed by the Church as the best possible means, outside of the Eucharist itself, by which the glorification of God and the sanctification of man may be achieved. However, at the same time, she insists, at first in general terms,[17] and then in more specific terms,[18] on the preeminent value and efficaciousness of its communal dimension, a dimension which must include all the People of God.[19]

The Church's view on this matter should, therefore, be abundantly clear. Outside of the Eucharist itself, and yet intimately related to it, it is the communal celebration of the Liturgy of the Hours by all the People of God which the Church views as the outstanding means to reestablish and strengthen that essential relationship within the life of every Christian, between life and prayer, between service to man and worship to God. Thus, complementing the Eucharist, the liturgical celebration of public praise and adoration rendered to the Father, in, with and through Christ, in the Hours, is seen as the most sacred and effective action which the Church can possibly perform to achieve these noble ends.[20]

It is precisely because of this conviction that the Church suggests to all pastors of souls that "whenever possible the more important Hours could be celebrated in common" within the local parish,[21] and then proceeds to strongly urge them to ensure "that the faithful are invited and helped by requisite instruction to celebrate the chief Hours in common, especially on Sundays and feasts."[22] And yet, despite the urgency of the situation, and the Church's specific directives and recommendation in this regard, there are still those who question the validity of the Liturgy of the Hours as a viable prayer for contemporary man.

All too often we hear the standard objections voiced repeatedly that although this reformed prayer may be ideal for use in religious communities, to attempt to reestablish the praying of the Hours on the parish level and to have it become something acceptable and valuable to the faithful would not only be impractical but futile as well. Many pastors claim that they have enough problems trying to get their people to come to Mass each Sunday and that expecting them to come to morning and evening prayer as well is unreal.[23] Such objections not only display an obvious disregard of the historical reality, but they also tend to ignore the signs of the times as the Church interprets them for her people.

In the very first chapter of this thesis we were made aware that it was precisely in the parishes that the Liturgy of the Hours originated and flourished for centuries. History reveals to us that it was particularly in the cathedral parishes where both clergy and laity actively participated in the communal celebration of the Daily Office consisting of morning and evening prayer.[24] The beautiful witness of Eusebius of Caesarea to the daily gathering of the faithful in all the churches of the Christian world at both sunrise and sunset for the offering up of hymns and praises to the Lord,[25] was echoed by St. Ambrose,[26] St. Augustine,[27] and many others,[28] all testifying to the common practice of the daily gathering of the faithful and clergy for the common celebration of the morning and evening Offices of the Church. And despite the eventual clericalisation and monasticisation of the cathedral Office, the faithful continued to participate, in varying degrees in the remnant of the cathedral Office, principally Matins before Mass and afternoon Vespers, down through the ages until relatively recent times.[29] Thus, there is a strong historical precedent in favor of the restoration of this venerable and valuable prayer to all the People of God, and it would be a tragic disservice to them and to the Church to refrain from doing so and to continue celebrating the Office as if it were still strictly a private clerical preserve.

Any hope for truly utilizing the Hours to their full advantage rests in faithful compliance with the principles so beautifully expressed in the *General Instruction.* These principles insist strongly that the liturgical leaders of the Church, namely bishops, priests and other sacred ministers, bear a grave obligation to do everything possible, sparing no effort to effectively lead their people in an appreciation of, and active participation in, this wonderful prayer wherein "they can have an impact on all men and contribute to the salvation of the whole world."[30] However, the only telling way in which this may be accomplished is if the bishops and pastors faithfully and fully assume their proper roles primarily as men of God and as the spiritual and liturgical leaders of their people.[31] The necessary element is that the day of each local community of faith be essentially centered in prayer.[32]

But not all the objections voiced against the introduction of the Divine Office on the parish level are directed against the Liturgy of the Hours per se, as a viable corporate prayer for all the faithful. Others, while agreeing upon the obvious value and need of this prayer for this purpose, have expressed skepticism that the Liturgy of the Hours, in its presently revised form, can be pastorally effective in this capacity.[33] The crux of their criticism rests upon the opinion that the reformed Hours continue to represent an essentially monastic and not a cathedral Office, and are consequently much better suited to be used for private devotion than as an expression of the communal, public worship of the faithful.[34] By far the most widespread and most serious of the reasons offered for arriving at this conclusion are the use of the *recitatio continua* of the psalter, or the monastic principle of the recitation of the entire psalter "in course," and the *lectio continua* of the rest of the sacred scriptures, which practices must presume upon the presence of the worshiper at every daily Office in order for it to make sense.[35] As far as public worship involving the laity is concerned, this arrangement is considered to be a totally unrealistic one.[36] Only a thorough historical knowledge of the development of the Divine

Office can serve to arrive at a full understanding of the problem and then to a satisfactory pastoral reform of the Hours today.[37]

Undoubtedly, the present form of the Office could use some adaptation in order to be more pastorally effective in its corporate, public celebration by the People of God. This is something which we will discuss at greater length later on in this chapter. However, we would like to underscore several points relevant to the criticisms voiced above. First of all, it seems that the intention of the Church in promoting the celebration of the Hours for all the faithful is principally centered upon the use of the chief Hours of Lauds and Vespers, "the two hinges upon which the daily Office turns," and the Hours which reflect most clearly the ancient cathedral Office.[38] Recognized as the Hours of the highest importance, full and active participation in their public and communal celebration is strongly encouraged for all the faithful.[39] Consequently, in the reform of Lauds and Vespers, the Church has made a serious, sincere and intelligent effort to design these Hours as effectively as possible for the specific purpose of celebration with the people, and in which the various elements comprising both Hours would be kept in harmony with the unique character of the Hours themselves.[40] Although the reformers have maintained the traditional monastic pattern of psalmody for the Office as a whole, they have also done everything possible to ensure that the psalms would be truly prayed rather than merely recited.[41] However, relative to the principal Hours of Lauds and Vespers, despite the rule of praying the psalms "in course," specific psalms have been chosen primarily for their suitability to the basic meaning of these Hours and to their public celebration with the people.[42] This is also true for the Hour of Compline seen as the ideal bedtime prayer for all Christians.[43]

On the other hand, there are those who feel that the very preponderance of psalms in themselves presents one of the principal difficulties with the Office and that people today find the psalter to be increasingly difficult to use as a form of Christian prayer.[44] As far as the merits and value of the psalms as Christian prayer are concerned, this has already been discussed in detail in Chapter III of this study,[45] and to repeat them now would be redundant. Therefore, at this point let us merely add some clarifying comments to this entire question.

The psalms, as the inspired word of God, have always been among the principal sources of prayer for the Christian community and as such have embedded themselves deeply into the entire tradition of the Church's prayer life. Although the psalms unquestionably need to be explained and understood in order to be most properly and effectively used as prayer in the Divine Office, they should not be neglected or casually abandoned unless every effort has first been made to implement the recommendations of the *General Instruction* proposed precisely for this very purpose.[46] While perhaps they could possibly be couched to a greater degree in the idiom of contemporary man, we can only talk about actually substituting some other prayers in place of the psalms when another form of prayer is available which is better suited to serve the needs of modern man, while at the same time maintaining the qualities of deep spirituality, poetic beauty and genuine prayerfulness so magnificently charterized by the psalms. Up to this point in time it seems that no such prayer has yet been composed or found. Therefore, despite the very real problem surrounding the effective use of the psalms in the revised Office, they still represent a most venerable form of Christian prayer which has proven itself to be of the greatest value for the spiritual enrichment and edification of the praying community of faith down through the ages. "From the very beginning they have had the power to raise men's minds to God, to evoke in them holy and wholesome thoughts, to help them give thanks in time of favor, and to bring consolation and constancy in adversity."[47]

Concerning the adoption of the *lectio continua* or the reading of the sacred scriptures "in course," this approach has always presented the Church with many problems. Since the Bible represents a large and very miscellaneous collection of books, a decision must be made in any reform whether to include the entire Bible, the *lectio continua,* or only certain parts of it, the *lectio electa.* Whichever choice is made, it always represents a very difficult one and is inevitably open to criticism of one form or another.[48] Although the present reform has seen fit to adopt the reading of the sacred scriptures "in course,"[49] it has also attempted to ensure the promotion of the overall spiritual and pastoral value, not only of the scriptural readings,[50] but of the other readings as well.[51]

The improvements made in this area over the past have been truly significant.

In addition to the criticisms voiced above, there is the accusation that the present Office is excessively formalistic and rigid in its overall structure and content, and that perhaps a balance should be sought between fixed formulas and improvisation.[52] However, once again the large number of possible variations offered by the new Office, if fully and properly utilized, could contribute greatly toward eliminating, or at least alleviating, such objections. As it now stands, the Liturgy of the Hours does provide a workable, stable structure which is necessary for any prayer which ordinarily is going to be used for public, communal worship on a regular basis. Anyone experienced in attempting to experiment with other structures or formats, spontaneous or otherwise, can vouch for the fact that sooner or later some stable structure is inevitably needed to fall back on. It becomes much too taxing for the participants' creative imaginations to consistently come up with viable new structures of quality and theological consistency each time the community gathers for prayer. The Liturgy of the Hours offers such a format as a stable and proven resource for the public, communal use of the faithful.[53]

While the criticisms which have been presented above do not exhaust all objections expressed relative to the reformed Office and its ability to serve the spiritual needs of the faithful in communal prayer, they do seem to represent the major objections voiced concerning this aspect of the Divine Office. We have not sought to enter in any way into a polemic on the merits and failings of these objections, but have simply sought to make the reader aware of them and at the same time to present some considerations on the Liturgy of the Hours relative to these objections, which would serve not so much to counter them as to present an overall more balanced view on the entire subject. All of these points in question have been dealt with before in one form or another in Chapter III of this study, however, it did seem necessary once again to recall the reader's attention at least to those more important concepts germane to this particular area of our development.

Overall, although the reformed Office seems to be a mixture of the older and newer traditions—cathedral and monastic—and although it is open to a certain amount of justifiable criticism, the reformers had sought to adapt it as well as possible to the needs of both clergy and laity. While this attempt seems to have been quite successful in relationship to the needs of the clergy, it does not seem to be quite as successful relative to the needs and the participation of the laity. With all the good efforts which have been expended to ensure the full, active participation of the faithful, the very multiplicity of elements of mixed literary forms make this prayer, most particularly Lauds and Vespers, a rather difficult one for easy adoption by the laity. However, the ability to use the Office with great flexibility should enhance the possibility of arriving at various solutions presented by the existing complexity of the Office.[54]

But similar to every new form of liturgy, the true virtues and defects of the revised Office will only be revealed when and if all the recommendations of the General Instruction are fully and effectively implemented and the communal celebration of the Office actually experienced by all the faithful on the parish level, over a considerable period of time. When this has been done, with the experiences having been fairly evaluated, and any parts of the Office are then found to be irrelevant or inadequate in any legitimate way, then the Church must seek to provide better forms and structures for the public prayer life of the faithful. The real danger lies in the possibility that this will not be done and that the people will not be given the necessary catchesis and leadership, as well as the opportunity to really experience the benefits of the celebration of the Hours in common. This would indeed be a tragedy for the Church, for all the faithful and clergy alike.

The Church has repeatedly expressed her confidence in the ability of this salutary prayer to serve contemporary man in a most significant manner.[55] For over six years there had been an enormous amount of research, study, consultation and experimentation on all levels of the Church, with the aid of many liturgical scholars and other experts as well, in order to meet the present-day spiritual needs of all the People of God. Because of this, the Church was very hopeful that this prayer would serve as a most wonderful means by which the glorified and risen Christ could continue to be authentically encountered throughout the Hours as an extension of the Eucharist, and as a true sacrifice of praise, thereby sanctifying the entire day of the Christian in prayer.[56] While the Church encourages private and spontaneous forms of prayer and sees them as necessary in the life of the Christian, rarely are these forms of prayer able to integrate an individual or community of believers into the liturgical cycle of the mystery of Christ in the Church Year as consistently and as effectively as the newly revised Liturgy of the Hours.[57] The particular form and structure of the new Office, despite its inevitable shortcomings, has the unique ability of being able to effectively accomplish this goal. This prayer can serve as a most valuable means by which the faithful would be united throughout the day with each other and with the Church as she moves progressively and logically through the continuous cycle of sacred time.

It has now been over fifteen years since the publication of *The General Instruction on the Liturgy of the Hours* in February 1971. As has already been stated in the previous chapter, the primary purpose for its publication, in anticipation of the appearance of the official four volume Latin edition of the reformed Divine Office, was to provide the means by which:

> . . . priests, religious and the faithful, whether individually or in groups gathered for study or prayer, may have the opportunity to familiarize themselves with the values of this new book of the Church, its special structure and the norms for celebrating the Liturgy of the Hours, as well as the spiritual benefits the People of God will gain from it.[58]

The appearance of the approved interim version of the Divine Office in English in 1971 provided a valuable means by which these directives could be put into practice while awaiting the publication of the definitive volumes of the Divine Office in the United States of America.[59] It has now been over eleven years since this publication has taken place and ten years since the publication of the one volume condensed edition. What has happened during this period of time, pastorally speaking, as far as the use of the Liturgy of the Hours on the parish level is concerned? Have pastors sought to promote this prayer among their people as recommended by the General Instruction?[60] Has there been a general acceptance among clergy and laity of the Liturgy of the Hours as a valuable means of solving the prayer gap within the lives of our Christian communities? These are not easy questions to answer with any great degree of detail and accuracy. However, on the basis of my own personal experience and investigations throughout the United States and Europe, I feel that it would be safe to say that while many pastors have indeed taken the initiative in this matter by introducing the Liturgy of the Hours to their people as effectively as possible, the vast majority have not.

That the Liturgy of the Hours is being used at all on the parish level, albeit in a limited fashion, is encouraging. However, while these positive developments may be reassuring in themselves, it seems that the negative aspect has the most to teach us. For this lack of implementation of the Liturgy of the Hours on the parish level demonstrates the essential fact that the marvelous potential of the Liturgy of the Hours to be able to fulfill, together with the Eucharist, the essential spiritual needs of the People of God, is remaining for the most part untapped. This should not be cause for undue alarm and discouragement as much as it should be an incentive for all concerned—laity and clergy—to begin now with renewed vigor to take the necessary steps to implement this prayer as fully and as quickly as possible into the everyday life of the Christian community.

Materials Now Available for the Communal Celebration of the Liturgy of the Hours

Since the publication of the *General Instruction on the Liturgy of the Hours* in February 1971, a wealth of material has appeared in the United States and elsewhere, relative to the Liturgy of the Hours and its celebration by all the People of God. Principal among these publications was the official four volume edition of the Divine Office.[61] However, despite its appearance and obvious great worth, it is certainly much too inconvenient and much too expensive an edition to lend itself to any widespread use by the faithful. It was precisely for these reasons that the Church, in special consideration of the needs of the laity, saw fit to authorize the publication of a much more practical and economical one volume edition of the Divine Office.[62] While the contents of these volumes vary according to the choice of the individual publisher, certainly fundamental to each of them are Morning Prayer and Evening Prayer, the two principal Hours upon which the entire Office revolves.[63] In addition to these two hinge Hours, there have been included in varying combinations, daytime prayer, night prayer (Compline), and the four week psalter for the Office of Readings, as well as a representative selection of hymns. It was hoped that, because of the availability of these one volume editions of the Office with their convenient size and economical cost in relation to the four volume edition, parishes throughout the country would thereby be more readily encouraged to use the Liturgy of the Hours as a communal prayer of praise and thanksgiving on a regular basis.

Over and above these official volumes there have also appeared good adaptations of Morning and Evening Prayer which represents a responsible, more simplified approach to the use of the Hours by the faithful,[64] as well as hymnals with special sections devoted to the Liturgy of the Hours,[65] and a substantial amount of hymnody and psalmody.[66] Therefore, the means are now available to fully and properly implement the Liturgy of the Hours on the parish level. The need to do so is as great and as important as ever. Consequently, both clergy and laity must put aside all unfounded fears, misgivings and excuses, and begin in earnest to familiarize themselves with the structure and contents of the Office in order to be able to move forward with the necessary knowledge, love, and determination toward achieving a full integration of the Prayer of the Hours into their parochial and communal lives.

Need for Adaptation in the Communal Celebration of the Liturgy of the Hours

However, while the new Liturgy of the Hours is certainly a most precious liturgical treasure, it remains extremely difficult to envision how this exceedingly rich and complicated prayer can ever be totally employed in the worship of the parish community on a regular basis except by a select minority. Both the *Constitution on the Sacred Liturgy* and the *General Instruction on the Liturgy of the Hours* place great emphasis upon the fact that Morning and Evening Prayer are the two most important Offices of the day.[67] In effect, this is a reaffirmation of the ancient cathedral Office, when aside from the Eucharist itself, these two Hours represented the principal daily and communal public prayer of the ancient Church. In the light of this pastoral emphasis, therefore, it seems that Morning and Evening Prayer should be restored once again to their original roles as ecclesiastical offices and consequently adapted as much as possible toward meaningful communal celebration with the laity. The entire cursus of seven Hours, while not totally excluded from the daily public participation of the laity, should be considered as the exception and certainly not the rule. There are those particular occasions when these prayers can be effectively employed within the Christian community and we will comment on this matter later in this discussion. But for the present, we are convinced that for Christians of today, with all the complexities of modern life, it would hardly be realistic to ask any more of them than that they once again reaffirm the practice of the cathedral Office in their lives by praying regularly, publicly, and communally, in the morning and in the evening. It is upon this premise that we will now proceed into our discussion of suggested guidelines which hopefully will serve both clergy and laity alike to achieve a meaningful and proper implementation of the Liturgy of the Hours within their communal parish prayer lives.

Practical Guidelines for the Implementation of the Liturgy of the Hours on the Parish Level

The following guidelines are presented as recommendations for the parish scene in general. To seek to draw up a list of guidelines that would be equally applicable to every parish would be both a presumptuous and impractical task. Therefore, the following recommendations must be adjusted and applied to the individual parish and its own particular characteristics and setting so that the very best results may be achieved.

A. *The Task of the Clergy:*

While the thrust of this entire study has centered upon the restoration of the laity to the public and communal celebration of the Divine Office, any hopes of successfully realizing such a goal is ultimately contingent upon the leadership, guidance, competence, and example of the clergy. The *Constitution on the Sacred Liturgy* affirms this in principle when, after stressing the necessity of the full cooperation of the faithful in order for the liturgy to produce its full effects, it goes on to insist that this will only happen when the clergy realizes its solemn duty to offer the necessary instruction and guidance.[68] Time and again the Constitution strongly reminds the sacred ministers of their obligation to promote the full and active participation of the laity in the liturgical celebrations of the Church, primarily through the advancement of the proper instruction as well as through the strength of personal example.[69]

The *General Instruction on the Liturgy of the Hours* reiterates these very same admonitions in a very specific application to the communal celebration of the Liturgy of the Hours when it declares the following:

> The task of those who are in sacred orders or who have a special canonical mission is to direct and preside over the prayer of the community; they should devote their labor to this end, that all those committed to their care may be of one mind in prayer. Pastors of souls should see to it that the faithful are invited and helped by requisite instruction to celebrate the chief Hours in common, especially on Sundays and feasts. They should teach them to draw sincere prayer from their participation and so help them to understand the psalms in a Christian way that they may gradually come to use and appreciate the prayer of the Church more fully.[70]

And yet, before the clergy can provide this requisite instruction and leadership in a truly effective manner, they must first be convinced of the ultimate value of the Liturgy of the Hours for their own personal prayer lives as well as for those of the faithful entrusted to them.[71] This calls for a radical change in the attitude of many priests and religious who for centuries, conditioned by legislation and tradition, have looked upon the Divine Office as a personal duty to be performed each day in its entirety under serious obligation and sanction, whenever and however this could be conveniently done. Unfortunately, for many the Office thus became more of a burdensome duty to be fulfilled privately, than a rewarding and inspiring prayer to be shared with their people.

Now, amid the pressures of their many pastoral duties, the Church is asking the clergy, not only to continue to recite the entire Office,[72] but to do so at a time most clearly corresponding to the true canonical time of each Hour,[73] and most importantly, to celebrate the chief Hours in common with their people.[74] In order to properly insure this, they are strongly urged to provide the proper catechetical instruction, leadership, and guidance.[75] This is certainly not an easy task for the clergy, but neither are these easy times in which we are living, and in order to promote and preserve a meaningful prayer life within our Christian communities, sacrifices must be made by all concerned, both clergy and laity alike. Convinced of the absolute necessity for such a program, and fired by a personal conviction in its innate value, the clergy must, therefore, seek to overcome all obstacles, be they real or imagined, to truly promote the communal celebration of the Liturgy of the Hours within their parishes. Once this program has been properly initiated, they will find the results both surprising and rewarding.

Consequently, the role of the clergy and their pastoral responsibility for the proper preparation of the Christian community in this matter remains absolutely essential, and without it the success of such a celebration, no matter how well intentioned, is doomed to failure. Presuming, therefore, upon the good will and the priestly zeal of the clergy, the process of providing the proper instruction to the laity may be initiated.

However, despite the very best of attitudes in this matter, one cannot give that which one does not possess. In ensuring the success of any catechetical program directed to the laity, "a prime need, is that attention be directed, first of all, to the liturgical instruction of the clergy."[76] The *Constitution on the Sacred Liturgy* makes particular recommendations in this regard for both seminaries and houses of religious as well as for priests, both secular and religious, who are already working in the Lord's vineyard.[77]

Relative to the revised Liturgy of the Hours, the clergy themselves must be well acquainted with the theology, history, composition, and meaning of the Hours in all their component parts, most especially the psalms.[78] This could possibly be accomplished by means of special clergy workshops, pastoral letters, printed educational material,[79] specially prepared cassette tapes on the topic,[80] a series of articles appearing in the diocesan newspaper, and any other viable means available.

Naturally, all this material will mean nothing unless the clergy is willing to use it for their own educational and pastoral development. The bishop, as the high priest of his flock, should ensure the promotion of this type of education within his diocese through the services of his Diocesan Liturgical Commission.[81]

What we have been underscoring in these past few pages is the essential role that the clergy must play in any such pastoral program, a role which must involve not only the willingness to instruct and lead the faithful, but which must also involve the proper personal conviction and preparation in order to be able to do so effectively. Assuming, therefore, that pastors have been well-prepared and that they are also well-disposed toward fulfilling their particular responsibilities in these matters, the ideal being stated, the proper catechesis of the People of God may then take place.

B. *Catechesis:*

Whether or not the public, communal celebration of the Liturgy of the Hours bears lasting fruit among the faithful depends in a large measure upon the degree of instruction and preparation which they have received in the process. Without this preparation and understanding, the Office will become simply another novelty which for lack of roots will quickly wither and fade away. The Diocesan Liturgical Commission must do everything possible to design a well-planned catechetical program for their people which each parish must then incorporate and adapt to its own particular make-up and needs.

Essentially, the entire catechesis should involve a basic development on prayer with special emphasis placed upon the revised Liturgy of the Hours, its history, theology, structure, form, contents, and importance for the lives of the faithful.[82] In addition, a simple instruction on biblical themes with an analysis of the psalms as Christian prayer should be emphasized as well. There are many fine texts now available which could be used for this purpose.[83] In order to most effectively accomplish this, the Diocesan Liturgical Commission could possibly sponsor evening or weekend workshops for the laity and religious on parish liturgy teams which can be a tremendous help to any busy pastor in promoting the proper implementation of the Liturgy of the Hours on all levels of parish life. Perhaps these workshops could then be duplicated on a regular basis, with some necessary modifications, on the individual parish level in the form of special seminars or classes in which the pastor and his assistants, together with the parish liturgy team, could then apply their workshop experience to the lives of those interested faithful of the parish.[84]

Another possible approach to this question which could prove to be most effective would be the practice of conducting small prayer services in the various homes of the faithful of the parish, to which small groups of fellow parishioners are invited. These meetings could be prefaced by a brief informal period during which some modest but essential instruction is imparted on the Office and its value for the prayer life of the Christian community. The fruit of these discussions could then be put to actual use in the celebration of an appropriate Hour. It would seem that in this intimate, communal setting much could be imparted, learned, and exchanged to everyone's mutual advantage. The idea would be to conduct these services in such a way so that eventually the entire parish membership would be covered, at least geographically, perhaps several times before the Liturgy of the Hours is initiated as an official parish program. Ideally, whatever is learned and experienced in these small, communal encounters in prayer, could then be imparted to the larger parochial communal service, and there integrated into the worship of the entire parish community. All of these means can collectively serve to instruct and prepare both clergy and laity in the very best possible way, not only to properly initiate the prayer of the Hours for the entire parish community, but also to guarantee that it will really be the meaningful and rewarding experience that it was meant to be.

C. *Liturgical Roles:*

"In liturgical celebrations each person, minister, or layman, who has an office to perform, should do all of, but only, those parts which pertain to his office by the nature of the rite and the principles of liturgy."[85] With these words the *Constitution on the Sacred Liturgy* reaffirms once again an ancient liturgical tradition reflective of a fundamental understanding of the make-up of the worshiping community of faith. The Christian community, although one in faith, represents many unique individuals, each responsible for assuming his or her own particular role and performing his/her own special function within the drama of Christian worship.

In the celebration of the Liturgy of the Hours as in other liturgical actions, whether as a minister or as one of the faithful, each person should perform his role by doing solely and totally what the nature of things and liturgical norms require of him.[86]

Through these recommendations the Church seeks to restore and to preserve the integrity of the hierarchical character of the liturgy wherein each individual is guaranteed the right and privilege of exercising his distinct charism and function within any liturgical celebration in which he may be participating. Thus both clergy and laity should faithfully discharge their own appropriate functions and, under normal circumstances, neither one should capitulate that function to another or others, or usurp someone else's function to himself.

Whenever the faithful are gathered together in Church to pray the Liturgy of the Hours in common, the bishop (ideally), or his representative, the pastor or one of his fellow priests, should "direct and preside over the prayer of the community."[87] In his role as the normative leader of the community, the priest or deacon must attempt, to the best of his ability by means of a good sense of celebration, to create an atmosphere conducive to prayer. This should be accomplished above all through the proper personal preparation, both rubrically and prayerfully, as well as through an awareness of the general effects of his presence, manner, and tone upon this community celebration. As leader, he will be responsible for the initiation of the action and for summing-up the reflections of the entire worshiping community. This would include beginning the Office with the introductory verse, initiating the Lord's Prayer, pronouncing the concluding prayer, greeting, blessing, and dismissing the people.[88]

However, there will be times when despite the very best of intentions a priest or deacon, for good pastoral reasons, may not be available at the scheduled time of celebration in church. It is in view of these occasions the General Instruction asserts that one of the faithful may preside provided he or she exercised this role as one among equals.[89] This also provides the opportunity for groups of the faithful to pray the Hours on other occasions whenever they are gathered together for whatever reason and there may be no priest or deacon present.[90] Certainly, a great degree of solemnity and beauty would be added to the celebration if the leader were able, at least on Sundays and principal feasts, to sing the texts of the various prayers and blessings designated to him.[91] And this takes us into a consideration of another important role in the public celebration of the Divine Office, namely that of the cantor.

The General Instruction informs us that "a cantor or cantors should begin the antiphons, psalms, and other songs,"[92] while the manner in which the psalms are sung can be varied according to the norms of nn. 121-125.[93] While the faithful are encouraged to sing the Hours as "the form which best accords with the nature of this prayer,"[94] they should sing only those parts which they are capable of singing without placing an undue strain or burden upon their resources and patience.[95] The cantor can do much to ensure the success of any such sung celebration of the Hours by leading and supporting the faithful to the extent that they may need his assistance, and by establishing a certain harmony of listening and responding between himself and the faithful. However, the cantor should never assume so great a musical responsibility that the role of the faithful is overly curtailed. The less the involvement of the faithful, the greater the danger of their losing interest and being reduced to passivity and non-participation.

Although ideally the cantor should possess a certain basic musical ability, he or she need not be a professional. With a pleasant voice and the proper training, the cantor should be able to perform his role with all necessary competence, dignity, and beauty to ensure a prayerful and rewarding service. If there should be no one capable of properly fulfilling this important role within the parish, then every effort should be made to find someone willing and able to assume this function and then to provide that person with the necessary training.[96] Properly exercised, the role of the cantor can be a most important means of ensuring the beauty and prayerfulness of any communal celebration of the Hours, since the pace and overall effect of any Hour is very much influenced by the manner and care with which the antiphons, opening verses of the psalms, hymns, and canticles are intoned.

Another very important role of the communal celebration of the Hours is that of the lector whose function is to proclaim the readings.[97] Fundamental to the effective exercise of this function is the proper amount of preparation. No matter how capable or how confident the lector may feel, the readings, be they long or short, should be well prepared in advance. Without this preparation the best of readers could prove to be ineffectual. Normally, unaccustomed to many of the biblical and theological terms and expressions found in readings, the lector, through the proper preparation and consultation, will ensure the elimination of any errors in his rendition.

The lector must also be able to proclaim the readings at the proper rate of speed, distinctly and loudly enough so that all assembled will be able to hear and to understand them clearly. Perhaps a public address system could be used advantageously for this purpose, especially if the service is being held in a large church or hall,[98] or if it is acoustically difficult to hear the readings clearly without it. It is also very important that the lector read with reverence and conviction while at the same time avoiding all traces of affectation in his delivery.

In any communal celebration of the Hours with the people it seems that the option of choosing longer and perhaps more suitable readings is to be recommended.[99] This will not only prove to be more beneficial to the faithful listeners, but will also serve to make the lector's task somewhat easier. In addition, if there is to be a homily, this will also afford the homilist a richer source of material for his reflection, commentary, and application.[100] The General Instruction goes on to tell us that "the lector should stand in a suitable place to proclaim the readings...."[101] Any such suitable place most assuredly will be a prominent location in full view of the assembly. Consequently, the lector should also be very much aware of his general appearance and bearing before the community. He should not slouch, read with his head down buried in the book, or in any way distract the faithful from listening attentively and devotedly to the readings being proclaimed. If these few basic rules are observed faithfully, then the lector's performance will be certain to enhance rather than impede the message of the sacred readings.

Other roles such as that of the acolytes, cross bearer, thurifer, and additional readers or cantors may be assumed as well. However, whether the entire number of roles be expanded or reduced will ultimately depend upon the size of the worshiping community, the particular needs of the parish, the measure of talents and creativity available and employable in the general organization of the service, and the degree of solemnity that one wishes to achieve. Whatever the role, it should have been assigned well in advance, and the person so delegated should be urged to prepare himself for it in the best possible manner.

Two practical points in the realm of human relations should be borne in mind. The assignment of roles should never be based on favoritism of any kind. The selection should always be made fairly and impartially, after consultation, and on the grounds of the proper qualifications, and these roles should be open to the possibility of rotation among other qualified members of the parish. It would also be wise to install these selected people into their particular roles within the context of some religious ceremony during which they could be introduced to the other members of the parish and their roles briefly explained. In addition, it would be advisable to award them with a religious medallion or some such object as a symbol of the particular liturgical role they have been called upon to fulfill.

D. *Singing in the Liturgy of the Hours:*

Sacred music has always held an exalted position within the Church's life of worship. It is in maintaining this venerable tradition that the *Constitution on the Sacred Liturgy* makes the following affirmation: "Liturgical worship is given a more noble form when the divine offices are celebrated solemnly in song, with the assistance of sacred ministers and the active participation of the people."[102] Relative to the Divine Office, it is in the light of the above statement that the General Instruction strongly recommends the sung form of the Office to all who celebrate it in choir or in common since it is more reflective of the true nature of this prayer, as well as more fully expressive of its solemnity and of the unity of hearts in the worshiping community.[103] Therefore, in planning for any communal celebration of the Office, everything possible should be done to provide the faithful with the suitable instruction and practices, so that they may be enabled to more fully participate in the sung parts of the Office which pertain to them.[104]

While it would be ideal to sing the entire Hour being celebrated, for many parishes this would be impractical and often impossible. Therefore, although the ideal should be a constant goal, consideration must always be given to the age, status, and way of life and degree of religious culture of the faithful.[105] Consequently, each parish must adapt according to its own musical strengths and weaknesses in attempting to achieve a considerable amount of variety augmented by a proper balance within each celebration, between the sung and recited sections, and the periods of reflective silence.[106] However, no matter how difficult it may be for the faithful to sing the entire Hour being celebrated, their particular role, although adjustable, should never be overly dominated by clergy, cantor, or choir. Each can help immeasurably in their own turn to ensure the success of any sung Hour, but the participation of the faithful in song must always be encouraged as much as possible.[107] Parishes should especially strive to sing the Office on Sundays and feast days, with preference given to the two principal Hours of Lauds and Vespers.[108]

The hymn can be a most effective pastoral tool for promoting the community's singing of the Divine Office for "they help to move the people taking part and draw them into the celebration."[109] Because of their very lyrical nature they are meant to be sung and not merely recited.[110] While for the sake of variety two series of hymns have been provided for each Hour, the option is also open for the selection of new hymns.[111] But the introduction of any new hymns should never be the result of an arbitrary process for they should always be reflective in some way of the spirit of the Hour, season, or feast.[112] While initially it would seem most practical to use hymns with which the community is familiar, parishes should never allow themselves to become entrapped in the two or three hymn syndrome. After a certain basic corpus of hymns has been learned, new hymns should be continually added in order to provide an additional richness of variety and meaning to the service while at the same time avoiding monotony and the unnecessary restrictions imposed on the community's creative prayer because of a limited repertoire of hymns.

Similar to the hymns, the canticles, responsories, and the psalms are of a lyrical nature and, consequently, they should be sung as well.[113] In fact, in order to fully understand many of the psalms it is especially appropriate that they be sung, and every effort should be made to do so particularly for the more important Hours.[114] This can be accomplished in a variety of ways as outlined by the General Instruction, not for any superficial reason, but in order that the meaning and spirit of the psalms may be more faithfully preserved.[115] There are many publications presently available which are able to provide any parish community with a wide variety of musical settings for hymns, psalms, and canticles.[116] Each parish should be certain to avail itself of those publications which it feels may be better suited to its particular needs. In addition, every effort should be made to discover those members of the parish who may be musically gifted, and to enlist their help and support in the promotion of the singing of the Hours. The conscientious promotion and use of liturgical singing in the parish can be an essential element in the development of a truly rewarding, exciting, and prayerful public celebration of the Liturgy of the Hours.

E. *The Use of Silence in the Liturgy of the Hours:*
In marked contrast to all the reading and singing which must be exercised in the communal celebration of the Hours, and yet in a very real and important way complementary to it, is the proper use of silence. Our modern society with all its movement and sound, is not accustomed to silence and in general is not very comfortable with it. And yet, silence should be an indispensable element of every liturgical celebration. The *Constitution on the Sacred Liturgy* makes this quite clear when it declares that in the promotion of the active participation of the faithful, not only should they be encouraged to take part by means of acclamations, responses, psalmody, antiphons, songs, actions, gestures, and bodily attitudes, but also by means of the proper use of silence.[117] The General Instruction reaffirms this in relationship to the Divine Office by stressing the need for providing the opportunity to observe reverent periods of silence in the celebration of the Liturgy of the Hours.[118]

Why such stress upon silence, upon the absence of words and of sound? Because a reverent period of silence represents much more than a mere absence of something. More than anything else it represents an attitude of mind, a spirit of sensitive receptivity which must be cultivated and used properly in order to effect a full and meaningful experience in prayer. The General Instruction explains it in this manner: "The purpose of this silence is to allow the voice of the Holy Spirit to be heard more fully in our hearts, and to unite our personal prayer more closely with the Word of God and the public voice of the Church."[119]

Such periods of silence may be effectively employed in the public celebration of the Hours in the following ways: after the psalms, once the antiphon has been repeated; after the reading, whether long or short; and before or after the responsory.[120] If there should be a brief homily, then certainly a period of silence would be more effective at its conclusion rather than after the reading which would precede it. These periods of silence must be well-integrated into the rhythm of the entire service. If the celebration is rushed then these silent pauses will seem unnatural and forced and thus meaningless. This valuable time of prayer must be a time for slowing down, for relaxtion and repose, for solace and recuperation of peace and strength. And yet, at the same time, we must avoid falling into the opposite excess of an indiscriminate multiplication or prolongation of silences which could, in effect, either deform the structure of the Office, or cause the faithful to be uncomfortable or bored.[121] The entire service should be well-balanced between those elements which are sung, those which are spoken, and those measured moments of silence.[122] Once again the clergy can play an important role in the laity's acceptance and proper use of silence in the Liturgy of the Hours if they possess a good pastoral sense of its use in the liturgy and also if they have already been making proper use of these periods of reflective silence called for in the Eucharistic liturgies celebrated throughout the year.[123] Therefore, through careful and gradual preparation, the faithful must be led to a deeper appreciation of the mystery of silence and its great value within their prayer lives, for these precious moments afford each individual worshiper the opportunity to personalize that which has been read, heard, and sung. Only in this way will the public celebration of the Liturgy of the Hours be assured of becoming a profound and living experience in prayer rather than merely an exercise in word and song.[124]

F. *Bodily Nature in the Liturgy of the Hours:*

Individuals express themselves by means of actions and all the movements of their minds and hearts are shown forth by their gestures and their bodily attitudes. Above all, this phenomenon is of special significance when the faithful are involved in the exercise of public and communal prayer. Thus the participation of the faithful in the public celebration of the Liturgy of the Hours should be an action which involves the whole person of each member of the worshiping community. Generally we have shown little concern for this particular aspect of worship and yet it should be given careful consideration in any planning of a communal, liturgical service. In recent years there has been a general reaction against all forms of rubricism and triumphalism in the Church, much of it for good reason. However, while the use of gestures and bodily attitudes should never be employed in a merely formalistic or ritualistic manner, used thoughtfully, prudently, and with dignity, these outward manifestations of prayer are able to contribute significantly to the success of any public liturgical celebration through the living worship of the whole person.[125]

Therefore, it is very important that we instill an understanding of, and appreciation for this bodily aspect of the liturgical celebration of the Hours in all our people. This should be accomplished primarily through a proper catechesis which would entail not only establishing why this involvement should be present, but most importantly underscoring that these actions and bodily attitudes constitute the necessary outward expression of the inner state of prayer, as well as the stimulus to the initiation of that very same prayer. The more profound the prayer, the greater the involvement of the whole person. These outward actions and gestures become prayers in themselves as through them we communicate with God. In turn, these same outward manifestations of prayer can stimulate, dispose, and evoke in us a deeper state of interior prayer.[126]

Translated into more specific terms, any planning of the public celebration of the Liturgy of the Hours should always give serious and careful consideration to this involvement of the whole person in prayer. The thoughtful use of processions involving candles, incense, song, and dramatic movement can be a most effective means of initiating the service and highlighting the solemnity of the occasion.[127] Such bodily attitudes as standing, kneeling, and sitting are all postures illustrative of the contribution which body language can make to the enhancement of a true atmosphere of prayer.

Standing at the introduction to the Office and at the introductory verse of each Hour is not only the sign of the initiation of a solemn period of prayer, but also a sign of respect for the bishop, priest, or other sacred ministers who may be entering the Church at the time.[128] Standing during the hymn, besides being very practical by facilitating full participation in the singing, also emphasizes the element of praise inherent in all the hymns.[129] Standing during the Gospel Canticle, during the prayers, the Lord's Prayer, and the concluding prayers also serves to illustrate the special attitudes of joy, respect, and belief which are inherent in these particular movements of the Hours.[130] Except for the Gospel, the entire community should always be seated during the readings for this is a position which best facilitates listening, meditation, and repose—attitudes most proper and conducive for deriving the full benefits from the word of God, as well as from the other selected readings.[131] Although the community may sit or stand according to custom, during the recitation of the psalms and other songs with their antiphons, it would seem most appropriate to be seated, since they are longer reflective prayers of praise.[132] Kneeling as a traditional posture of penitence and petition, can be used most effectively during any particular celebration where these two elements need to be emphasized, or during the penitential seasons of the Church's liturgical year, most particularly during the concluding prayers of the service.

All of these bodily attitudes, as well as any other appropriate actions or hand gestures such as a sign of peace, or the sign of the cross,[133] are part and parcel of the community's prayer and consequently should always be performed gently, with dignity and conviction.

In this entire question of the proper use of action, movement and gestures, a good sense of timing is also very important. Being able to sense when it is the proper time to move, to remain still, to speak, or to remain silent, are all essential factors contributing to the overall effectiveness of the service. Allowing the community enough time to sit, stand, settle down, or to find their places in the breviary before intoning a prayer, hymn, antiphon, psalm, or reading, may seem like a simple enough thing to do, yet it is a very necessary thing which requires a certain degree of sensitivity essential to good order and harmony. Therefore, the full movement of the bodily nature of each participant in the Liturgy of the Hours, coupled with a basic understanding of its meaning, can be a most effective means of involving the whole person in worship and contributing significantly to the overall quality and success of the celebration.

However, it is most important to note that whenever discussing these bodily attitudes in the liturgy, we must seek to convince the people that when the presence of God in the midst of the praying community is accepted as a real, vibrant, and active life force, then the actions, gestures, and other bodily attitudes relating to this transcendent God will be truly religious and worshipful. But when the immediacy and vitality of God's presence ceases to be a reality for the praying community, then the actions will become forced, theatrical, and devoid of any real significance.[134]

G. *The Setting for the Liturgy of the Hours:*

The setting for the celebration of the Hours by the parish community could possibly involve holding the service in various locales, however, it is recommended that the parish church be the principal setting, just as it is for the Eucharistic liturgy. The arrangement of the sanctuary should be simple, dignified, and uncluttered. While it would be ideal to have the community seated in a manner that would facilitate rather than hinder the interaction of prayer,[135] many churches in the United States of America are not open to such options since they have fixed pews facing forward. However, one must adapt as best as possible to these situations.

The use of such elements as light or darkness, candles, holy water, incense, or banners, should all be decided upon and planned well in advance. The utilization of any multi-media, audio-visual elements can also be very effective if well-planned. But before the initiation of the actual service, all the necessary equipment should be in place, pretested, in good working order, and ready to be used at the proper time without hesitation, awkwardness, or unnecessary delays. The celebration itself is certainly not the place for experimentation. Unless this is

done extremely well, with prudence and good judgment, it could prove
to be a great obstacle to prayer rather than a contribution.[136]

Any vestments to be used by the ministers in the service, such as a
stole over the alb or surplice, a cope, or a dalmatic,[137] should all be
determined and prepared well in advance for ready use in the celebration. It is also important, as a sign of reverence and respect, that all
such vestments be clean and presentable. Although, many of these
elements may seem to be of little importance in themselves they all
contribute to the creation of the proper setting for the celebration and
its possible success or failure. If not planned well, prepared well, and
used properly, these same elements can contribute to the overall
breakdown of the service, rather than to the creation of a truly
prayerful experience.

H. *The Scheduling of the Liturgy of the Hours:*

The question of the proper scheduling of these prayer services
requires much thought, discussion and pastoral awareness. We know
that there are parishes presently celebrating morning prayer within
the context of the morning Eucharistic service. While the coupling of
the Hours with the Eucharistic celebration is certainly an option
provided for by the General Instruction, nevertheless, it is offered with
reservations, urging that special precautions be taken to ensure that
this type of liturgical practice does not prove to be pastorally
harmful.[138]

For the Hours not only serve as an excellent preparation for the
Eucharist but also, through the sanctification of time, complement the
Eucharist as they extend its saving effects throughout the course of the
day.[139] It would seem that if overdone this practice of joining an Hour
to the Eucharist would vitiate those dimensions of that particular
Hour and would tend to rob, or at least diminish, both the Hour and
the Eucharist of some of their individual uniqueness and pastoral
effectiveness. However, used prudently, with moderation and for a
good pastoral reason, according to the rubrics outlined by the General
Instruction, it can serve on occasion to meet a real pastoral need.[140] It
may also be possible to effectively combine the celebration of the
Office with such other traditional Catholic devotions as the recitation

of the rosary, or with Benediction of the Blessed Sacrament, or with the exposition of the Blessed Sacrament for a Holy Hour devotion.[141]

We know that there are other parishes that have scheduled the celebration of morning prayer with relative success about twenty minutes to one half hour before the principal morning Eucharistic liturgy. While idealistically speaking it would be better to avoid such liturgical overloading as the above forms of scheduling seem to represent, nevertheless these particular options do seem to offer some practical solutions for most parishes in the very difficult pastoral problem of proper scheduling.[142] Evening prayer offers a greater possibility of choice in this matter since the evenings are generally more open for people to attend. There is also a greater opportunity to develop more elaborate liturgies, with the involvement of more liturgical roles and the more extensive use of such elements as lightness and darkness, incense, song, and ceremony, which morning prayer does not normally offer. Certainly, Sunday Vespers would be especially suited for such a full-scale evening service.

Concerning the frequency of celebration, perhaps initially the celebration of Lauds and Vespers could be introduced on Sundays and special feasts, and then only gradually expanded to a daily celebration as people become more accustomed to these prayers and as they assume more and more of a place in the prayer life of the community. However, no matter how well-planned the scheduling of the Hours may be, we must never delude ourselves into thinking that the entire parish community will be present. Even if there is initially just a small representative group in attendance for any celebration of the Hours, the important thing is that the prayer of the Church is being celebrated publicly, at fixed times, and that throughout the course of the week there are some faithful present who could serve as a core group which would help to establish and eventually influence the participation of more members of the parish community in this celebration.[143] Ultimately, the entire difficult question of scheduling must be a decision left up to the careful pastoral judgment of the local pastor in consultation with the parish liturgy team, with the faithful of the parish, and always in consideration of the particular character and needs of the local community.

I. *Other Occasions for the Use of the Liturgy of the Hours:*

Aside from Lauds and Vespers as the two principal Hours of celebration for the entire Christian community, any other Hour could be celebrated as well according to the pastoral needs and opportunities of each parish. Normally, within the life of any parish, there are many such opportunities to utilize the Liturgy of the Hours, especially for smaller groups of the faithful outside of the context of the entire parish community. Gatherings of youth groups, sodalities, seminars, and any other type of select parish congregation, meeting for prayer, the apostolate or for some other purpose, could provide the occasion for the celebration of some part of the Divine Office.[144] Depending upon the particular time of the day at which these gatherings take place, the appropriate Hour could be planned for and celebrated as the indispensable element of prayer central to any such meetings.[145]

However, fundamental to any effective prayer either by the entire parish community or by smaller groups as mentioned above, and indispensable for the survival of the parish and the growth of the Church, is family prayer. "As the domestic sanctuary of the Church," the family would certainly be a most fitting and appropriate milieu for the celebration of that prayer which will unite it more closely to the Church.[146] This is an area which needs much pastoral attention and catechesis, and any program for the restoration of the Hours on the parochial level should certainly include first and foremost, a promotion of prayer in general within the individual families of the parish where religious attitudes are formed and nourished. For it is within the family unit that the individual is better able to learn, appreciate, and assimilate Christian values as well as to express himself in relationship to them, thus developing true Christian maturity.[147]

Once good habits of prayer have been well-established within the Christian home, then certainly it would be appropriate to include some part of the Liturgy of the Hours within this life of prayer. What could be more inspirational than to witness a Christian family—father, mother, and children—gathered together at the end of each day, or at least as often as possible, united with Christ and with the entire Church, for the recitation of Compline as their nighttime prayer? What a marvelous example and experience for the children in each family, and how important and crucial for the building-up of the love of prayer within their young lives. It is here that the prayer life of the parish must find its meaning and strength. And since the family is the community within which we first experience the presence of God, it is only fitting that within this same community we learn to thank him and to praise him for his love and for his countless gifts of grace.[148]

This beautiful practice of home prayer could certainly grow out of the small group prayer meetings conducted throughout the parish as part of the preparation for the praying of the Hours on the parish level, and then could continue to be practiced as a vital part of the home prayer life of each family member in attendance. The Liturgy of the Hours as the prayer of the entire parish community could then be built, supported, and strengthened from the basic family unit, through the various group units, and on up to the principal parish unit of the entire worshiping community of faith. Thus, inaugurated in this manner, the Liturgy of the Hours would have penetrated all levels of parish life.

J. *The Order of Celebration for the Liturgy of the Hours:*[149]

Because of the complexity, variability and expense of the present form of the revised Liturgy of the Hours, it would seem both practical and realistic to initiate the celebration of the principal Hours of Lauds and Vespers on the parish level in a much more simplified and uninvolved manner. Therefore, initially the order of celebration should be kept simple, with a more or less standard format, while at the same time adhering to the essential thrust and structure of the official Office.[150] This can be accomplished by fully utilizing those recommendations of the General Instruction which permit and encourage adaptation of the Liturgy of the Hours to the particular needs of the Christian community in their public worship. Eventually, once the community becomes well-adapted to this order of celebration, perhaps a more elaborate format may be introduced.

The structure of this parish Office should more closely emulate the ancient cathedral Office of the Church. Therefore, after the introductory verse and response invoking God's help and blessing,[151] the following basic order of service should be followed:

1. *The Opening Hymn*: This hymn could be taken from any authorized source provided that it suits the spirit of the Hour, season, or feast. It is recommended that it be sung. Therefore, both text and music should always be made available.[152]

2. *The Antiphons:* An antiphon is said, or sung at the beginning of each psalm and may be repeated at the conclusion of the psalm.[153]

3. *The Psalms:* The psalms, and the Old and New Testament canticles, may be recited or sung in various ways; either with alternate verses or strophes recited or sung by two choirs or two separate groups of the congregation, or in responsorial fashion, that is with the choir, or the entire body of the faithful, answering the cantor, who sings or recites the psalms, with a simple refrain.[154]

4. *The Readings:* These readings from Sacred Scripture should be proclaimed from a suitably prominent position by a well-qualified lector, or some other delegated person.[155] Other appropriate readings may be used as well, but only to supplement and never to substitute for the scriptures. Although the service is to be kept simple, it is recommended that, especially in celebrations with the people, a longer selection from the sacred scriptures be read and that a brief commentary or homily be given.[156] The readings, or homily, should be followed by a period of meditative silence.[157]

5. *The Gospel Canticle:* These canticles are expressive of the entire community's praise and thanksgiving for its redemption. At morning prayer this includes the Canticle of Zechariah, or the *Benedictus* (Lk. 1:68-79); while at evening prayer the Canticle of the Blessed Virgin Mary, the *Magnificat* (Lk. 1:46-55), is used.[158]

6. *The Intercessions:* These are prayers of petition, intercession, and thanksgiving offered up for everyone. At morning prayer they are characterized by a spirit of offering and consecration of the entire day to God; while at evening prayer they are characterized by a spirit of petition and thanksgiving, with a special final intention for all the faithful departed.[159]

7. *The Lord's Prayer:* Made sacred by tradition, this model prayer

serves as a most fitting conclusion to the worshiping community's celebration of morning and evening prayer. It is recommended that it be sung standing.[160]

8. *The Concluding Prayer, Final Blessing, and Dismissal:* A concluding prayer brings to completion the celebration of the Hours. This summary prayer, as well as the final blessing and dismissal, traditionally pertain to the priest or deacon. However, if both should be absent, another form of dismissal which does not imply authority may be employed by one of the faithful. This final blessing and dismissal by the leader calls down God's blessing upon the praying community and sends it forth in hope, joy, and confidence under his protective power.[161]

A simple, inexpensive Office could be drawn up from the above structure for use on the parish level which would involve a minimal amount of material and expense. Since, as we have already noted, the opening hymn may be taken from any authorized source,[162] use can be made of those church hymnals already available for parochial use. Because the antiphons need not be repeated after each psalm,[163] they could be recited or intoned by a cantor or by some other designated person.[164] Ideally, the readings should be *listened to*, therefore, since they will be proclaimed by the lector, it would be best not to place a copy of them in the hands of the worshiping community.[165] Both parts of the intercessions may be recited by the priest or minister and need only involve the faithful to the point of repeating an invariable response after each intercession, or to simply pause in silence.[166] The Lord's Prayer is well-known to everyone and can certainly be recited from memory, while the concluding prayer, final blessing, and dismissal pertain to the priest or minister.[167] Therefore, at least initially, all that the people would need would be an economical copy of the psalter properly arranged according to the Hours, a copy of the Old and New Testament Canticles used in Lauds and Vespers, and a copy of the *Benedictus* and the *Magnificat*, in order to be able to participate fully and actively in the celebration of the Liturgy of the Hours.[168]

In planning for any communal celebration of the Hours, it is essential that the praying community be made to feel as comfortable and as familiar as possible with what they are going to be doing. If the faithful come to the service knowing little or nothing of what to expect, this could lead to uneasiness, embarrassment, and discouragement, and could very well vitiate all the good efforts previously expended in the proper preparation. It is essential, therefore, that they have a clear indication of exactly what is expected of them at each point of the celebration. This objective could be effected in various ways. Prior to the actual initiation of the Office, the order of service should be distributed to the entire assembly. This would include all of those directives necessary for the full and active participation of the people including the proper posture. All of this could be printed on a simple card and enclosed in the people's copy of the psalms and canticles. As a further help it could also be printed in the parish bulletin. All other variable information such as hymn numbers, could be posted in church where all could clearly see it, or announced verbally just before the service.

It is also important that the people be exhorted to be present in church at least five minutes before the scheduled time for the Hour in order that some more proximate preparation or instruction may be actively shared in. This will allow the community time to adjust to any last minute changes or announcements and will also offer the opportunity for a brief but very valuable practice during which the hymns and any other sung portions of the Office may be quickly rehearsed. But the people must not only be impressed with the need for punctuality, but primarily for their presence and active participation as elements vital to the support of the community and the ultimate success of the celebration. The clergy themselves can give the best example in this regard. Tardiness can lead to rushing, confusion, and frustration and can consequently destroy the atmosphere necessary for fruitful prayer, while absenteeism can weaken the very structure of community which is so essential to this communal gathering for prayer.

Finally, once the praying community is gathered in church and ready to begin the service, allow a brief period of silence so that everyone may become recollected and properly disposed for this encounter with the Lord.[169] For no matter how well prepared the community may be, and no matter how perfectly designed the order of service may be, ultimately the success or failure of the service will depend upon each individual present, clergy and laity alike, who will be primarily responsible for the degree and quality of his participation. His daily personal life of faith and prayer will greatly determine the quality and intensity of his encounter with Christ in this particular Hour. Thus, if the Office truly becomes a profound experience of prayer for any individual, it is undoubtedly because prayer already occupied a precious portion of his personal life. But the liturgy also has the power to foster and to nourish prayer in the life of the Christian. Therefore, the individual's openness, and his life of charity toward God and neighbor will be the greatest assurance that this communal gathering of prayer will be truly a fruitful, rewarding, and faith-filled experience. Now, let the celebration of the Liturgy of the Hours begin.

Conclusion

In the face of a very real crisis of faith and prayer in the world today, there is a pressing hunger for prayer among those who are genuinely concerned. The Spirit is working to preserve and to strengthen his Church and the Liturgy of the Hours can serve to fill this need for prayer in a most salutary way. The Church feels that this is so and has offered its faithful this renewed Divine Office as a precious gift recommending that it once again become a very special prayer for all believers.

The clergy has a most important role to play in this entire religious drama. The People of God will respond generously and enthusiastically to a celebration of the Hours that is thoroughly well-prepared, well-celebrated and initiated through a lively and wholehearted conviction of its value for the Christian life. The Divine Office, however, must never be reduced to a perfunctory performance of formalistic, external forms. Rather, it should become a marvelous sign of the very real encounter between God and his people in word, song, and action. It should never, however, remain merely a sign, but it must become a sacramental sign in that it truly effects what it signifies, namely, the very real union of the spirit of man with that of God.

All clergy, awakened to the new possibilities of this wonderful prayer, must not presume upon a spontaneous outpouring of the Holy Spirit but must instead be true leaders who will see to it that their people receive the proper instruction and guidance needed to understand and to participate meaningfully in the celebration of the Hours. Necessarily this will demand preparation which in turn will require a genuine understanding of the people and a sensitivity to their needs. It will also demand that the leaders of prayer must generously give of themselves in this entire endeavor and seek to truly involve themselves in the sorrow and pain, joy and hope of their people. True leadership, therefore, must embody a personal awareness of that conviction to the community of faith, not only through words, but primarily through the personal witness of lives immersed in prayer. If this is done, then the People of God will truly be receiving the proper leadership necessary for the promotion of meaningful prayer in the richest, fullest way possible.

In turn the People of God must respond generously to the initiatives of the Church in the renewal of the Liturgy of the Hours. They must be open to the leadership and instruction of the clergy and they must recognize the value of the Divine Office in their lives as a sanctification of all their time, not in a generic, abstract sense, but in a very real and specific sense. They must see the Liturgy of the Hours as a most valuable source of strength and inspiration for personal prayer. They must recognize the vital link that exists between the Liturgy of the Hours and the Eucharist realizing that through the Hours the sacramental presence of the Eucharistic Christ is prolonged throughout the day and the Paschal Mystery complemented and therefore continued to be actively experienced and shared. They must also be open to the initiatives and privileges which the Church has rightfully restored to them in declaring the Liturgy of the Hours to be a prayer for all of its faithful members. Finally, they must be open to see the newly reformed Divine Office in its proper light discovering therein its theological and spiritual richness. Only in this manner will the Liturgy of the Hours be able to genuinely fulfill its role as the public and communal prayer of the entire Church.

Today the Church has seen the necessity for the reformation of the Liturgy of the Hours. This study has attempted to explore at length not only the reasons motivating this reform but also its present state and future consequences in the lives of the faithful. Since we initiated this treatise with a quotation from *Laudis Canticum, The Apostolic Constitution on the Beviary,* it is also fitting that we now conclude with another quotation from that very same document expressing in beautiful and meaningful terms the Church's hopes and aspirations regarding the reformed Liturgy of the Hours and its place in the Christian life.

By means of the new book of the Liturgy of the Hours, which we now establish, approve and promulgate by our Apostolic Authority, let divine praise ring out, therefore, more splendidly and beautifully in the Church of our times. Let it unite with the praise of the Saints and the Angels resounding in the heavenly mansions and, growing in perfection, let it approach more and more, in the days of this earthly exile, that full praise that is given forever to Him who sits upon the throne and to the Lamb.

(Pope Paul VI, AAS 63, 1971, 534).

Notes

Introduction

[1]*Acta Apostolicae Sedis* 63, 1971, 527-535. (Hereafter cited as AAS).

[2]"The Constitution on the Sacred Liturgy—Sacrosanctum Concilium," *Vatican Council II—The Conciliar and Post Conciliar Documents*, ed. A. Flannery (Dublin: Dominican Publications, 1975), para. 83-101, pp. 24-28.

[3]AAS 63, 1971, 529.

[4]A. Bugnini, "Introduction," *The Liturgy of the Hours—The General Instruction on the Reform of the Breviary*, trans. P. Coughlan, P. Purdue (London: Geoffrey Chapman, 1974), p. 16.

[5]See page 77 of the commentary of A. M. Roguet in the work cited above in n. 4.

[6]"The General Instruction on the Liturgy of the Hours," *The Divine Office—The Liturgy of the Hours According to the Roman Rite*, vol. I (London: William Collins Sons and Co. Ltd., 1974), para. 1, 5-8. Hereafter cited as GILH.

[7]GILH 28-32. However, this obligation must now be seen more in the sense of duty and of an essential need rather than in a quantitative and juridical sense.

[8]GILH 20-23, 32.

[9]GILH 1.

[10]GILH 12, 14.

[11]GILH 9.

[12]GILH 10.

[13]AAS 63, 1971, 527.

[14]GILH 10, 11.

[15]AAS 63, 1971, 531-532.

Chapter I

[1]Pope Paul VI, *Apostolic Constitution on the Breviary—Laudis Canticum*, AAS 63, 1971, 527-535.

[2]For a most interesting and learned study of this entire question see C. W. Dugmore, *The Influence of the Synagogue Upon the Divine Office* (Westminster: The Faith Press Ltd., 1964).

[3]Cf. L. Bouyer, *Rite and Man: Natural Sacredness and Christian Liturgy* (Notre Dame: University of Notre Dame Press, 1963), pp. 1-37. See also M. Eliade, *Images and Symbols: Studies in Religious Symbolism*, trans. P. Mairet (New York: Sheed and Ward, 1969), pp. 57-91.

[4]Prayers within the Jewish family circle were always a very important part of the prayer life of Israel. Concerning the personal piety of the individual Israelite Psalm 4 has traditionally been seen as an evening prayer, and Psalm 5 as a morning prayer. Judith prayed at the hour when the evening sacrifice of incense was being offered in the Temple (Jdt. 9:1). Daniel prayed three times a day (Dn. 6:11), and Psalm 55:18 tells us that the Israelites prayed in the evening, in the morning and at noon. See W. W. Simpson, *Jewish Prayer and Worship* (New York: The Seabury Press, 1967), pp. 16-22.

[5]From the first historical texts to the book of Deuteronomy there is a continuous line of evidence to show that this type of sacrifice was prevalent in Israel. Among the more ancient witnesses are: Jgs. 6:26, 28, 13:15-20; 1 Sm. 6:14, 7:9, 10:8, 13:9f.; 2 Sm. 6:17f.; 1 Kgs. 3:4, 9:25, 18:38. Therefore there is a real line of continuity between the holocausts of the pre- and post-exilic periods, only in the post-exilic period they grew in importance. Cf. R. DeVaux, *Ancient Israel: Its Life and Institutions*, trans. J. McHugh (London: Darton, Longman and Todd, 1962), p. 432f.

[6]Cf. 1 Chr. 16:40; 2 Chr. 13:11, 31:3; also DeVaux, *op. cit.*, pp. 468-469.

[7]Cf. L. Hartman, *Encyclopedic Dictionary of the Bible*, trans. B. Woordenboek (New York: McGraw-Hill Book Company, Inc., 1963), cols. 1020, 1914. See also DeVaux, *op. cit.*, p. 416.

[8]*Ibid.*, pp. 415-456.

[9]J. J. Castelot, "Religious Institutions of Israel," *The Jerome Biblical Commentary*, ed. R. Brown, J. Fitzmyer, R. Murphy (Englewood Cliffs, New Jersey: Prentice-Hall, Inc., 1968), vol. II, col. 2, p. 725; also Hartman, *op. cit.*, col. 1897.

[10]DeVaux, *op. cit.*, p. 458.

[11]A number of the prayers now found in the Book of Psalms, such as Ps. 130, were most likely composed during this period of exile by anonymous authors. Cf. B. Anderson, *Understanding the Old Testament*, 2nd ed. (Englewood Cliffs, NJ: Prentice-Hall, Inc., 1966), p. 378.

[12]Such scholars as A. Tricot in "The Jewish World at the Time of Our Lord," *Guide to the Bible*, ed. A. Robert, A. Tricot, trans. E. Arbey, M. McGuire (Tournai: Desclee and Co., 1955), vol. II, p. 284; and W. Simpson, *op. cit.*, p. 17, claim that most certainly these meetings were the direct forerunners of the synagogue.

[13]Anderson, *op. cit.*

[14]DeVaux, *op. cit.*, pp. 343-344.

[15]Simpson, *op. cit.*, pp. 16-17.

[16]A. Hamman, *Prayer: The New Testament*, trans. P. J. Oligny (Chicago: Franciscan Herald Press, 1971), p. 66. See also S. H. Hooke, "Emergence of Christianity," *Judaism and Christianity—The Age of Transition*, ed. W. O. E. Oesterley (New York: KTAV Publishing House, 1969), pp. 272-273.

[17]Cf. L. Bouyer, "Jewish and Christian Liturgies," *True Worship*, ed. L. Sheppard (Baltimore: The Helicon Press, 1963), pp. 34-35. See also W. O. E. Oesterley, *The Jewish Background of the Christian Liturgy* (Oxford: The Clarendon Press, 1925), pp. 16-35 and Dugmore, *op. cit.*, pp. 11-12. Extremely valuable in the study of this entire area are the works of I. Elbogen, in particular *Der judische Gottesdienst in seiner geschichtlichen Entwicklung*, 3rd ed. (Frankfurt am Main, 1931).

[18]Cf. J. Bonsirven, "From the Exile to the Destruction of Jerusalem," *Guide to the Bible*, vol. II, pp. 233-234. Also Hartman, *op. cit.*, col. 2375; and Oesterley, *op. cit.*, p. 37.

[19]The establishment of the practice of reading the Torah publicly before the people is credited to Ezra according to Neh. 8:18. In ancient Israel the priest was the man of the Torah; to him was entrusted the task to interpret the Law for the people by teaching and practice. However, from the time of the Exile onward, they ceased to be the sole teachers of the Torah. With the development of the synagogues, a new class of scribes and teachers of the Law arose. This class was open to all, priests and Levites and lay people as well, eventually displacing the priestly caste in the work of teaching. Cf. DeVaux, *op. cit.*, pp. 354-355; Hamman, *op. cit.*, p. 66.

[20]The *shema* and the *amidah* have always formed the two chief elements of Jewish daily morning and evening prayer. Cf. Dugmore, *op. cit.*, p. 16; Hartman, *op. cit.*, cols. 2195-2196.

[21]This creed was called the *shema*, "Listen" after the opening words of Dt. 6:4, "Listen, O Israel!" Cf. Oesterley, *op. cit.*, p. 42.

[22]It is highly probable that the words of this injunction "at your lying down or at your rising" gave rise to the custom of beginning and ending each day with the confession of the one God. It became a general Jewish practice in pre-Christian times, wherein all men and boys beginning with their twelfth birthday, were required to recite it regularly. Cf. J. Jeremias, *The Prayers of Jesus*, trans. J. Bowden, C. Burchard, J. Reumann (Norwich: SCM Press Ltd., 1976), pp. 66-69. Also see E. Mally, "The Gospel According to Mark," *The Jerome Biblical Commentary*, vol. II, art. 42, col. 1, p. 49.

[23]G. von Rad, *Deuteronomy: A Commentary*, trans. D. Barton (London: SCM Press Ltd., 1966), p. 63.

[24]Cf. K. Hruby, "Les Heures de Prière dans le Judaisme à l'Epoque de Jésus," *La Prière des Heures* — Semaine d'Etudes Liturgiques de Saint Serge, Juillet 1961, Lex Orandi 35 (Paris: Les Editions du Cerf, 1963), pp. 63, 76-81. See also L. Bouyer, *Eucharist*, trans. C. U. Quinn (Notre Dame: University of Notre Dame Press, 1968), p. 69; and Oesterley, *op. cit.*, pp. 44-51; Dugmore, *op. cit.*, pp. 20-21.

[25]It was always known as the *amidah* (standing) since the congregation always stood for its recitation. Cf. Hamman, *op. cit.*, pp. 66-67; Bouyer, *Eucharist*, pp. 70-78; Oesterley, *op. cit.*, p. 54.

[26]Cf. G. Hebert, "Worship in the Old Testament," *True Worship*, pp. 14-28. See also Dugmore, *op. cit.*, pp. 3-4.

[27]Bouyer, *Eucharist*, p. 70.

[28]*Ibid.*, pp. 70-78. Also by Bouyer see "Jewish and Christian Liturgies," *True Worship*, pp. 40-41. See also Oesterley, *op. cit.*, pp. 51-67; and Dugmore, *op. cit.*, pp. 114-127.

[29]Oesterley, *op. cit.*, pp. 52-53.

[30]Anderson, *op. cit.*, p. 467. See also L. H. Vincent, "The Temple of Jerusalem," *Guide to the Bible*, pp. 87-90.

[31]Anderson, *op. cit.*, pp. 467-468. See especially the developments made in this area of study by such scholars as S. Mowinckel, *The Psalms in Israel's Worship*, I-II, trans. D. R. Ap-Thomas (New York: Abingdon, 1962), and H. Gunkel, J. Begrich, *Einleitung in die Psalmen* (HKAT, Gottingen, 1933). See also R. E. Murphy's commentary in *The Jerome Biblical Commentary*, vol. I, pp. 569-576.

[32]L. Sabourin, *The Psalms, Their Origin and Meaning* (New York: Alba House, 1974), p. 39. Some examples of such psalms would be: Ps. 24; 68:24-25; 78; 89:15; 118:27; 149:3.

[33]Sabourin, *op. cit.*, pp. 175-214. See also Murphy, *op. cit.*, p. 572. Some of the psalms belonging to this first category would be: Ps. 95; 117; 145; 148; 149; and 150.

[34]Sabourin, *op. cit.*, pp. 215-334. See also Anderson, *op. cit.*, p. 467, and Murphy, *op. cit.*, pp. 572-573. Some of the psalms belonging to this second category would be: Ps. 10; 35-36; 42; 43; 63; 64; 74; 79; 106; 120; 137; and 140.

[35]See DeVaux, *op. cit.*, pp. 484-506 for a good coverage of the Festivals of Israel.

[36]Anderson, *op. cit.*, p. 485.

[37]It is fairly certain that the *Hallel*, consisting of psalms of thanksgiving

sung on certain festivals (Ps. 113-118), was an ancient element of the synagogue service. See Dugmore, *op. cit.*, pp. 14-15; and Oesterley, *op. cit.*, pp. 73-76.

38Sabourin, *op. cit.*, pp. 47-48.

39Cf. Simpson, *op. cit.*, pp. 16-22.

40The prerogative of preaching on the Sacred Scriptures eventually was opened to any male person present in the assembly who wished to offer a few words of exhortation (Acts 13:5; Mt. 4:23; Lk. 4:4). See Hartman, *op. cit.*, col. 2375; Tricot, *op. cit.*, pp. 284-285; and Dugmore, *op. cit.*, pp. 22, 109.

41Hamman, *op. cit.*, p. 70.

42It is most likely that elements from the Temple services were incorporated into the synagogue after the destruction of the Temple. See S. E. Johnson, "The New Testament and the Christian Community," *The Interpreter's One Volume Commentary on the Bible*, ed. C. M. Laymon (New York: Abingdon Press, 1971), p. 1119.

431 Chr. 24:7-18; Lk. 1. See also Castelot, *op. cit.*, pp. 708-710; and DeVaux, *op. cit.*, pp. 345-405 for an excellent development on this entire subject concerning the hebraic priestly office.

44In this later age only two services were held each day in the Temple, in the morning and in the evening. See DeVaux, *op. cit.*, p. 458; Hruby, *op. cit.*, pp. 64-69; and Jeremias, *op. cit.*, pp. 70-71.

451 Kg. 8:44-48. This custom of turning toward Jerusalem, which was sanctioned by later Judaism, eventually influenced the orientation of the synagogues toward Jerusalem. See DeVaux, *op. cit.*

46J. Pinell, *La Liturgia delle Ore* (Padova: Istituto di Liturgia Pastorale, 1975), p. 37.

47Dugmore, *op. cit.*, pp. 43-44.

48Cf. R. Aron, *The Jewish Jesus*, trans. A. Forsyth, A. M. de Commaille (Maryknoll: Orbis Books, 1971), pp. 49-91.

49In reference to the Temple see: Mt. 8:4; 23:16-24; and the force of Jesus' argument in Mt. 12:6-8, relies upon the value and respect which he holds for the Temple. See also Mk. 11:15-17. In reference to the synagogue see: Mt. 4:23; 9:35; 12:9; 13:54; Mk. 1:21-22, 39; 3:1; 6:2; Lk. 4:15-27; 44; 6:6; 13:10f.; Jn. 6:59; 18:20.

50For an excellent coverage of this entire area see Cassien, "La Prière dans le Nouveau Testament," *La Prière des Heures—Lex Orandi*, pp. 18-25. Also J. Jeremias, *The Prayers of Jesus*, pp. 72-78.

51L. Duchesne, *Christian Worship: Its Origin and Evolution* (London: S.P.C.K., 1912), p. 446. See also Mt. 18:19-20; Lk. 18:1f.; Acts 1:14; 2:1, 42-47; Eph. 6:18-20.

⁵²Cf. Lk. 24:52-53; Acts 2:46; 3:1; 21:26-27; 22:17.

⁵³Cf. Acts 6:9-10; 9:20; 13:5, 14-15; 15:21; 17:2, 10, 17; 18:4, 19, 26; 19:8. Most of these references refer to Paul and his relationship with the synagogues of the diaspora.

⁵⁴Duchesne, *op. cit.* Oesterley, *op. cit.*, pp. 84-90.

⁵⁵Dugmore, *op. cit.*, p. 113.

⁵⁶This seems to have developed into a regularly observed pattern by New Testament times. The Acts of the Apostles attest to the observance of afternoon prayer at three in the afternoon (Acts 3:1; 10:3, 30) and J. Jeremias also affirms in *The Prayers of Jesus*, p. 79, that Paul's continued perseverance in prayer (Rom. 12:12; Col. 4:2) should be interpreted as meaning "faithfully to observe a rite." See also Duchesne, *op. cit.*, p. 447.

⁵⁷Jeremias, *The Prayers of Jesus*, p. 72. See also Dugmore, *op. cit.*, pp. 60-61.

⁵⁸Cf. Mk. 1:35; 6:46-48; 14:32-42; Lk. 5:16; 6:12; 9:18, 28; Acts 10:9; 12:5, 12; 16:25; 2 Cor. 6:5; 11:27; Eph. 6:18. See also Cassien, "La Prière dans le Nouveau Testament," *La Prière des Heures—Lex Orandi*, 20-21; and Jeremias, *op. cit.*, pp. 73-76f.

⁵⁹Cf. Acts 2:42, 46; 20:7-11; 1 Cor. 11:17-34; 14:26-40. Concerning the passages from Acts and their Eucharistic overtones see R. Dillon, J. Fitzmyer, "Commentary on the Acts of the Apostles," *The Jerome Biblical Commentary*, pp. 165-214; and also E. Kilmartin, *The Eucharist in the Primitive Church* (Englewood Cliffs, NJ: Prentice-Hall Inc., 1965), pp. 144-148.

⁶⁰Cf. Acts 1:12-14, 24-25; 2:1f.; 4:23-24; 12:12; 13:1-3; 18:7-8. See also P. Vicenti, "Dimensione Orante della Chiesa e Liturgia delle Ore," *Liturgia delle Ore, Documenti Ufficiali e Studi* (Torino-Leuman: Elle Di Ci, 1972), pp. 136-140.

⁶¹Cf. Acts 2:47; 4:24f.; Eph. 5:19; Col. 3:16; 1 Cor. 14:26. See also Cassien, *op. cit.*, pp. 28-29.

⁶²Cf. Acts 20:7f.; 28-23; 31; 1 Cor. 14:26f.

⁶³Cf. G. Cuming, "The New Testament Foundation for Common Prayer," *Studia Liturgica*, II, 2 (1976), 89-102. Jn. 4:23; Rom. 8:26; 1 Cor. 14:26-33; Acts 2:42-47; 4:32-35.

⁶⁴Dugmore, *op. cit.*, pp. 2-5, 79, 103.

⁶⁵Cf. Jn. 2:13-22; Heb. 5:1-4; 6:19-20; 7:18-19; 9:1-10.

⁶⁶Cf. 1 Thess. 5:16-18; 2 Thess. 2:1-17.

⁶⁷Cf. Oesterley, *op. cit.*, pp. 109-154.

⁶⁸Chap. 8, J. Quasten, J. Plumpe, ed. "The Didache, The Teaching of the Twelve Apostles," *Ancient Christian Writers*, 6th ed. (Westminster: The Newman Press, 1948), p. 19.

[69]J. Jeremias, *op. cit.*, pp. 78-81. Hamman, *op. cit.*, pp. 105-108.

[70]D. Y. Hadidian, "The Background and Origin of the Christian Hours of Prayer," *Theological Studies*, 25 (1964), p. 60.

[71]Tertullianus, "De Oratione," (PL I, 1300-1301), CC I, 272-273.

[72]Duchesne, *op. cit.*, p. 447.

[73]Hadidian, *op. cit.*

[74]Tertullianus, "Ad Uxorem," (PL I, 1408), CC I, 389.

[75]Cyprianus, "De Oratione Dominica," PL IV, 560; CSEL 3, 292.

[76]*Ibid.*

[77]Cf. J. Quasten, *Patrology*, vol. II (Westminster, Maryland: The Newman Press, 1964), pp. 163-207.

[78]Chap. 41, B. Botte, ed. *La Tradition Apostolique de Saint Hippolyte* (Munster, Westfalen: Aschendorffsche Verlagsbuchhandlung, 1963), p. 89. See also Chap. 35, p. 83. Hereafter cited as: Botte, *La Tradition.*

[79]*Ibid.*, Chap. 39, p. 87.

[80]In his commentary on this text in "Les Heures de Prière dans la 'Tradition Apostolique' et les Documents Dérivé," *La Prière des Heures—Lex Orandi*, pp. 104-105, B. Botte asserts that while these meetings called for the daily appearance of the clergy, they did not necessarily include the presence of the entire community, at least on the same daily basis. The bishop would designate each day as the occasion for a reunion in a particular location and he would call together his priests and deacons. The bishop's purpose for changing the location for prayer seems to have been for the purpose of providing all Christians with the opportunity of listening to the word of God and receiving instruction as frequently as possible. Their presence was encouraged when the location selected for the reunion was not too distant from their homes. Consequently, each meeting was expected to accommodate only those faithful who found the location convenient and accessible.

[81]Chap. 36, p. 83. Botte, *La Tradition.*

[82]*Ibid.*, Chap. 41, p. 91. See also Mk. 15:25 (only the Gospel of Mark indicates specifically the third hour as that of the crucifixion).

[83]Cf. Botte, *La Prière des Heures—Lex Orandi*, p. 105.

[84]Chap. 41, p. 91, Botte, *La Tradition.* See also Mk. 15:33; Lk. 23:44; Mt. 27:45.

[85]Chap. 41, pp. 91-93, Botte, *La Tradition.* See also Jn. 19:34.

[86]While prayer in the evening before retiring is enjoined, nothing is said about any public assembly at that hour outside of the reference to the *lucenarium*. See Chap. 25, pp. 64-67, Botte, *La Tradition.* Hippolytus gives evidence that the common liturgical evening meal (agape) was introduced by

the blessing of light (*luxvikov, lucernarium*), and responsorial psalmody; the people sang Alleluia in response. The introductory *lucernarium* has all but disappeared from the Roman rite, remaining most prominently in the Easter Vigil service. In the East it has survived to this day both in the Byzantine and Armenian rites and was formerly prominent in the Vesper services of the Coptic and Ethiopic rites. In the West, it is still present in the Vesper services of the Mozarabic and Ambrosian rites. See G. Podhradsky, *New Dictionary of the Liturgy*, ed. L. Sheppard (New York: Alba House, 1966), pp. 197-198. G. Dix, *The Shape of the Liturgy*, (London: Dacre Press, 1970), p. 87.

[87]Chap. 41, pp. 93-95, Botte, *La Tradition*.

[88]*Ibid.*, Chap. 41, p. 97.

[89]Although the hours for prayer in the synagogue were three, there is no way to verify that they corresponded to the Christian hours of Terce, Sext, and None. See C. W. Dugmore, "Canonical Hours," *A Dictionary of Liturgy and Worship*, ed. J. G. Davies (London: SCM Press Ltd., 1972), p. 114; Hadidian, *op. cit.*, p. 65.

[90]Duchesne, *op. cit.*, p. 447.

[91]Dugmore, *The Influence of the Synagogue Upon the Divine Office*, p. 67. Once these hours of Terce, Sext, and None had been added to the regular and better established morning and evening Office, they quickly became part of the regular cycle of prayer for all the faithful.

[92]Cf. P. Battifol, *Histoire du Breviaire Romain* (Paris: Auguste Picard, 1911), pp. 15-16; and J. A. Jungmann, *The Early Liturgy*, trans. F. A. Brunner (Notre Dame: University of Notre Dame Press, 1959), p. 105.

[93]Cf. Dugmore, *The Influence of the Synagogue Upon the Divine Office*, p. 47. See also Duchesne, *Christian Worship: Its Origin and Evolution*, pp. 446-448, who asserts that while morning and evening prayer were essentially private prayers for the early Christians, nevertheless, they do admit to communal prayer "confined to those days and hours fixed for assembly."

[94]Tertullianus, "De Oratione," (PL I, 1300-1301); CC I, 272-273.

[95]Cyprianus, "De Oratione Dominica," (PL IV, 541, 559-560); CSEL 3, 1, 292.

[96]Origenes, "Homilia in Genesim," PG XII, 215-218. Upon examining the terminology Origen usually employs when specifically referring to the Eucharist ("Commentarius in Psalmos," PG XII, 1386), it seems quite certain that in these particular cited instances above, he is not referring to a Eucharistic celebration but to a daily prayer service marked by the reading of the Sacred Scriptures, a homily and prayer.

[97]Chaps. 39, 41, pp. 87, 89, Botte, *La Tradition*.

[98]For a good survey of this question see Dugmore, *op. cit.*, pp. 47-50.

[99]Origenes, *op. cit.* See also F. van der Meer, C. Mohrmann, *Atlas of the Christian World*, trans. and ed. M. F. Hedlund, H. H. Rowley (London: Thomas Nelson and Sons Ltd., 1959), p. 47.

[100]J. G. Davies, *The Early Christian Church* (New York: Holt, Rinehart and Winston, 1965), pp. 115-119. See also A. H. M. Jones, *Constantine and the Conversion of Europe* (New York: Collier Books, 1967), pp. 35-58 and Dix, *op. cit.*, pp. 305-306.

[101]Eusebius, "Historia Ecclesiastica," PG XX, 346-347, English translation G. A. Williamson, *The History of the Church* (Middlesex: Penquin Books Ltd., 1965), pp. 382-383. Jones, *op. cit.*, pp. 73-90.

[102]Dix, *op. cit.*, p. 305.

[103]While we have already assumed that the faithful did assemble publicly for these prayers in the late second and early third centuries, (see footnotes 93-98), we can now affirm it for the fourth century with a greater degree of certitude.

[104]Eusebius, "Commentarius in Psalmos," PG XXIII, 639.

[105]Epiphanius, "Adversus Haereses," PG XLII, 829-830.

[106]Chrysostomos, "In Epistolam Primam ad Timotheum, Commentarius," PG LXII, 530.

[107]Jungmann, *op. cit.*, p. 280. See also J. Mateos, "The Morning and Evening Office," *Worship*, XLII (January, 1968), p. 31.

[108]"Constitutiones Apostolicae," PG I, 742-743; also *Didascalia et Constitutiones Apostolorum*, ed. F. X. Funk, vol. I (Paderbornae, Schoeningh, 1905), pp. 170-172.

[109]P. Salmon, "La Prière des Heures," *L'Eglise en Prière*, ed. A. G. Martimort (Tournai: Desclée, 1961), pp. 801-802. Hereafter cited as: Salmon, *L'Eglise*.

[110]What we have come to know as Lauds for centuries was known as *Matutinum* or Matins. It seems most probable that this was the very same morning Hour which had constituted the morning prayer service at least in episcopal churches, both in the East and in the West, since the fourth century with the evening prayer service of Vespers as its counterpart. These were the two Hours in which the people participated freely in varying numbers while the other Hours, such as Terce, Sext, and None played little part in public worship at least until the fourth century. See J. A. Jungmann, *Pastoral Liturgy* (New York: Herder and Herder, 1962), p. 123.

[111]As to exactly who the *monazontes* and *parthenai* may be, we have no clear evidence. However, since Egeria does distinguish them from ordinary lay people, whom she refers to as secular men and women, it seems that they

were most likely ascetics or *ferventes*. While Egeria uses different words to describe people who have set themselves apart from the world for religious motives, her vocabulary is too confused to make it possible for us to distinguish with any great precision the exact meaning attached to the various technical terms she employs. See J. Wilkinson, *Egeria's Travels* (London: S.P.C.K., 1971), pp. 33-35. Also consult this same work for a good English translation of the entire *Itinerarium Egeriae*.

[112]*Itinerarium Egeriae*, CC 175, 67-68. See also Wilkinson, *op. cit.*, pp. 65-68 for a further elaboration of *Lychnicon* or *Lucernare*.

[113]*Itinerarium Egeriae*, CC 175, 67-68.

[114]Dugmore, *op. cit.*, p. 51.

[115]See footnote 111 above. See also F. L. Cross, ed., *The Oxford Dictionary of the Christian Church* (London: Oxford University Press, 1966), pp. 93-94.

[116]*Itinerarium Egeriae*, CC 175, 67-69.

[117]Cf. A. Baumstark, *Liturgie Comparée* (Gembloux: J. Duclot, 1932), pp. 118-121. The term "monastic" is used here in a qualified sense since at this period of time monasticism is still in its early stages of development and is not yet a fully formed institution.

[118]Cf. Baumstark, *op. cit.*, and Wilkerson, *op. cit.*, pp. 54-69.

[119]For an excellent survey of the origins of monasticism see J. A. Mohler, *The Heresy of Monasticism* (New York: Alba House, 1971). The author has called the work "The Heresy of Monasticism," not in the modern pejorative sense, but rather in the root meaning of an option, choice, way of life, or sect. For an excellent bibliography on the subject see pp. 241-250 of this same work as well as Cross, *The Oxford Dictionary of the Christian Church*, pp. 914-915.

[120]Mohler, *op. cit.*, pp. 31-76.

[121]B. Luykx, "L'influence des moines sur l'office paroissial," LMD, 51 (1957), 67-74.

[122]A. Schememann, *Introduction to Liturgical Theology* (London: Faith Press, 1966), p. 107.

[123]Cf. Luykx, *op. cit.*, 60-67; *Itinerarium Egeriae*, CC 175, 67-68; Salmon, *L'Eglise*, p. 804.

[124]H. Dalmais, *Introduction to the Liturgy*, trans. R. Capel (Baltimore: Helicon Press, 1961), p. 144. The gatherings of bishops with their clergy and the faithful throughout the fourth and fifth centuries in both the East and West was a phenomenon which has clearly been attested to. See footnotes 96, 108, 109, and 112 of this chapter, as well as the following: Ilario di Poitiers, "Tractatus in Psalmum LXIV," (PL IX, 420), CSEL 22, 243-244. In turn,

during this same period, "monastic" communities, in both East and West, were celebrating in common, with far greater frequency and regularity, a full cursus of liturgical prayer. See the following: Cassien, "De Coenobiorum Institutis II, III," (PL XLIX, 83-84; 112-152), CSEL 17, 32-45. O. Rousseau, "La Prière des Moines au Temps de Jean Cassien," *La Prière des Heures—Lex Orandi*, pp. 117-138. S. Baumer, *Histoire du Bréviaire*, vol. I, trans. R. Biron (Rome: Herder, 1967), pp. 141-150; 209-214.

[125] Baumstark, *op. cit.*

[126] Jungmann, *Pastoral Liturgy*, p. 154.

[127] In the greater city centers of Christendom the Hours were distributed among the principal churches while in smaller towns they were not celebrated at all. At the same time not all clerics participated in the entire Office but took turns according to episcopal directions. See S. J. P. Van Dijk, J. H. Walker, *The Origins of the Modern Roman Liturgy* (Westminster: The Newman Press, 1960), pp. 16-17.

[128] Salmon, *L'Eglise*, pp. 808-809.

[129] Salmon, *The Breviary Through the Centuries*, trans. S. D. Mary (Collegeville: The Liturgical Press, 1962), pp. 107-108. Hereafter cited as: Salmon, *The Breviary*.

[130] *Itinerarium Egeriae*, CC, 175, 67-68.

[131] Jungmann, *Pastoral Liturgy*, pp. 122-157.

[132] Ambrosius, "Expositio in Psalmum CXVIII," (PL XV, 1479), CSEL, 62, 438-439.

[133] Augustinus, "Confessiones," (PL XXXII, 714), CSEL 33, 104.

[134] Augustinus, "De Civitate Dei," (PL XLI, 765), CC 48, 820.

[135] Augustinus, "Enarratio in Psalmum LXVI," PL XXXVI, 805. See also F. Van der Meer, *Augustine the Bishop*, trans. B. Battershaw, G. R. Lamb (New York: Harper and Row, 1961), pp. 325-337.

[136] Ambrosius, "Epistolae Classis I," PL XVI, 1054. "De Elia et Jejunio," (PL XIV, 752), CSEL 32, 2, 444-445. P. Borella, *Il Rito Ambrosiano* (Brescia: Morcelliana, 1964), pp. 225-271, and A. King, *Liturgies of the Primatial Sees* (Milwaukee: The Bruce Publishing Company, 1957), pp. 286-453.

[137] Jungmann, *Pastoral Liturgy*, p. 152.

[138] J. D. Crichton, *Christian Celebration—The Prayer of the Church* (London: Geoffrey Chapman, 1976), p. 40.

[139] "Liber diurnus III," PL CV, 71.

[140] Concile d'Agde (506 A.D.), *Histoire des Conciles*, ed. C. J. Hefele, H. Leclercq, vol. IIa, Can. 21, 30 (Paris: Letouzey et Ané, 1908), pp. 990, 992. Hereafter cited as: Hefele-Leclercq. Concile a Tarragone (516 A.D.), Hefele-

Leclercq, vol. IIa, Can. 7, p. 1028. Deuxième Concile de Braga (563 A.D.), Hefele-Leclercq, vol. III, Can. 1, 2, p. 179. For a more complete list of these councils see Salmon, *The Breviary*, pp. 133-134.

[141]Justinianus, "De Episcopis et Clericis," *Codex Juris Civilis*, I, Tit. III, vol. II, ed. P. Krueger (Berolini: Weidmannos, 1877), p. 28. See also H. Leclercq, "Office Divin," *Dictionnaire d'archéologie chrétienne et de Liturgie*, vol. XII, pars VI (Paris: 1936), col. 1962.

[142]Salmon, *The Breviary*, pp. 108-109.

[143]Luykx, *op. cit.*, pp. 67f. These "monks" and "monasteries" should not be thought of as expressive of the fully formed monastic communities and monasteries of the later ages.

[144]Salmon, *The Breviary*, pp. 104-105. Mateos, *op. cit.*, p. 41.

[145]Salmon, *The Breviary*, pp. 104-105.

[146]Duchesne, *Christian Worship: Its Origin and Evolution*, p. 452.

[147]Salmon, *The Breviary*, p. 105.

[148]Chrysostomos, "Homilia IV de Anna," PG LIV, 667.

[149]Jungmann, *Pastoral Liturgy*, pp. 151-157.

[150]See pages 43-45 of this chapter especially: Ambrosius, "Expositio in Psalmum CXVIII," (PL XV, 1479), CSEL 62, 438-439; Augustinus, "Confessiones," (PL XXXII, 714), CSEL 33, 104; "De Civitate Dei," (PL XLI, 765), CC 48, 820; "Enarratio in Psalmum LXVI," PL XXXVI, 805. See also Luykx, *op. cit.*, pp. 31-51; Crichton, *op. cit.*, pp. 39-41.

[151]Crichton, *op. cit.*, p. 43.

[152]Van Dijk, Walker, *The Origins of the Modern Roman Liturgy*, pp. 16-17.

[153]*Ibid.*, p. 17. Salmon, *L'Eglise*, p. 818.

[154]"Vita Sancti Caesarii Episcopi," PL LXVII, 1006-1007. "Historica episcoporum Antissiodorensium," PL CXXXVIII, 231-236, 243-245.

[155]Cf. B. Capelle, "L' 'Opus Dei' dans la Règle de Saint Benoit," *La Prière des Heures—Lex Orandi*, pp. 144-147. See also J. Lechner, L. Eisenhofer, *The Liturgy of the Roman Rite*, trans. A. J. Peeler, E. F. Peeler, ed. H. E. Winstone (New York: Herder and Herder, 1961), pp. 442-443.

[156]Although well-known from the sixth century there is no conclusive evidence to affirm that all the monasteries of Rome exclusively adopted the Benedictine rule, at least not before the influence of Cluny in the tenth century. See Salmon, *The Breviary*, p. 105.

[157]I. H. Dalmais, "Origine et Constitution de l'Office," LMD, 51 (1950), p. 37. This process was a very slow one being only gradual in Italy and Gaul where for a long time it continued to compete with Columban usages which it

eventually ousted. See also Crichton, *op. cit.*, p. 43.

[158]Jungmann, *Pastoral Liturgy*, p. 154. Salmon, *L'Eglise*, pp. 817-818.

[159]Lechner, Eisenhofer, *op cit.*, pp. 441-442. Baumer, *Histoire du Bréviaire*, pp. 242-257. Crichton, *op. cit.*, pp. 42-44.

[160]Salmon, *The Breviary*, pp. 105-106.

[161]Pinell, *La Liturgia delle Ore*, pp. 79-83. Duchesne, *op. cit.*, p. 452.

[162]Beda, "Historia Ecclesiastica Anglicana," PL XCV, 52-54.

[163]*Ibid.*, 173-175, 199-200.

[164]Cross, *Oxford Dictionary of the Christian Church*, p. 184. Baumer, *op. cit.*, p. 327.

[165]Up to the early ninth century, the complete Office was celebrated solely in the basilicas of Rome, in those churches which had "monasteries" attached to them, and in those abbeys following the rules of Saint Columban, Saint Benedict or others who possessed a full cursus of prayer. See Salmon, *The Breviary*, p. 106.

[166]*Ibid.*, p. 8.

[167]T. Klauser, *A Short History of the Western Liturgy*, trans, J. Halliburton (London: Oxford University Press, 1969), p. 46. See also Baumer, *op. cit.*, pp. 327-329.

[168]"Capitulare Ecclesiasticum," PL XCVII, 180, 248. "Capitulare Duplex in Theodonis Villa Promulgatum," PL XCVII, 283.

[169]Salmon, *The Breviary*, pp. 105-106. Baumer, *op. cit.*, p. 378.

[170]B. Luykx, "L'influence des moines sur l'office paroissial," LMD, 51 (1957), 61-81. Capelle, *op. cit.*, pp. 140-141. I. Schuster, *La Regula Monasteriorum—San Benedetto* (Torino: Societa Editrice Internazionale, 1942), Chap. XLIII, pp. 291-292.

[171]While the obligation for the celebration of the daily Office had been previously treated in many instances, it was made formal and explicit by the Council of Aix-la-Chapelle (816 A.D.), *Monumenta Germaniae Historica*, ed. F. Maassen (Hannover, Hahn, Berlin: Weidmann, 1826ff.), Leges, Concilia Aevi Karolini, Can. 131, I, p. 408; see also Can. 126, p. 403.

[172]Van Dijk, Walker, *op. cit.*, p. 20. See also Cross, *op. cit.*, pp. 304-305.

[173]Salmon, *The Breviary*, p. 106.

[174]Amalarius, "Regula Canonicorum et Sanctimonialium," "Eclogae de Officio Missae," "Epistolae," PL CV, 816-1340.

[175]Salmon, *L'Eglise*, p. 836. See also Lechner, Eisenhofer, *op. cit.*, 442-443.

[176]Abelardus, "Epistola X," PL CLXXVIII, 340. However, in the eleventh century, the Office celebrated by the Pope and his court in the Papal Chapel remained substantially the old, Roman monastic Office.

[177]Cf. M. Andrieu, *Les Ordines Romani du Haut Moyen Age* (Louvain, 1931), I, p. 519, footnote 1.

[178]Cf. Salmon, *L'Eglise*, p. 836.

[179]Cf. E. Bishop, *Liturgica Historica* (Oxford: Clarendon Press, 1918), pp. 211-237; and Lechner, Eisenhofer, *op. cit.*

[180]Pinell, *op. cit.*, p. 83.

[181]Van Dijk, Walker, *op. cit.*, pp. 91-112.

[182]Cf. Salmon, *L'Eglise*, pp. 835-836; and Van Dijk, Walker, *op. cit.*, pp. 1-12, 20-21.

[183]Cf. Crichton, *op. cit.*, p. 49.

[184]Cf. Van Dijk, Walker, *op. cit.*, 113-117, 129-237.

[185]Cf. Klauser, *op. cit.*, pp. 94-96.

[186]Salmon, *L'Eglise*, p. 837.

[187]*Ibid.* For a contrary opinion concerning the Breviary see Van Dijk, Walker, *op. cit.*, pp. 30-31.

[188]Salmon, *The Breviary*, pp. 13-20.

[189]Jungmann, *Pastoral Liturgy*, pp. 201-202.

[190]Lechner, Eisenhofer, *The Liturgy of the Roman Rite*, p. 445.

[191]Jungmann, *Pastoral Liturgy*, pp. 200-214.

[192]For an excellent analysis of the Breviary of Cardinal Quinonez see: V. Raffa, "Dal Breviario del Quinonez alla Liturgia delle Ore di Paulo VI," *Liturgia delle Ore, Documenti Ufficiali e Studi*, pp. 290-320. See also Baumer, *Histoire du Bréviare*, pp. 126-149.

[193]Lechner, Eisenhofer, *op. cit.*

[194]*Ibid.*, p. 446.

[195]H. Denzinger, A. Schonmetzer, *Enchiridion Symbolorum Definitionum et Declarationum de rebus fidel et morum*, editio XXXV (Freiburg im Breisgau: Verlag Herder KG, 1965), no. 1749, p. 410; no. 1759, p. 411. While this particular reference is in specific relationship to the use of the vernacular in the Mass, nevertheless, it is being quoted here because of its obvious pastoral implications concerning the use of the vernacular in the Divine Office as well.

[196]Dugmore, "Canonical Hours," *A Dictionary of Liturgy and Worship*, p. 117.

[197]L. J. Puhl, ed., *The Spiritual Exercises of Saint Ignatius*, (Chicago: Loyola University Press, 1951), p. 157.

[198]B. Neums, "Liturgy of the Hours," *Celebration—Monthly Newsletter of the Liturgical Commission of Baltimore*, 73 (1976), 8. See also Salmon, *L'Eglise*, pp. 848-849.

[199]Saint Francois de Sales, *Introduction à la Vie Dévote* (Paris: Nelson Editeurs, 1961), pp. 105-106.

[200]For an excellent account of the nature and development of these devotional books read: E. Bishop, *Liturgica Historica*, Chapter IX entitled "On the Origin of the Prymer," pp. 211-237.

[201]W. G. Storey, "Parish Worship—The Liturgy of the Hours," *Worship*, XLIX (January, 1975), p. 5.

[202]Salmon, *L'Eglise*, pp. 850-851.

[203]See footnote 195 above. A great degree of this attitude on the part of the council fathers could be accounted for by the very complex and perilous times in which the Church found herself due to the Protestant Reformation.

[204]Denzinger, Schonmetzer, *op. cit.*, no. 2486, p. 406; no. 2666, p. 536.

[205]Cf. Lechner, Eisenhofer, *op. cit.*, pp. 446-447. Salmon, *L'Eglise*, pp. 849-853. Some of these efforts at reform we have already noted in footnotes 202 and 203 above.

Chapter II

[1]B. Neunheuser, "Il Movimento Liturgico: Panorama Storico e Lineamenti Teologici," *Anamnesis 1, La Liturgia, momento nella storia della salvezze*, a cura di S. Marsili (Torino: Casa Editrice Marietti, 1974), pp. 11-20.

[2]Lechner, Eisenhofer, *op. cit.*, pp. 446-447.

[3]Acta Sanctae Sedis, 36, 1903, 329-339. Hereafter cited as ASS.

[4]*Ibid.*, pp. 329-331.

[5]ASS 38, 1905, 400-406.

[6]J. H. Miller, *Fundamentals of the Liturgy* (Notre Dame: Fides Publishers, Inc., 1959), p. 325.

[7]V. Raffa, "Dal Breviario del Quinonez alla Liturgia delle ore di Paolo VI," *Liturgia delle Ore. Documenti Ufficiali e Studi* (Torino-Leuman: Elle Di Ci, 1972), p. 340.

[8]AAS 3, 1911, 633-638.

[9]E. Cattaneo, *Introduzione alla Storia della Liturgia Occidentale* (Roma: Centro di Azione Liturgica, 1969), p. 414.

[10]L. Bouyer, *Liturgical Piety* (Notre Dame: University of Notre Dame Press, 1954), pp. 58-59.

[11]*Ibid.*, p. 61.

[12]L. Beauduin, Liturgy, *The Life of the Church*, trans. V. Michel (Collegeville: The Liturgical Press, 1926), p. 45.

[13]*Ibid.*, pp. 2-3.

[14]*Les Questions Liturgiques et Paroissiales*, Louvain: Abbaye du Mont-Cesar, (1910 et suiv.).

[15]Cf. *Mélanges Liturgiques: Recueillis parmi les Oeuvres de Dom Lambert Beauduin, O.S.B. a l'occasion de ses 80 ans, (1873-1953)* (Louvain: Centre Liturgique-Abbaye du Mont-Cesar, 1954), p. 13.

[16]For a good survey of the Belgian Liturgical Movement see S. A. Quitslund, *Beauduin, A Prophet Vindicated* (New York: Newman Press, 1973), pp. 17-36. See also A. Haquin, *Histoire du renouveau liturgique belge, 1882-1914* (Louvain, 1966) and by the same author, *Dom L. Beauduin et le renouveau liturgique*, (Gembloux, 1970).

[17]Bouyer, *op. cit.*, p. 65.

[18]AAS 21, 1929, 39-40.

[19]T. Klauser, *A Short History of the Western Liturgy* (London: Oxford University Press, 1969), p. 122.

[20]AAS 35, 1943, 193-248.

[21]*Ibid.*, p. 218.

[22]AAS 37, 1945, 65-67.

[23]*Ibid.*, p. 67.

[24]AAS 39, 1947, 521-595.

[25]Neunheuser, *op. cit.*, p. 27.

[26]AAS 39, 1947, 528-529.

[27]B. Capelle, "The Pastoral Theology of the Encyclicals *Mystici Corporis* and *Mediator Dei*," *The Assisi Papers* (Collegeville: The Liturgical Press, 1957), p. 36.

[28]AAS 39, 1947, 552.

[29]*Ibid.*, p. 573.

[30]*Ibid.*, pp. 575-576. Reinforcing this recommendation, the Sacred Congregation of Rites issued an instruction entitled, *De musica sacra, Sacred Music and the Sacred Liturgy*, (AAS 50, 1958, 630-663) in which it was emphasized (p. 646) that the singing of Vespers on Sundays and feast days was not to fall into disuse because of the newly introduced evening Masses.

[31]AAS 39, 1947, 592.

[32]AAS 45, 1953, 15-24.

[33]AAS 47, 1955, 838-847.

[34]AAS 47, 1955, 218-219.

[35]AAS 48, 1956, 713-714. For a complete review of the entire Congress see, LMD, 47-48, 1956, 9-327.

[36]AAS 51, 1959, 68.

[37]For an excellent coverage of the immediate background of *The Constitu-*

tion on the Sacred Liturgy consult P. M. Gy, "Esquisse Historique," LMD 76 (1963) 7-17.

[38]Cf. *Acta Synodalia Sacrosancti Concilii Oecumenici Vaticani II*, Volumen II, Periodus Secunda, Pars V, Congregatio Generalis LXXIII, 22 November 1963, (Roma: Typis Polyglottis Vaticanis, MCMLXXVI), pp. 699-768; *Il Concilio Vaticano II*, a cura di G. Caprile, vol. 3 (Roma: Edizioni "La Civilta Cattolica," 1966), pp. 322-324; A. Bugnini, EL 78, 1964, 3-14.

[39]The English translations used for these three documents, namely *The Dogmatic Constitution on the Church—Lumen Gentium, The Pastoral Constitution on the Church in the Modern World—Gaudium et Spes, The Decree on the Apostolate of the Laity—Apostolicam Actuositatem*, as well as for *The Constitution on the Sacred Liturgy—Sacrosanctum Concilium*, will be taken from *Vatican Council II, The Conciliar and Post Conciliar Documents*, ed. A. Flannery (Dublin: Dominican Publications, 1975).

[40]H. Fesquet, *The Drama of Vatican II*, trans. B. Murchland (New York: Random House, 1967), p. 565.

[41]AAS 39, 1947, 521-595.

[42]AAS 335, 1943, 193-248.

[43]Neunheuser, *op. cit.*, pp. 19-20.

[44]LG 9.

[45]*Ibid.*

[46]*Ibid.*

[47]LG 4.

[48]LG 5.

[49]P. Hebblethwaite, *The Theology of the Church* (Notre Dame: Fides Publishers, Inc. 1969), p. 24.

[50]K. Rahner, "The Church," *Encyclopedia of Theology—The Concise Sacramentum Mundi*, ed. K. Rahner (New York: The Seabury Press, 1975), p. 212.

[51]LG 10.

[52]S. Marsili, "La Liturgia, Momento Storico della Salvezza," *Anamnesis 1*, pp. 109-110.

[53]LG 10. For an excellent survey of this entire concept see C. Vaggagini, *Theological Dimensions of the Liturgy*, trans. J. Doyle, W. A. Jurgens (Collegeville: The Liturgical Press, 1976), pp. 143-156; and S. Marsili, *Anamnesis 1*, pp. 127-129.

[54]LG 11. Cf. A. Grillmeier's commentary in *Commentary on the Documents of Vatican II*, vol. I, ed. H. Vorgrimler (New York: Herder and Herder, 1967), pp. 159-164.

[55]LG 12.

[56]Marsili, *Anamnesis 1*, p. 127.

[57]LG 11.

[58]LG 30.

[59]LG 31. Thus according to the Dogmatic Constitution on the Church, "The term 'laity' is here (and throughout this entire study as well) understood to mean all the faithful except those in Holy Orders and those who belong to a religious state approved by the Church." (Chap. IV, para. 31).

[60]LG 32. Cf. F. Klostermann's commentary in *Commentary on the Documents of Vatican II*, vol. I, ed. H. Vorgrimler, pp. 238-240.

[61]LG 32.

[62]LG 33.

[63]LG 37.

[64]LG 39.

[65]LG 40.

[66]LG 10. Cf. S. Marsili, *Anamnesis 1*, p. 110.

[67]Concerning this question see the first eighteen pages of this chapter.

[68]Cf. *The Dogmatic Constitution on the Church, The Pastoral Constitution on the Church in the Modern World, The Consititution on the Sacred Liturgy*, and the *Decrees on Ecumenism, Life in the Missions*, and *Christian Education* are among the most notable.

[69]See the previous section of this chapter devoted to an analysis of this document.

[70]AA 2; LG 9.

[71]AA 2; LG 32.

[72]AA 2; LG 31.

[73]AA 3; LG 11.

[74]AA 3; LG 9.

[75]AA 3; LG 11, 33.

[76]AA 3; LG 33.

[77]AA 4.

[78]AA 9.

[79]AA 10.

[80]*Ibid.*

[81]LG 32.

[82]SC 1.

[83]These two documents referred to are *The Dogmatic Constitution on the Church—Lumen Gentium*, and the *Decree on the Apostolate of the Laity—Apostolicam Actuositatem*.

[84]GS 3.

[85]GS 4.

[86]GS 5.

[87]GS 10.

[88]GS 19.

[89]GS 11-22. For a good background to these articles see J. Ratzinger's commentary in *Commentary on the Documents of Vatican II*, vol. 5, ed. H. Vorgrimler, pp. 115-163.

[90]GS 16.

[91]GS 17.

[92]GS 23-32. See also O. Semmelroth's commentary in *Commentary on the Documents of Vatican II*, vol. 5, ed. H. Vorgrimler, pp. 164-181.

[93]GS 26.

[94]GS 27, 28, 29.

[95]GS 31, 32.

[96]SC 9, 10.

[97]GS 2, 40.

[98]LG 1.

[99]LG 8.

[100]GS 21.

[101]*Ibid.*

[102]AA 3, 9; LG 11; SC 2, 7.

[103]A. Verheul, *Introduction to the Liturgy* (Collegeville: The Liturgical Press, 1968), p. 92.

[104]SC 1.

[105]LG 1-8. While the encyclicals *Mystici Corporis* and *Mediator Dei* of Pope Pius XII both stressed the concept of the Church viewed as the Mystical Body of Christ, *Lumen Gentium* and *Sacrosanctum Concilium* carried this idea to a much greater depth of meaning.

[106]SC 7.

[107]SC 9.

[108]SC 10.

[109]*Ibid.*

[110]SC 11.

[111]J. Jungmann, *Commentary on the Documents of Vatican II*, vol. I, ed. H. Vorgrimler, p. 17.

[112]SC 14.

[113]ASS 36, 1903, 329-339.

[114]L. Bouyer, *The Revised Liturgy, A Doctrinal Commentary of the Concil-*

iar Constitution on the Liturgy (London: Darton, Longman and Todd, Ltd., 1965), pp. 91-92.

[115]SC 18.

[116]SC 19.

[117]Jungmann, *op. cit.*, p. 19.

[118]SC 21.

[119]SC 23.

[120]LG 1-8.

[121]Cyprianus, "De Ecclesiae Unitate," CSEL 3, 215-216.

[122]SC 26, 2, 7; AA 4.

[123]SC 27.

[124]SC 28.

[125]Jungmann, *op. cit.*, p. 22.

[126]LG 10.

[127]SC 29.

[128]SC 30.

[129]SC 21-25.

[130]SC 31.

[131]G. Sloyan, "Commentary," *The Constitution on the Sacred Liturgy* (Glen Rock, NJ: The Paulist Press, 1964), p. 19.

[132]J. D. Crichton, *The Church's Worship—Considerations on the Liturgical Constitution of the Second Vatican Council* (London: Geoffrey Chapman, 1965), p. 106.

[133]SC 33.

[134]SC 34.

[135]SC 36, (1).

[136]SC 36, (2).

[137]AAS 39, 1947, 545.

[138]SC 36, (3).

[139]SC 36, (4).

[140]SC 37.

[141]SC 38.

[142]SC 39-40.

[143]LG 11.

[144]SC 41.

[145]SC 42; PO 9, AAS 39, 1947, 592.

[146]SC 47.

[147]SC 10; LG 11.

[148]Cf. AAS 39, 1947, 552.

[149]SC 48, 10; LG 11.

[150]SC 49-50.

[151]SC 51.

[152]SC 52.

[153]SC 53.

[154]SC 54.

[155]SC 55.

[156]SC 56.

[157]SC 59-62.

[158]SC 63-69; 71-81.

[159]SC 83.

[160]AAS 39, 1947, 573.

[161]SC 84; PO 5.

[162]*Ibid.*, J. Pasher in EL 78, 1964, 339, feels that the justification for regarding this participation by the laity in the recitation of the Divine Office as truly liturgical, stems from the fact that even though there might be no *deputatio* for them, they certainly have a *vocatio* through the Church.

[163]SC 85.

[164]SC 86.

[165]SC 87.

[166]SC 88.

[167]SC 89, (a).

[168]SC 89, (b, c, d, e).

[169]SC 90.

[170]SC 92, (a, b, c).

[171]SC 93.

[172]SC 94.

[173]SC 95, (a, b, c).

[174]SC 96. For a comparative survey of this legislation see H. Schmidt, EL 78, 1964, 352-354.

[175]SC 98; J. Jungmann, *Commentary on the Documents of Vatican II*, p. 67.

[176]SC 99.

[177]*Ibid.*

[178]SC 100; AAS 39, 1947, 575-576; AAS 50, 1958, 646.

[179]Cf. H. Schmidt, *Constitution de la Sainte Liturgie—Genese et Commentaire* (Bruxelles: Editions Lumen Vitae, 1966), p. 179.

[180]Jungmann, *op. cit.*, p. 68.

[181]SC 101, (1).

[182]SC 101, (2).

[183]SC 101, (3).

[184]Crichton, *op. cit.*, p. 193.

[185]SC 113.

[186]SC 114, 118, cf. 28, 30.

[187]SC 124.

[188]Schmidt, *op. cit.*, pp. 204-205. The word *participare, participatio, participer,* participation is repeated on twenty-five different occasions throughout the Constitution in articles 11, 12, 14 (twice), 17, 19, 21, 26, 27, 30, 33, 41, 48, 50, 53, 55, 56, 79, 90, 106, 113, 114, 121, 124, as well as in the title of section II, Chapter I. Throughout these same articles this word is at various times modified, defined and clarified by such words and phrases as: active 11, 14 (twice), 19, 21, 26, 27, 30, 41, 48, 50, 79, 113, 114, 121, 124; full 14 (twice), 21, 41; conscious 14, 48, 79; knowingly 11; easily 79; devotedly 48, 50; fruitfully 11; internal and external 19; a total community 21; with total commitment of spirit 17.

[189]Schmidt, *op. cit.*, pp. 203-204. Cf. SC 14, 28; LG 11, 30; AA 3.

[190]SC 26, cf. Schmidt, *op. cit.*, p. 205. "Participation in the liturgy is, by virtue of baptism, the right and duty of all the faithful (art. 14), of all the people (art. 14), of the Christian people (art. 21), of all the holy People of God (art. 21), of the universal assembly of the faithful (art. 114), of the entire assembly of the people (art. 121), of each member of the Church (art. 26), of the people (art. 30, 53, 113), as well as priests and all the others (art. 90)."

[191]SC 95, 96.

[192]SC 84; AAS 39, 1947, 573.

[193]SC 100.

[194]SC 84.

[195]*Ibid.*

[196]SC 84, 95, 96.

[197]Cf. L. Sheppard, *Blueprint for Worship* (Westminster, Maryland: The Newman Press, 1964), pp. 75-76.

[198]SC 88, 94.

[199]SC 36, 101.

[200]SC 100.

[201]Schmidt, *op. cit.*, pp. 203-207.

[202]SC 21.

[203]SC 26, 42.

Chapter III

[1]SC 84.

[2] SC 87.

[3] SC 88.

[4] SC 89 (a).

[5] SC 89 (b).

[6] SC 89 (c).

[7] SC 89 (d).

[8] SC 89 (e).

[9] SC 91.

[10] SC 92.

[11] SC 100.

[12] AAS 56, 1964, 139-144.

[13] E. Cattaneo, *Il Culto Cristiano in Occidente*, ed. 3 (Roma: C. L. V.— Edizioni Liturgiche, 1978), pp. 637-639.

[14] V. Raffa, "Dal Breviario del Quignonez alla Liturgia delle Ore di Paolo VI," *Liturgia delle Ore, Documenti Ufficiali e Studi* (Torino-Leuman: Elle Di Ci, 1972), pp. 358-362.

[15] AAS 61, 1969, 299-301. Thus the former Congregation of Rites was now divided into two separate Congregations: the Congregation for Divine Worship—*Congregatio Cultu Divino*, and the Congregation for Saintly Causes—*Congregatio Causis Sanctorum*.

[16] Cf. Rivista Liturgica 55, (1968) 1, pp. 117-126.

[17] Cf. V. Raffa, *op. cit.*, also Rivista Liturgica 56, (1969), 5-6, p. 693.

[18] *Prière du Temps Présent, Nouvel Office* (Mame, Desclée, 1969).

[19] In Great Britain: *The Prayer of the Church* (London: Geoffrey Chapman, 1970). In the United States of America: *The Prayer of Christians* (New York: Catholic Book Publishing Company, 1971).

[20] AAS 63, 1971, 527-535.

[21] *Institutio Generalis de Liturgia Horarum* (Rome: Typis Polyglottis Vaticanis, 1971).

[22] *Liturgia Horarum Iuxta Ritum Romanum* (Rome: Editio Typica, Typis Polyglottis Vaticanis, 1971-1972).

[23] *The Divine Office—The Liturgy of the Hours According to the Roman Rite* (London: William Collins Sons and Co. Ltd., 1973-1974). This was followed in May 1975 with the publication in the United States of America of: *The Liturgy of the Hours According to the Roman Rite* (New York: Catholic Book Publishing Company, 1975-1976).

[24] SC 83-101.

[25] AAS 56, 1964, 139-144.

[26] *Ibid.*, p. 140.

[27] *Ibid.*

[28] *Ibid.*, SC 19.

[29] AAS 56, 1964, 141; SC 45, 46.

[30] AAS 56, 1964, 142-143; SC 98.

[31] AAS 56, 1964, 143; SC 101, 36c, d.

[32] AAS 56, 1964, 877-900.

[33] *Ibid.*, p. 877.

[34] *Ibid.*

[35] *Ibid.*, p. 878.

[36] *Ibid.*, SC 10.

[37] AAS 56, 1964, 878; SC 9.

[38] AAS 56, 1964, 879; SC 10.

[39] AAS 56, 1964, 879-881; SC 15-18.

[40] AAS 56, 1964, 881; SC 42.

[41] AAS 56, 1964, 884; SC 28.

[42] SC 36.

[43] AAS 56, 1964, 143.

[44] AAS 56, 1964, 885-886.

[45] *Ibid.*, pp. 895-896; SC 95.

[46] AAS 56, 1964, 886; SC 97.

[47] AAS 56, 1964, 896-897; SC 98-99.

[48] AAS 56, 1964, 897; SC 101.

[49] SC 84, 87, 90, 100, 101.

[50] AAS, 59, 1967, 300-320.

[51] *Ibid.*, p. 301; SC 113.

[52] AAS 59, 1967, 301; SC 114.

[53] AAS 59, 1967, 304; SC 26, 41-42.

[54] AAS 59, 1967, 304; SC 14.

[55] AAS 59, 1967, 304; SC 11.

[56] AAS 59, 1967, 304; SC 30.

[57] AAS 59, 1967, 305; SC 30.

[58] AAS 59, 1967, 305-306. Cf. Instruction on the Sacred Congregation of Rites, *Inter Oecumenici*, AAS 56, 1964, 881.

[59] AAS 59, 1967, 301.

[60] *Ibid.*, p. 304; SC 14.

[61] AAS 59, 1967, 311. Cf. AAS 39, 1947, 575-576; SC 90, 100.

[62] AAS 59, 1967, 311.

[63] *Ibid.*, pp. 311, 312, 316, 317; SC 101.

[64] L. Deiss, *Spirit and Song of the New Liturgy*, trans. L. Haggard, M.

Mazzarese (Cincinnati: World Library of Sacred Music, 1970), p. 9.

[65] AAS 59, 1967, 442-448.

[66] *Ibid.*, p. 442.

[67] *Ibid.*, pp. 446-447.

[68] *Ibid.*, p. 448; SC 36.

[69] AAS 63, 1971, 527-535.

[70] *Ibid.*, p. 529.

[71] *Ibid.*, pp. 529-530; SC 88.

[72] AAS 63, 1971, 530.

[73] *Ibid.*; SC 91.

[74] AAS 63, 1971, 530-531; SC 92 (a).

[75] AAS 63, 1971, 531; SC 92 (b).

[76] AAS 63, 1971, 531; SC 92 (c).

[77] AAS 63, 1971, 531. Cf. Chap. 8, "The Didache—The Teaching of the Twelve Apostles," *Ancient Christian Writers*, ed. J. Quasten, J. Plumpe (Westminster, Maryland: The Newman Press, 1948), p. 19.

[78] AAS 63, 1971, 531-532.

[79] *Ibid.*, p. 532; CS 83-84; AAS 39, 1947, 522.

[80] AAS 63, 1971, 532.

[81] *Ibid.*, pp. 532-533; SC 24.

[82] AAS 63, 1971, 533.

[83] *Ibid.*, pp. 533-534.

[84] *Ibid.*, p. 534.

[85] *Ibid.*, p. 527.

[86] Cf. SC 14; LG 11.

[87] A. Bugnini, "Introduction," *The Liturgy of the Hours—The General Instruction on the Reform of the Breviary*, trans. P. Coughlan, P. Purdue (London: Geoffrey Chapman, 1974), p. 16.

[88] *Institutio Generalis de Liturgia Horarum* (Rome: Typis Polyglottis Vaticanis, 1971). The English translation of the *General Instruction on the Liturgy of the Hours* (hereafter cited as GILH) will be taken from: *The Divine Office—The Liturgy of the Hours According to the Roman Rite*, vol. I (London: William Collins Sons and Co. Ltd., 1974), pp. xix-xcii. In the official title of this Instruction, the term "breviary" has been dropped in favor of "The Liturgy of the Hours." This change is significant for truly understanding the meaning of the reform. The Hours have been restored to their traditional sequence of time through which the public and common prayer of the whole Church is meant to sanctify the entire day for all the People of God.

[89] GILH 1.

[90]*Ibid.*, cf. Acts 1:14; 3:1; 4:24; 10:9; 12:5; 16:25; Eph. 5:19-21. See also the section entitled "The Development of Public Prayer in the Early Church" in Chapter I of this thesis.

[91]GILH 3, 4, 5, 6. Cf. SC 83; J. Jeremias, *The Prayers of Jesus* (Norwich: SCM Press, Ltd., 1976), pp. 64-65. T. Federici, "Liturgia: Creativita, Interiorizzazione, attuazione," *Notitiae* 127, 1977, pp. 83-84.

[92]GILH 7; cf. LG 10.

[93]GILH 7; cf. J. D. Crichton, *Christian Celebration—The Prayer of the Church* (London: Geoffrey Chapman, 1976), pp. 16-28.

[94]GILH 8; Lk. 10:21; Rom. 8:15. For an excellent survey of this entire concept read C. Vagaggini, *Theological Dimensions of the Liturgy*, trans. J. Doyle, W. A. Jurgens (Collegeville: The Liturgical Press, 1976), pp. 191-246.

[95]GILH 9; cf. Acts 1:14, 4:32.

[96]GILH 9; cf. Acts 2:42.

[97]GILH 9; cf. Mt. 18:20.

[98]GILH 10; cf. SC 83, 84, 94. See also L. Bouyer, *Rite and Man—Natural Sacredness and Christian Liturgy* (Notre Dame: University of Notre Dame Press, 1963), pp. 189-205; and E. Bargellini "Liturgia delle Ore: Pregare nel ritmo del Tempo," *La Preghiera nel Tempo*, Vita Monastica, Camaldoli, n. 123 (1975), pp. 277-293.

[99]GILH 11. Cf. SC 88.

[100]GILH 12-17. Cf. SC 33.

[101]GILH 18-19. Cf. SC 2, 10; and J. Pinell *La Liturgia delle Ore* (Padova: Istituto di Liturgia Pastorale, 1975), pp. 104-108.

[102]GILH 20; SC 26.

[103]GILH 20; SC 41.

[104]GILH 21. Cf. SC 42; AA 10.

[105]GILH 22. Cf. SC 26, 84.

[106]SC 100.

[107]SC 84.

[108]GILH 22. Cf. Commentary of A. M. Roguet in *The Liturgy of the Hours—The General Instruction on the Reform of the Breviary*, trans. P. Coughlan, P. Purdue (London: Geoffrey Chapman, 1974), pp. 95-96.

[109]GILH 23; SC 90, 100; PO 5.

[110]GILH 24.

[111]GILH 25, 26; SC 99.

[112]GILH 27, SC 100; AA 16; John 4:23.

[113]GILH 27; AA 11.

[114]GILH 28; SC 41, 90; Cf. LG 21, 26, 41; PO 5, 13.

[115]GILH 29; SC 88, 89, 94.

[116]GILH 30; Cf. AAS 59, 1967, 703.

[117]GILH 31; Cf. AAS 56, 1964, 895.

[118]GILH 32; SC 100.

[119]F. O'Leary, "The Liturgy of the Hours," *Furrow* 22, (1971), p. 425. See also SC 95, 96. As has already been stated in the Introduction to this thesis, the concept of obligation or deputation must be seen more in the sense of duty and of an essential need rather than in a quantitative and juridical sense.

[120]GILH 33; SC 27.

[121]GILH 37; SC 89, 100.

[122]GILH 40.

[123]GILH 42.

[124]GILH 43.

[125]GILH 44, 45, 46.

[126]GILH 47.

[127]GILH 48.

[128]GILH 49.

[129]GILH 50.

[130]GILH 51.

[131]GILH 52.

[132]GILH 55.

[133]GILH 57-59; SC 89 (c).

[134]SC 89 (e).

[135]GILH 76; Cf. 27.

[136]GILH 77; Cf. SC 89 (e).

[137]GILH 84; Cf. SC 89 (b).

[138]GILH 27; AA 11.

[139]GILH 88.

[140]GILH 93.

[141]GILH 94, 99.

[142]GILH 100. Cf. F. Mancini, "L'uso dei Salmi nei secoli," *La Preghiera nel Tempo*, Vita Monastica, Camaldoli, n. 124-125 (1976), pp. 19-42. See also L. Bouyer, *The Meaning of Sacred Scripture* (Notre Dame: University of Notre Dame Press, 1958), pp. 224-241.

[143]GILH 101. Cf. R. G. Weakland, "The Divine Office and Contemporary Man," *Worship* 43 (1969), pp. 214-218.

[144]GILH 102; SC 90. Certainly what is probably the most complete and up-to-date, reliable study of the Psalms in English is L. Sabourin's *The Psalms—Their Origin and Meaning* (New York: Alba House, 1974). On a

much simpler and practical level see M. H. Shepherd Jr., *The Psalms in Christian Worship—A Practical Guide* (Minneapolis: Augsburg Publishing House, 1976).

[145]Most assuredly great care and study should be and has been exercised in the proper translation of the psalms into the vernacular languages. See P. Beauchamp's article, "Les Psaumes Aujourd'hui—Pratique et Problemes de la Traduction," LMD 118, 1974, 49-75.

[146]GILH 108, 104. Cf. AAS 59, 1967, 300-320; SC 99, 113; L. Deiss, *Spirit and Song of the New Liturgy*, pp. 11-19.

[147]GILH 105, 106.

[148]GILH 107.

[149]GILH 108.

[150]GILH 109. Cf. B. Fischer, "Le Christ dans les Psaumes, " LMD 27 1951, 86-109; and by the same author, "Les Psaumes, Prière Chrétienne. Témoignages du IIe Siècle," *La Prière des Heures*—Semaine d'Etudes Liturgiques de Saint Serge, juillet 1961, Lex Orandi 35, ed. Cassien, B. Botte (Paris: Les Editions du Cerf, 1963), pp. 85-99. See also J. Danielou, *The Bible and the Liturgy* (Notre Dame: University of Notre Dame Press, 1956), pp. 177-190; and P. Salmon, *The Breviary Through the Centuries*, trans. D. Mary (Collegeville: The Liturgical Press, 1962), pp. 42-61.

[151]GILH 110.

[152]GILH 111.

[153]GILH 114.

[154]GILH 113-120. Cf. P. Salmon, "La Prière des Heures," L'Eglise en Prière, ed. A. G. Martimort (Tournai, Desclée and Cie, Editeurs, 1961), pp. 822-823; also J. Gélineau, *Voices and Instruments in Christian Worship*, trans. C. Howell (Collegeville: The Liturgical Press, 1964), pp. 107-108.

[155]GILH 121-125.

[156]SC 91.

[157]GILH 126. Cf. J. Tarruel, "La nouvelle destribution du Psautier dans la Liturgia Horarum," EL 87, 1973, 325-382; also J. Pascher, "Il nuovo ordinamento della salmodia nella Liturgia romana delle Ore," *Liturgia delle Ore—Documenti Ufficiali e Studi* (Torino-Leuman: Elle Di Ci, 1972), pp. 161-184.

[158]GILH 127.

[159]GILH 129-130, 134.

[160]GILH 131. The three psalms omitted from the psalter are: Ps. 57, 82, 108. The particular psalm verses omitted have been indicated at the beginning of the psalm, for example: The Office of Readings, Friday, First Week of Ordinary Time, Psalm 34, verses 4-9 have been omitted.

[161]GILH 131. Cf. Commentary of A. M. Roguet in *The Liturgy of the Hours—The General Instruction on the Reform of the Breviary*, trans. P. Coughlan, P. Purdue, pp. 116-117.

[162]GILH 132.

[163]GILH 100-102. Cf. Pascher, *op. cit.*, p. 184.

[164]T. Merton, *Praying the Psalms* (Collegeville: The Liturgical Press, 1955), p. 5.

[165]GILH 136-139. Cf. J. D. Crichton, *Christian Celebration—The Prayer of the Church* (London: Geoffrey Chapman, 1976), pp. 67-68.

[166]GILH 140. Cf. J. Lengeling, "Le Letture Bibliche e i loro Responsori nella nuova Liturgia delle Ore," *Liturgia delle Ore—Documenti Ufficiali e Studi*, pp. 185-219.

[167]GILH 143-155. Cf. 55-69; SC 89 (c).

[168]GILH 141-142.

[169]GILH 143, 154, 157, 158.

[170]GILH 143.

[171]GILH 159-160. Cf. 64-67. See also H. Marot, "La Place des Lectures Bibliques et Patristiques dans l'Office Latin," *La Prière des Heures*—Semaine d'Etudes Liturgiques de Saint Serge, Lex Orandi 35, ed. Cassien, B. Botte (Paris: Les Editions du Cerf, 1963), pp. 149-165.

[172]GILH 161-162. Cf. SC 92 (b); and H. Ashworth, "The New Patristic Lectionary," EL 85, 1971, 306-322, or by the same author, "Il Lesionario patristico del nuovo Ufficio divino," *Liturgia delle Ore—Documenti Ufficiali e Studi*, pp. 221-227.

[173]GILH 163-164. Cf. J. D. Crichton, *op. cit.*, p. 69. The author feels that in the face of modern scriptural exegesis many of the commentaries prove to be somewhat unsatisfactory.

[174]GILH 165.

[175]GILH 166.

[176]Cf. J. D. Crichton, *op. cit.*, pp. 69-70; and A. Amore "Le Letture agiografiche nella Liturgia delle Ore," *Liturgia delle Ore—Documenti Ufficiali e Studi*, pp. 229-230.

[177]GILH 167. Cf. SC 92 (c); AAS 63, 1971, 531.

[178]Cf. SC 8. For a good review of the tradition of the Church in relation to the cult of the saints, see P. Jounel, "Le Culte des Saints," L'Eglise en Prière, pp. 766-785.

[179]Cf. SC 104, 111; LG 49-51.

[180]GILH 167. Cf. Amore, *op. cit.*, pp. 230-234.

[181]GILH 169-170.

[182]GILH 172. Cf. Lengeling, *op. cit.*, pp. 206-210.

[183]GILH 173-174, 42. Cf. Salmon, *L'Eglise en Prière*, pp. 798-799, 824-826.

[184]GILH 173. Cf. SC 30; AAS 59, 1967, 305.

[185]GILH 175-176. Cf. SC 93.

[186]GILH 177. Cf. J. Gelineau, "Are New Forms of Liturgical Singing and Music Developing?" *Concilium*, 52 (New York: Herder and Herder, 1970), pp. 37-46; and also H. Hucke, "Towards a New Kind of Church Music," *Concilium*, 62, 1971, pp. 87-97.

[187]GILH 179. Cf. AAS 63, 1971, 531. Although in reality of very ancient origin and use, these prayers had fallen into neglect and disuse over the ages. For a good assessment of this question see F. Morlot, "Le Preces delle Lodi e dei Vespri," *Liturgia delle Ore—Documenti Ufficiali e Studi*, pp. 241-242.

[188]GILH 179; 182.

[189]GILH 180, 182. Cf. SC 53, and the commentary of W. Jurgens in *The General Instruction on the Liturgy of the Hours* (Collegeville: The Liturgical Press, 1975), pp. 139-140; as well as the commentary of A. M. Roguet in *The Liturgy of the Hours—The General Instruction on the Reform of the Breviary*, trans. P. Coughlan, P. Purdue, pp. 119-120.

[190]GILH 183.

[191]GILH 180-182, 186.

[192]GILH 184-188.

[193]GILH 183. Cf. Morlot, *op. cit.*, p. 246.

[194]GILH 189-193.

[195]Cf. Morlot, *op. cit.*, p. 249.

[196]GILH 194. This practice follows the example of the old Monastic Office. See Chap. 13, *The Rule of Saint Benedict*, ed. and trans. J. McCann (London, 1972), p. 57.

[197]GILH 195-196. Cf. AAS 63, 1971, 531. In reciting this prayer three times daily the Church has reestablished one of its ancient customs as testified to in the eighth chapter of the *Didache—The Teaching of the Twelve Apostles*. See footnote 68 in the first chapter of this study.

[198]GILH 197-200. Cf. A. Duman, "Le Orazioni dell'Ufficio feriale nel Tempo per annum," *Liturgia delle Ore—Documenti Ufficiali e Studi*, pp. 251-268.

[199]GILH 201-203. Cf. SC 30; Roguet, *op. cit.*, pp. 124-125.

[200]GILH 207.

[201]AAS 39, 1947, 575-576.

[202]SC 100.

[203]SC 28.

[204]GILH 253-254.
[205]GILH 255-258.
[206]SC 99.
[207]AAS 59, 1967, 310.
[208]GILH 268-269; SC 113.
[209]GILH 270-271.
[210]GILH 272-273, 277-284. Cf. SC 89 (a).
[211]GILH 275-276. Cf. AAS 59, 1967, 312, 315-317. See also Jurgens, *op. cit.*, pp. 169-173.
[212]GILH 279.
[213]LG 9.
[214]LG 11.
[215]GILH 21, 22.
[216]SC 42.
[217]GILH 23; SC 14.
[218]SC 100.
[219]GILH 27; SC 100; AA 16.

Chapter IV

[1]Cf. SC 84, 85, 90.
[2]Cf. GS 4-10.
[3]Cf. GS 7.
[4]GS 4.
[5]A. Bergomini, *Il Breviario per Tutti* (Bologna: Edizioni Dehoniane, 1971), pp. 11-12.
[6]*Ibid.*, p. 12.
[7]Papa Paolo VI, Lettera Enciclica, *Lo Sviluppo Die Popoli*, (Populorum progressio), (Rome: Tipografia Poliglotta Vaticana, 1967), pp. 29-30.
[8]SC 7.
[9]SC 14.
[10]GILH 13.
[11]SC 2.
[12]SC 9.
[13]SC 10.
[14]*Ibid.*
[15]SC 83. Also see GILH 10, 13.
[16]GILH 10, 12.
[17]SC 41.
[18]GILH 20.
[19]GILH 20-27; SC 21, 26, 27. For a good review of this communal aspect of

the Liturgy of the Hours see A. Cuva, *La Liturgia delle Ore* (Rome: Edizioni Liturgiche, 1975), pp. 40-44.

[20]Cf. GILH 18.

[21]GILH 21; SC 99.

[22]GILH 23; SC 100.

[23]Cf. W. G. Storey, "Parish Worship: The Liturgy of the Hours," *Worship* 49, (1975), p. 8. Over the past three years we have had the opportunity to question many pastors and parish priests on this matter and although some positive answers were received, the negative responses reflected at this point of the study were by far the most prevalent.

[24]Cf. J. Jungmann, *Pastoral Liturgy* (New York: Herder and Herder, 1962), pp. 122-157. See also footnotes 130-138 of Chapter I of this thesis.

[25]Eusebius, "Commentarios in Psalmos," PG XXIII, 639.

[26]Ambrosius, "Expositio in Psalmum CXVIII," (PL XV, 1479), CSEL 64, 438-439.

[27]Augustinus, "Confessiones," (PL XXXII, 714), CSEL 33, 104; "De Civitate Dei," (PL XLI, 765), CC 48, 820; "Enarratio in Psalmum LXVI," PL XXXVI, 805.

[28]Cf. footnotes 105, 106, 108, and 112 of Chapter I of this study.

[29]Cf. W. G. Storey, "The Liturgy of the Hours: Cathedral versus Monastery," *Christians at Prayer*, ed. J. Gallen (Notre Dame: University of Notre Dame Press, 1977), p. 74. See also C. W. Dugmore, "Canonical Hours," *Dictionary of Liturgy and Worship*, ed. J. G. Davies (London: SCM Press Ltd., 1972), p. 117.

[30]GILH 254.

[31]Cf. GILH 23.

[32]Cf. GILH 9, 10, 11. See also R. Morhaus, "Monastic Liturgy in Progress," *Liturgy* 18 (1973), p. 23.

[33]Cf. W. J. Grisbrooke, "A Contemporary Liturgical Problem: The Divine Office and Public Worship," *Studia Liturgica* 8 (1971-1972), pp. 129-168; 9 (1973), pp. 3-18, 18-106; Storey, "The Liturgy of the Hours: Cathedral versus Monastery," *Christians at Prayer*, pp. 61-82.

[34]*Ibid.*, pp. 74-75; Grisbrooke, *op. cit.*, pp. 130-131.

[35]*Ibid.*

[36]*Ibid.*, pp. 91-96.

[37]*Ibid.*, pp. 130-131.

[38]GILH 37.

[39]GILH 26, 40; SC 100. Outside of Compline the other Hours, such as those of Readings, Terce, Sext, and None, can realistically be considered as the

exception and not the rule for daily, communal and public use by the laity.

⁴⁰Cf. GILH 38, 39, 42, 54, 126, 127, 136, 137, 138, 172, 173, 175, 176.

⁴¹GILH 110-125.

⁴²GILH 42-43, 126-127.

⁴³GILH 88, 128.

⁴⁴Cf. R. Weakland, "The Divine Office and Contemporary Man," *Worship* 43, (1969), pp. 215-216.

⁴⁵Cf. Chapter III of this study.

⁴⁶GILH 101-125.

⁴⁷GILH 100.

⁴⁸Cf. Grisbrooke, *op. cit.*, pp. 84-90.

⁴⁹GILH 126.

⁵⁰GILH 55-57, 63-67, 140-158; SC 89 (c), 92.

⁵¹GILH 159-165; SC 92.

⁵²Cf. Weakland, *op. cit.*, p. 217.

⁵³Cf. G. T. Broccolo, "The Praying People of God," *A Statement on Prayer* (Chicago: The Liturgical Commission, 1970), p. 9.

⁵⁴Cf. J. D. Crichton, *Christian Celebration: The Prayer of the Church* (London: Geoffrey Chapman, 1976), pp. 64-65.

⁵⁵Cf. GILH 11, 14, 18.

⁵⁶Cf. GILH 10, 12, 13, 15.

⁵⁷Cf. GILH 6, 7, 9.

⁵⁸*The Liturgy of the Hours: The General Instruction on the Reform of the Breviary*, trans. P. Coughlan, P. Purdue (London: Geoffrey Chapman, 1974), p. 16.

⁵⁹On this entire subject refer to the first three pages of Chapter III of this study.

⁶⁰GILH 23; SC 100.

⁶¹The English edition of the Divine Office published in the United States is *The Liturgy of the Hours According to the Roman Rite*, 4 vols. (New York: Catholic Book Publishing Company, 1975-1976).

⁶²In the United States there have been five individual versions of the one volume official edition of the Liturgy of the Hours published with the contents of each volume varying according to the choice of the individual publisher. They are as follows:

1. Catholic Book Publishing Company, (two editions), New York, 1976.
2. Daughters of St. Paul, Boston, 1976.
3. Helicon Press, Baltimore, 1976.
4. The Liturgical Press, Collegeville, 1976.

[63]GILH 37.

[64]*Morning Praise and Evensong: A Liturgy of the Hours in Musical Setting*, edited and arranged by W. G. Storey, F. C. Quinn, D. F. Wright (Notre Dame: Fides Publishers Inc., 1973). "Morning and Evening Prayer," *The Catholic Liturgy Book*, gen. ed. R. A. Keifer (Baltimore: Helicon Press, 1975), pp. 539-621. *Morning and Evening Prayer*, ed. Rev. D. Joseph Finnerty, Rev. George J. Ryan (Collegeville: The Liturgical Press, 1980). *Praying With Christ—A Seasonal Form of Morning and Evening Prayer for Parish Participation* (Collegeville: The Liturgical Press, 1981). In addition to the above selections the Federation of Diocesan Liturgical Commissions, Washington, D.C. has published the following works: *Advent Evening Prayer*, (Evening Prayer II, Sunday Week II with Advent antiphons and hymns). *Evening Prayer for Lent*, (Evening Prayer II, Sunday Week II with Lenten antiphons and ten Lenten hymns). *Obedient Unto Death*, (Office of Readings for Good Friday with music). *The Easter Triduum*, (Holy Thursday Night Prayer; Good Friday Morning and Evening Prayer; Holy Saturday Morning Prayer, all with accompanying music). *Behold Your Mother: Evening Prayer for Feasts of Mary*, (Evening Prayer II from the Common of the Blessed Virgin Mary). *Sing Praise to the Lord*, (Evening Prayer II, Sunday Week I).

[65]*The Catholic Liturgy Book*, gen. ed. R. A. Keifer (Baltimore: Helicon Press, 1975).

[66]L. Deiss, *Biblical Hymns and Psalms*, 2 vols. (Cincinnati: World Library of Sacred Music Publications, Inc., 1965-1970). J. Gelineau, *The Grail Gelineau Psalter* (Chicago: G.I.A. Publications, Inc., 1963). *Christian Prayer—The Liturgy of the Hours—Organ Accompaniment* (Washington, D.C., The International Commission on English in the Liturgy, 1976-1978). This volume contains the organ accompaniment to the hymns and service music found in *Christian Prayer* the one volume edition of the Liturgy of the Hours. Further musical aids may be found in cassette recordings of the service music for the new Liturgy of the Hours as published by the National Association of Pastoral Musicians, Washington, D.C., which include the music found in the one volume edition of the Hours as well as a select number of hymns found in the four volume edition of the Liturgy of the Hours.

[67]SC 100; GILH 37.

[68]SC 11.

[69]SC 14, 19.

[70]GILH 23.

[71]GILH 19, 28, 29; SC 14, 90.

[72]GILH 28.

[73]GILH 11; SC 88.

[74]GILH 23.

[75]Ibid.

[76]SC 14.

[77]SC 16, 17, 18.

[78]GILH 23.

[79]Printed material such as that already referred to in footnote 62 of this Chapter, and none better than the General Instruction on the Liturgy of the Hours.

[80]W. G. Storey, "Morning Praise and Evensong for Parishes," NCR Cassettes (Kansas City: National Catholic Reporter Publishing Company, 1974).

[81]Cf. SC 41.

[82]Certainly the General Instruction on the Liturgy of the Hours itself, with a good commentary would be best suited for this instruction. Especially recommended are the following: The Liturgy of the Hours—The General Instruction on the Reform of the Breviary, with a commentary by A. M. Roguet, trans. P. Coughlan, P. Purdue (London: Geoffrey Chapman, 1974), and General Instruction on the Liturgy of the Hours, trans. and with commentary by W. A. Jurgens (Collegeville: The Liturgical Press, 1975). The Archdiocese of Chicago and Archdiocese of New York have published some excellent catechetical material on this subject in order to promote the communal use of the Hours. See Liturgy 70, vol. 7, no. 8 (Chicago: The Office for Divine Worship, 1976), also J. Connolly, J. Baxendale, The New Office (New York: The Liturgical Commission, 1972). See also The Liturgy of the Hours, Study Text VII, Bishop's Committee on the Liturgy, (United States Catholic Conference, Washington, D.C.), 1981.

[83]Some books which can serve admirably as texts for this particular phase of instruction are: J. Danielou, The Bible and the Liturgy (Notre Dame: University of Notre Dame, 1956); A. Bloom, Beginning to Pray (New York: Paulist Press, 1970); M. H. Sheppard, The Psalms in Christian Worship—A Practical Guide (Minneapolis: Augsburg Publishing House, 1976); T. Merton, Praying the Psalms (Collegeville: The Liturgical Press, 1955).

[84]There are publications containing such liturgy training programs presently in circulation and ready for use by any pastor or parish liturgy team. See "Prayer Life of the Church," Liturgy in the Seventies (Chicago: Archdiocesan Liturgical Commission, 1971).

[85]SC 28.

[86]GILH 253.

[87]GILH 21, 23, 254.

[88]GILH 256, 257.

[89]GILH 258.

[90]GILH 22.

[91]GILH 271, 284.

[92]GILH 260.

[93]Cf. GILH 279.

[94]GILH 268.

[95]Cf. GILH 273.

[96]The Music Commission of the Archdiocese of Chicago has been providing special programs specifically designed for the training of cantors.

[97]GILH 259.

[98]Cf. GILH 262.

[99]Cf. GILH 46, 248, 249, 251.

[100]GILH 47.

[101]GILH 259.

[102]SC 113.

[103]GILH 268; SC 99; AAS 59, 1967, 310.

[104]GILH 269; SC 30; AAS 59, 1967, 305. Although designed primarily for the sacramental liturgies the following publication can be a great help in the guidance and the encouragement of the faithful to sing in church. B. Tamblyn, *Sing Up* (London: Geoffrey Chapman, 1971).

[105]Cf. art. 18, *The Instruction on Music in the Liturgy—Musicam Sacram*, AAS 59, 1967, 305-306.

[106]GILH 273.

[107]Cf. GILH 270.

[108]Cf. GILH 271-272.

[109]GILH 173.

[110]Cf. GILH 269, 277, 279, 280.

[111]GILH 175, 176, 177, 178.

[112]GILH 178.

[113]GILH 269, 277.

[114]GILH 278.

[115]GILH 279. See also 121-123.

[116]While there are many such resource books presently available, the following represent a limited sampling of some of the better qualified texts. L. Deiss, *Biblical Hymns and Psalms*, 2 vols. (Cincinnati: World Library of Sacred Music Publications, Inc., 1965-1970). J. Gelineau, *The Grail Gelineau Psalter* (Chicago: G.I.A. Publications, Inc., 1963). S. Somerville, *Psalms for*

Singing, 2 vols. (Cincinnati: World Library of Sacred Music Publications, Inc., 1960). *Morning Praise and Evensong—A Liturgy of the Hours in Musical Setting*, ed. and arranged by W. G. Storey, F. C. Quinn, D. F. Wright (Notre Dame: Fides Publishers, Inc., 1973). *The Catholic Liturgy Book*, ed. R. A. Keifer (Baltimore: Helicon Press, 1975). *Cantor Book* (Cycles A, B, C) (Cincinnati: World Library of Sacred Music Publications, Inc., 1970). *People's Mass Book* (Cincinnati: World Library of Sacred Music Publications, Inc., 1970). *F. E. L. Hymnal* (Los Angeles: F. E. L. Publications Ltd., 1972). *Christian Prayer—The Liturgy of the Hours—Organ Accompaniment* (Washington, D.C., The International Commission on English in the Liturgy, 1978).

[117]SC 30.

[118]GILH 201.

[119]GILH 202.

[120]*Ibid.*

[121]*Ibid.*

[122]GILH 273.

[123]Cf. art. 23, "General Instruction on the Roman Missal," ed. A. Flannery (Dublin: Dominican Publications, 1975), p. 168. See also AAS 66 (1974), pp. 30-46.

[124]Cf. Commentary of A. M. Roguet in *The Liturgy of the Hours—The General Instruction on the Reform of the Breviary*, trans. P. Coughlan, P. Purdue (London: Geoffrey Chapman, 1974), p. 124.

[125]Cf. H. L. deLenval, *The Whole Man at Worship* (New York: Desclee Company, 1961).

[126]Cf. A. Verheul, *Introduction to the Liturgy* (Collegeville: The Liturgical Press, 1964), pp. 117-130.

[127]J. P. Mossi, "The Procession," *Modern Liturgy Handbook*, ed. J. P. Mossi (New York: Paulist Press, 1976), pp. 174-177.

[128]Cf. GILH 263 (a).

[129]*Ibid.*, 263 (b).

[130]*Ibid.*, 263 (c, d).

[131]GILH 264.

[132]GILH 265.

[133]GILH 266.

[134]Cf. P. D. Jones, *Rediscovering Ritual* (New York: Newman Press, 1973), pp. 1-7.

[135]Cf. *Morning Praise and Evensong—A Liturgy of the Hours in Musical Setting*, ed. Storey, Quinn, Wright, p. vii.

[136]Cf. G. Collopy, "The Use of Slides in Liturgy," *Modern Liturgy Handbook*, ed. J. P. Mossi (New York: Paulist Press, 1976), pp. 117-119.

[137]Cf. GILH 255.

[138]GILH 93.

[139]GILH 12.

[140]GILH 94-98.

[141]Cf. J. D. Crichton, *Christian Celebration—The Prayer of the Church* (London: Geoffrey Chapman, 1976), p. 121.

[142]P. Duggan, "The Liturgy of the Hours," *Worship* 51, (1977), p. 309.

[143]Cf. *La Vita Liturgica nella Communita Christiana*, Ufficio Liturgico Diocesano di Torino (Torino-Leuman: Elle Di Ci, 1973), p. 45.

[144]GILH 27. See also SC 100.

[145]Cf. B. Neunheuser, "Das Stundengebet, Gebet Auch der Laien," *Notitiae* 143-144 (1978), 264-266. R. H. Oldershaw, *Morning Prayer and Evensong* (Chicago: Liturgy Training Program, 1973), p. 1.

[146]GILH 27.

[147]Cf. P. Duggan, *op. cit.*, p. 313. W. G. Storey, "Parish Worship: The Liturgy of the Hours," *Worship* 49 (1975), p. 11.

[148]Cf. I. Pratt, "Prayer in the Home—A Mother's Testimony," *Concilium— Prayer and Community*, vol. 52, ed. H. Schmidt (New York: Herder and Herder, 1970), pp. 87-91. W. A. Jurgens, "Commentary," *General Instruction on the Liturgy of the Hours*, pp. 45-47. B. Neunheuser, *op. cit.*, pp. 266-268. M. E. Moynahan, "Going Home: Rediscovery and Defence of Family Liturgy," *Modern Liturgy Handbook*, pp. 209-216. See also Chapters VII and VIII of this last mentioned text which are devoted to children's liturgies and worship in the home, pp. 181-228.

[149]Special acknowledgement is to be given to the following authors and works for their contribution toward the formation of this particular section: R. Oldershaw, "Morning and Evening Prayer," *Liturgy 70—Liturgy of the Hours*, vol. 7 (Chicago: Liturgy Training Program, 1976), pp. 4-8, and by the same author *Morning Prayer and Evening Song* (Chicago: Liturgy Training Program, 1973), p. 8. *Morning Praise and Evensong—A Liturgy of the Hours in Musical Setting*, ed. Storey, Quinn, Wright, pp. VII-XI. J. Connolly, J. Baxendale, *The New Office* (New York: The Liturgical Commission, 1972).

[150]GILH 33.

[151]GILH 34.

[152]GILH 42, 178.

[153]GILH 123.

[154]GILH 121, 122, 260.

[155]GILH 259.
[156]GILH 46, 47, 248, 249, 251.
[157]GILH 48.
[158]GILH 50, 138, 261, 266.
[159]GILH 51, 179-193.
[160]GILH 52, 194, 195, 196.
[161]GILH 53, 54, 197-200.
[162]GILH 42, 178.
[163]GILH 113, 123.
[164]GILH 260.
[165]GILH 259.
[166]GILH 193.
[167]GILH 54, 197.
[168]Cf. Crichton, *op. cit.*, p. 122.
[169]Cf. GILH 202.

A Selected Bibliography

Andrieu, M. *Les Ordines Romani du Haut Moyen Age*. Louvain, 1931 et suiv., vol. I.

Ashworth, H. "The New Patristic Lectionary," EL 85 (1971), 306-322.

Battifol, P. *Histoire du Bréviaire Romain*. Paris: August Picard, 1911.

Baumer, S. *Histoire du Bréviaire*. 2 vols. Trans. R. Biron. Rome: Herder, 1967.

Baumstark, A. *Liturgie Comparée*. Gembloux: J. Duclot, 1932.

Beauduin, L. *La piété de l'Eglise*. Louvain: Monte-Cesar, 1914. English trans. *Liturgy, The Life of the Church*. 2nd ed. Trans. V. Michel. Collegeville: The Liturgical Press, 1929.

Bishop, E. *Liturgica Historica*. Oxford: Clarendon Press, 1918.

Borella, P. *Il Rito Ambrosiano*. Brescia: Morcelliana, 1964.

Botte, B. "Les Heures de Prière dans la 'Tradition Apostolique' et les Documents Dérivés," *La Prière des Heures*—Semaine d'Etudes liturgiques de Saint Serge, Juillet 1961, Lex Orandi 35, ed. M. Cassien, B. Botte. Paris: Les Editions du Cerf, 1963.

Bouyer, L. *Eucharist*. Trans. C. U. Quinn. Notre Dame: University of Notre Dame Press, 1968.

——"Jewish and Christian Liturgies," *True Worship*. Ed. L. Sheppard. Baltimore: The Helicon Press, 1963.

——*Liturgical Piety*. Notre Dame: University of Notre Dame Press, 1954.

——*Rite and Man: Natural Sacredness and Christian Liturgy*. Notre Dame: University of Notre Dame Press, 1963.

——*The Meaning of Sacred Scripture*. Notre Dame: University of Notre Dame Press, 1958.

——*The Revised Liturgy. A Doctrinal Commentary of the Conciliar Constitution on the Liturgy*. London: Darton, Longman and Todd, Ltd., 1965.

Brasso, G. M. *Liturgy and Spirituality*. Trans. L. J. Doyle. Collegeville: The Liturgical Press, 1960.

Bugnini, A. "Da Sacra Liturgia in Secunda Sessione Concilii Oecumenici Vatican II," EL 78 (1964), 3-14.

——"Introduction," *The Liturgy of the Hours—The General Instruction on the Reform of the Breviary.* Trans. P. Coughlan, P. Purdue. London: Geoffrey Chapman, 1974.

Capelle, B. " 'L'Opus Dei' dans la Règle de Saint Benoit," *La Prière des Heures—Lex Orandi.*

——"The Pastoral Theology of the Encyclicals *Mystici Corporis* and *Mediator Dei," The Assisi Papers.* Collegeville: The Liturgical Press, 1957.

Cross, F. L. ed. *The Oxford Dictionary of the Christian Church.* London: Oxford University Press, 1966.

Cuming, G. J. "The New Testament Foundation for Common Prayer," *Studia Liturgica* 10, 3/4 (1974), 88-105.

Danielou, J. *The Bible and the Liturgy.* Notre Dame: University of Notre Dame Press, 1956.

Deiss, L. *Biblical Hymns and Psalms.* 2 vols. Cincinnati: World Library of Sacred Music Publications, Inc., 1965-1970.

——*Early Sources of the Liturgy.* Trans. B. Weatherhead. New York: Alba House, 1967.

DeVaux, R. *Ancient Israel: Its Life and Institutions.* Trans. J. McHugh. London: Darton, Longman and Todd, 1962.

"Didache—The Teaching of the Twelve Apostles," *Ancient Christian Writers.* 6th edition. Ed. J. Quasten, J. Plumpe. Westminster, MD: The Newman Press, 1948.

Didascalia et Constitutiones Apostolorum. Ed. F. X. Funk. Vol. 1. Paderborn: Schoeningh, 1905.

Dix, G. *The Shape of the Liturgy.* London: Dacre Press, 1970.

Dolan, J. P. *History of the Reformation.* New York: Desclee Company, 1964.

Duchesne, L. *Christian Worship: Its Origin and Evolution.* S.P.C.K., 1912.

Duggan, P. "The Liturgy of the Hours," *Worship 51* (1977), 307-315.

Dugmore, C. W. "Canonical Hours," *A Dictionary of Liturgy and Worship.* Ed. J. G. Davies. London: SCM Press Ltd., 1972.

——*The Influence of the Synagogue Upon the Divine Office,* Westminster: The Faith Press Ltd., 1964.

Eliade, M. *Images and Symbols: Studies in Religious Symbolism.* Trans. P. Mairet. New York: Sheed and Ward, 1969.

Fischer, B. "Le Christ dans les Psaumes," LMD 27 (1951), 86-109.

——"Les Psaumes Prière Chrétienne Témoignages du IIe Siècle," *La Prière des Heures—Lex Orandi.*

Gelineau, J. "Are New Forms of Liturgical Singing and Music Developing?" *Concilium 52.* Ed. H. Schmidt. New York: Herder and Herder, 1970.

——*The Grail Gelineau Psalter.* Chicago: G. I. A. Publications, Inc., 1963.

——*The Liturgy Today and Tomorrow.* Trans. D. Livingstone. London: Darton, Longman and Todd, 1978.

——*Voices and Instruments in Christian Worship.* Trans. C. Howell. Collegeville: The Liturgical Press, 1964.

Grisbrooke, W. J. "A Contemporary Liturgical Problem: The Divine Office and Public Worship," *Studia Liturgica* 8 (1971-1972), 129-168; 9 (1973), 3-18, 18-106.

Gy, P. M. "Esquisse Historique," LMD 76 (1963), 7-17.

Hamman, A. *Prayer: The New Testament.* Trans. P. J. Oligny. Chicago: Franciscan Herald Press, 1971.

Haquin, A. *Dom L. Beauduin et le renouveau liturgique.* Gembloux, 1970.

——*Histoire du renouveau liturgique belge,* 1882-1914. Louvain, 1966.

Hefele, C. J., Leclercq, H. ed. *Histoire des Conciles.* Vols. IIa, III. Paris: Letouzey et Ané, 1908.

Hippolytus. *La Tradition Apostolique de Saint Hippolyte.* Essai de Reconstitution par B. Botte. Munster, Westfalen: Aschendorffsche Verlagsbuchhandlung, 1963.

Hruby, K. "Les Heures de Prière dans le Judaisme a l' Epoque de Jésus," *La Prière des Heures—Lex Orandi.*

Jeremias, J. "La prière quotidienne dans la vie du Seigneur et dans l' Eglise primitive," *La Prière des Heures—Lex Orandi.*

——*The Prayers of Jesus.* Trans. J. Bowden, C. Burchard, J. Reumann. Norwich: SCM Press Ltd., 1976.

Jounel, P. "Le Culte des Saints," *L' Eglise en Prière.* Ed. A. G. Martimore. Tournai: Desclée Company, 1961.

Jungmann, J. A. "Commentary on the Constitution on the Sacred Liturgy," *Commentary on the Documents of Vatican II.* Ed. H. Vorgrimler.

——*Pastoral Liturgy.* New York: Herder and Herder, 1962.

——*The Early Liturgy.* Trans. F. A. Brunner. Notre Dame: University of Notre Dame Press, 1959.

Kilmartin, E. *The Eucharist in the Primitive Church.* Englewood Cliffs, New Jersey: Prentice—Hall, Inc., 1965.

King, A. *Liturgies of the Primatial Sees.* Milwaukee: The Bruce Publishing Company, 1957.

Lechner, J., Eisenhofer, L. *The Liturgy of the Roman Rite.* Trans. A. J. Peeler, E. F. Peeler, ed. H. E. Winstone. New York: Herder and Herder, 1961.

Leclercq, H. "Office Devin," *Dictionnaire d' Archeologie chrétienne et de Liturgie.* Vol. XII. Paris: 1936. Cols. 1962-2017.

Luykx, B. "L'influence des moines sur l'office paroissial," LMD 51 (1975), 55-81.

Magrassi, M. "La spiritualita dell' Ufficio divino," *Liturgia delle Ore— Documenti Ufficiali e Studi.*

Mancini, F. "L'uso dei Salmi nei secoli," *La Preghiera nel Tempo.* Vita Monastica Camaldoli, nn. 124-125 (1976), 19-42.

Marot, H. "La Place des Lectures Bibliques et Patristiques dans l' Office Latin," *La Prière des Heures—Lex Orandi.*

——*Spirit and Song of the New Liturgy.* Trans. L. Haggard, M. Mazzarese. Cincinnati: World Library of Sacred Music, 1970.

Marsili, S. "La Liturgia, Momento storico della Salvezza" *Anamnesis 1, La Liturgia, momento nella storia della salvezza.* A cura di S. Marsili. Torino: Casa Editrice Marietti, 1974.

Martimort, A. G. "La Institutio Generalis e la Nuova Liturgia Horarum," *Liturgia delle Ore—Documenti Ufficiali e Studi.*

Mateos, J. "The Morning and Evening Office," *Worship 42* (1968), 31-47.

Merton, T. *Praying the Psalms.* Collegeville: The Liturgical Press, 1955.

Mowinckel, S. *The Psalms in Israel's Worship.* 2 vols. Trans. D. R. Ap-Thomas. New York: Abingdon Press, 1962.

Murphy, R. "Psalms," *The Jerome Biblical Commentary.*

Neunheuser, B. "Il Movimento Liturgico: Panorama Storico e Lineamenti Teologici," *Anamnesis 1, La Liturgia, momento nella storia della salvezza,* a cura di S. Marsili. Torino: Casa Editrice Marietti, 1974.

——"Das Stundengebet, Gebet auch der Laien," *Notitiae* 143/144 (1978), 259-269.

Nocent, A. "L' Ufficio divino in trasformazione," *Studi Francescani 65,* (1968) 172-184.

Parsch, P. *Il Breviario Romano.* Torino: Marietti, 1958.

Pinell, J. *La Liturgia delle Ore.* Padova: Istituto di Liturgia Pastorale, 1975.

——"Le Collette Salmiche," *Liturgia delle Ore—Documenti Ufficiali e Studi.*

Quasten, J. *Patrology*. 3 vols. Westminster, Maryland: The Newman Press, 1964.

Raffa, V. "Dal Breviario del Quignonez alla Liturgia delle Ore di Paolo VI," *Liturgia delle Ore—Documenti Ufficiali e Studi*.

Rahner, K., LeGuillou, M. J. "The Church," *Encyclopedia of Theology—The Concise Sacramentum Mundi*. Ed. K. Rahner. New York: The Seabury Press, 1975.

Ratzinger, J. "Commentary on the Pastoral Constitution on the Church in the Modern World," *Commentary on the Documents of Vatican II*. Ed. H. Vorgrimler.

Rousseau, O. "La Prière des Moines au Temps de Jean Cassien," *La Prière des Heures—Lex Orandi*.

Sabourin, L. *The Psalms, Their Origin and Meaning*. New York: Alba House, 1974.

Salmon, P. "La Prière des Heures," *L' Eglise en Prière*.

——*The Breviary Through the Centuries*. Trans. S. D. Mary. Collegeville: The Liturgical Press, 1962.

Schmidt, H. *Constitution de la Sainte Liturgie—Genèse et Commentaire*. Bruxelles: Editions Lumen Vitae, 1966.

——"De Officio Divino," EL 78 (1964), 341-356.

Semmelroth, O. "Commentary on the Pastoral Constitution on the Church in the Modern World," *Commentary on the Documents of Vatican II*. Ed. H. Vorgrimler.

Shepherd, M. H. *The Psalms in Christian Worship—A Practical Guide*. Minneapolis: Augsburg Publishing House, 1976.

Tricot, A. "The Jewish World at the Time of Our Lord," *Guide to the Bible*, vol. II.

Trimeloni, L. *Tempo di Preghiera—Liturgia delle Ore*. Torino: Marietta, 1971.

Vaggagini, C. *Theological Dimensions of the Liturgy*. Trans. J. Doyle, W. A. Jurgens. Collegeville: The Liturgical Press, 1976.

van der Meer, F., Mohrmann, C. *Atlas of the Christian World*. Trans. and ed. M. F. Hedlund, H. H. Rowley. London: Thomas Nelson and Sons Ltd., 1959.

——*Augustine the Bishop*. Trans. B. Battershaw, G. R. Lamb. New York: Harper and Row, 1961.

Van Dijk, S. J. P., Walker, J. H. *The Origins of the Modern Roman Liturgy.* Westminster, MD: The Newman Press, 1960.

Vicentin, P. "Dimensione Orante della Chiesa e Liturgia delle Ore," *Liturgia delle Ore—Documenti Ufficiali e Studi.*

Von Allmen, J. J. "The Theological Meaning of Common Prayer," *Studia Liturgica* 10, 3/4 (1974), 125-136.

Wilkinson, J. *Egeria's Travels.* London: S.P.C.K., 1971.

Index